DEDICATED TO THOSE WHO DREAM OF UFOs, E.Ts, TIME WARPS...AND A BRIGHTER TOMORROW

Vargas Interprets the Women of the Future for the Screen's Science-Fiction Sesation . . .

WORLD Without END

ALLIED ARTISTS PICTURE starring HUGH MARLOW NANCY GATES PRODUCED BY RICHARD HEERMANCE WRITTEN AND DIRECTED BY EDWARD BERNUDS

Filmed in **CINEMASCOPE**
Color by TECHNICOLOR

TOP 100 SCI-FI MOVIES. Copyright © Gary Gerani, 2011. All rights reserved. Published by IDW in association with Fantastic Press. IDW Publishing, a division of Idea and Design Works, LLC. Editorial Offices: 5080 Sante Fe Street, San Diego, CA 92109. All rights reserved. None of the contents of this publication may be reprinted without the permission of Idea and Design Works, LLC.

ISBN 978-1-60010-879-2   14 13 12 11 1 2 3 4
First printing, April 2011. Printed in Korea.

COVER COLLAGE: an original illustration by Steven Chorney celebrates the top six sci-fi movies as ranked by this book. 1st PAGE: Space visitors Gort and Klaatu from *The Day the Earth Stood Still* (20th Century Fox, 1951). ABOVE: Popular artist Vargas takes on a trio of beauties from *World Without End* (Allied Artists, 1957).

FANTASTIC PRESS

presents

TOP 100

SCI-FI
MOVIES

Written, Edited and Designed by

GARY GERANI

KEN RUBIN

Production Coordinator

FANTASTIC PRESS

IDW

POSTER/PHOTO CREDITS. Columbia Pictures (8,9,42,43,44,58,59,116,117,157), Paramount Pictures (10,12,13,16,17,45,46,63,64,71,102,104, 105,106,107,136,137,138,139,148,149,150,194, back cover), 20th Century Fox (11,66,67,75,76,77,78,80,81,100,101,120,121,128,129,130, 131,142,143,150,151,152,153,158,159,165,166,167,182,183,194, back cover), Jack H. Harris (14, 15), Allied Artists (2, 18, 19, 22, 23, 24, 52, 53, 163, 164), United Artists (20, 28, 29, 34, 49, 79, 103, 109, 110, 111), DCA (21, 50, 51), American International (25, 27, 145), Genie Productions (30), Cinema 5 (31), Universal Studios (12, 13, 32, 33, 36, 40, 41, 54, 55, 56, 57, 60, 61, 62, 65, 70, 98, 99, 112, 113, 114, 115, 118, 126, 127, 132, 146, 147, 154, 155, 156, 195, 198, 199, 200, back cover), Metro-Goldwyn-Mayer (4, 7, 26, 35, 88, 180, 181, 184, 185, 188, 189, 190, 191, 192, 193, 194, 195, back cover), Exclusive Films (37, 68), Lippert (38, 39), Warner Bros. (2, 4, 7, 18, 19, 47, 48, 52, 53, 72, 73, 74, 86, 87, 88, 93, 94. 95, 119, 134, 135, 162, 170, 171, 172, 173, 180, 181, 184, 185, 188, 189, 190, 191, 192, 193, 194, back cover), Orion (69, 168, 169, 177, 178, 179, back cover), Toho (50, 51, 84, 85), Tri-Star Pictures (5, 89, 140, 141, 194), Buena Vista (96, 97), Anthos Films (108), Eagle Lion (124, 125), J. Arthur Rank (133), British Lion (82, 83), Corolco (140, 141), Focus Features (144), Lucasfilm (158, 159, 182, 183, 194, back cover), London Film (160, 161), UFA (174, 175, 176), King Bros. (90, 91, 92), Hammer (186, 187), National Pictures (122, 123).

PHOTO SOURCES: The Gary Gerani Photo and Poster Collection, Photofest (special thanks to Buddy Weiss); Jerry Ohlinger's Movie Material Store, Hollywood Movie Posters (Ronald V. Borst), Hollywood Book and Poster (Eric Caiden), Porkepyn, Stephen Sally, other sources.

SPECIAL THANKS to a plethora of first-rate sci-fi film historians who keep interest in the genre alive with their ongoing commentary and research: Ronald V. Borst, Bill Warren, Tom Weaver, David J. Schow, Tim Lucas, Lucy Chase Williams, David Skal, Steve Haberman, Scott MacQueen, among others, with a special tip of the space helmet to Mr. Forrest J Ackerman, who started it all. EXTRA SPECIAL THANKS to Greg Goldstein and Ted Adams of IDW, supporters and encouragers of Fantastic Press, managing editor Justin Eisinger, and graphic artist Robbie Robbins.

RIGHT: An alien mothership hovers over South Africa in Neill Blomkamp's offbeat, Best Picture-nominated *District 9* (TriStar Pictures, 2009).

Table of Contents

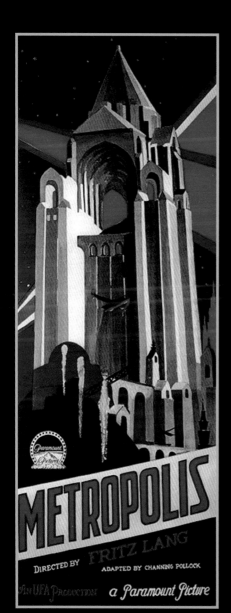

OPPOSITE PAGE: Astronaut Dave Bowman (Keir Dullea), now a wizened old man, faces the enigmatic monolith of Stanley Kubrick's speculative masterpiece *2001: A Space Odyssey* (MGM, 1968).

INTRODUCTION
JOHN CARPENTER

I've always loved science fiction stories involving the fantastic. I suppose it goes directly back to childhood, the passionate interests we all have as kids that ultimately shape who we become. How many times did I see *The Thing from Another World*, the brilliant 1951 Howard Hawks' film? Or the first *Godzilla*? Or *Forbidden Planet*? What was it about these science fiction movies that made them so indelible?

They were modern-age fairy tales, that's certainly true, with atomic mutations and reborn dinosaurs replacing dragons, giants and ogres. And then there was their subversive appeal. "He's been reading those trashy science fiction magazines again!" says the mother in *Invaders from Mars*, the William Cameron Menzies film from 1953. Parents and authority figures considered this kind of entertainment bad medicine, like comic books ("Seduction of the Innocent") and, worst of all, rock and roll. So naturally, that only added to the genre's growing appeal.

Science fiction allows the filmmaker to express truths in an imaginative, highly enjoyable way, and this tends to make these stories more universal and timeless. That's probably why we're still watching *The Twilight Zone* after all these years. Most people would say *They Live!* is an example of a movie with a political theme within the context and parameters of a science fiction thriller. But there are thoughts and ideas being expressed in *Dark Star* that run just as deep. People see things in the character relationships of *The Thing* that they recognize in their own lives. But the science fiction aspect of that story makes it more intriguing, more powerful perhaps than a straightforward study of paranoia might be.

So this genre offers much to an artist with the hunger to express something in joyously original storytelling terms. I'll always be a fan of science fiction films, an appreciator of the form in all permutations, from *Godzilla* to *2001*, anxious to lose myself in a wonder world somebody very talented has sweated his soul to conceive.

For us movie addicts, it really doesn't get much better than that.

John Carpenter, 2011

OVERVIEW
GARY GERANI

Back in the redefining, socially-relevant '60s, *Castle of Frankenstein* editor Calvin Beck declared science fiction the greatest of all movie genres (for you youngsters, *CoF* was the "high brow" competition for Forry Ackerman's seminal *Famous Monsters* magazine). The colorful Mr. Beck was actually on to something. Science Fiction (or "sci-fi") calls for everything any good story or movie must have: a solid and interesting plot, believable characters you care something about, and a theme of legitimate freshness and worth. But it also requires the pure staring bliss of human imagination, an audacious flight of fancy conceived to awe and excite, depicted on screen through special effects. If this "high concept" can somehow reflect incisive truths about our perplexing species, the science fiction tale has fully succeeded in doing its creative job. The specific nature of this far-out fantasy can range from an indestructible fabric to a mass invasion of suction-cup-fingered Martians. If nothing else, imagination is versatile.

Thanks, Calvin. And Forry. And Frederick S. Clarke (creator/editor of the original *Cinefantastique* magazine). You guys knew from Day One that science fiction had it all, and were happy to share that insight with us. With fanciful planets, advanced technology and alien entities as creative assets, the pleasures of this movie genre will always resonate. Here's to the future, ladies and gents!

Gary Gerani, 2011

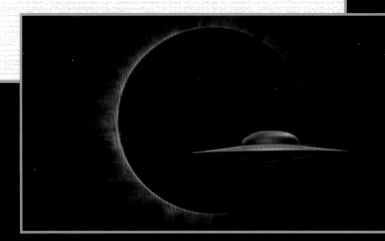

KEY TO UNDERSTANDING

97   **1.85**

Clock: Running time
Monitor: Aspect Ratio
Full headphone: Stereo soundtrack
Half headphone: Mono soundtrack

ABOUT THE BOOK

The 100 movies you're about to read about represent my choices for the cinema's most significant science fiction endeavors. Sorry, no comic book superhero or animated features in this line-up, as they belong to very active subgenres (and hopefully future studies) of their own. Ranking is a subjective party game, of course, a fun way to stimulate some spirited debate. But really, all of the movies showcased here are worth experiencing, from the celebrated classics to way-below-the-radar obscurities and foreign efforts.

ABOUT THE AUTHOR

First professional writing assignment: impersonating the *Creature from the Black Lagoon* for *The Monster Times* (1972), a monthly tabloid devoted to scary movies. Book #1: 1977's *Fantastic Television* is the very first to explore sf/horror/fantasy on the small screen. A lifelong creative relationship with the Topps Company yields books, magazines, sticker albums, and hundreds of trading card sets for over four decades, including cult fave *Dinosaurs Attack!* Finally, co-writing the screenplay for Stan Winston's *Pumpkinhead* results in a brand new, snaggle-fanged, rubber-suited Famous Monster of Filmland. In 2010, launches *Bram Stoker's Death Ship* – the nightmarish story of Dracula's voyage to London – in graphic novel form.

100 EARTH VS. THE FLYING SAUCERS 1956 85 1.85

WHO MADE IT:

Columbia Pictures (U.S.). Director: Fred F. Sears. Producers: Sam Katzman, Charles H. Schneer. Writers: George Worthing Yates & Bernard Gordon, based on a screen story by Curt Siodmak and a book by Donald E. Keyhoe. Special effects: Ray Harryhausen. Cinematography (b/w): Fred Jackman Jr. Music: Mischa Bakaleinikoff (uncredited). Starring: Hugh Marlowe (Dr. Russell A. Marvin), Joan Taylor (Carol Marvin), Donald Curtis (Major Huglin), Morris Ankrum (Brig. Gen. John Hanley), John Zaremba (Prof. Kanter), Thomas Browne Henry (Vice Adm. Enright), Paul Frees (alien voice; uncredited).

WHAT IT'S ABOUT:

Rocket scientist Dr. Russell Marvin is inexplicably buzzed by a flying saucer, which, unknown to him, has left a message on his tape machine at accelerated speed. Soon after, an unexpected visit from space visitors at Operation Skyhook results in the military base's total destruction. Having solved the mystery of this alien attack after a slowed-down tape clarifies their message, Russell meets directly with the invading extraterrestrials, and is told that mankind's total capitulation is the only way to avoid planetary bloodshed. Instead of surrendering, humanity endures a series of punishing atmospheric convulsions and frustrates the enemy with a new anti-gravity device developed by Dr. Marvin. A spectacular battle in the skies and streets of Washington D.C. succeeds in repelling an attempted saucer takeover.

WHY IT'S IMPORTANT:

Clearly inspired by the success of George Pal's *War of the Worlds*, *Earth vs. the Flying Saucers* offers a similar scenario in glorious black-and-white and on a lower budget, with Pal's graceful manta-ships replaced by Ray Harryhausen's grim, more energetic spinners. The result is an entertaining space attack movie in its own right, allowing Harryhausen an opportunity to experiment with non-living animation subjects for the first time in a feature. Accordingly, he invests his grey-metal warships with semi-human personality; these relentless discs are malevolent, thundering speed-demons that delight in obliterating cherished national landmarks. They became so iconic over time that filmmakers ranging from Orson Welles (in *F For Fake*) and Tim Burton (in *Mars Attacks!*) saw fit to celebrate them.

Then there's the story itself, essentially a set-up for exotic combat scenes. Events begin enigmatically with a botched alien message regarding a saucer landing, which results in the annihilation of military base Skyhook. That original message finally playing on an accidentally slowed-down tape provides an eerie, ironic moment, suggesting that Skyhook's Pearl Harbor-style obliteration may have been caused by a simple mistake. From there, the plot proceeds along conventional lines, with the building of an anti-saucer weapon and the physical nature of the aliens becoming key points. The latter pretty much adheres to Wells' notion of a genetically-weak species that relies heavily on advanced technology for both survival and offensive operations.

With a capable cast headed by Hugh Marlowe (last seen in *The Day the Earth Stood Still*) and Joan Taylor (soon to be seen in *20 Million Miles to Earth*), *Earth vs. the Flying Saucers* remains reasonably diverting and visually inventive throughout, a more than serviceable sci-fi vehicle for stop-motion maestro Harryhausen.

ABOVE: Captured General Hanley (Morris Ankrum) is mind-probed by the inquisitive extra-terrestrials after they leave Earth's orbit. This sequence aboard the flying saucer is especially well-directed and photographed, with dramatic up angles and impressive-for-their-day special effects.

LEFT, TOP: An early set-piece depicting the annihilation of American military forces establishes the level of raw power these extra-terrestrials have at their command. Almost as iconic as the saucers themselves are the armored aliens that pilot them.

After shooting a Saucerman and removing his helmet. Dr. Marvin and company discover that the aliens are physically fragile life forms, their senses amplified by organic, electrically-charged body suits.

RIGHT: Most of Washington D.C.'s iconic landmarks take a beating during the climactic saucer attack. One of them even splashes down in the Potomic.

Ray Harryhausen was required to animate collapsing buildings in addition to saucers, a budget consideration that negated the use of high-speed photography.

WHO MADE IT:

Security Pictures (U.K.)/Paramount (U.S.). Director: Andrew Marton. Producers: Philip Yordan, Lester A. Sansom, Bernard Glasser. Writers: Jon Manchip White & Julian Zimet. Cinematography (Technicolor): Manuel Berenguer. Music: John Douglas. Starring: Dana Andrews (Dr. Stephen Sorenson), Janette Scott (Dr. Maggie Sorenson), Kieron Moore (Dr. Ted Rampion), Alexander Knox (Sir Charles Eggerston), Peter Damon (John Masefield), Jim Gillen (Rand).

WHAT IT'S ABOUT:

Hoping to hit reserves of magma, acclaimed scientist Stephen Sorenson ignores the dire warnings of colleague and personal rival Ted Rampion (jilted lover of Sorenson's beautiful young wife, Maggie) and sinks a nuclear bomb deep into the planet's core. Magma is indeed struck, but this explosion also causes a devastating crack in the Earth's crust that threatens to encircle the world and ultimately destroy it. Working against time, Sorenson and his team desperately try to halt the fantastic destruction they've unleashed. Only an unexpected

breakaway, resulting in the birth of a second moon, saves the Earth from total annihilation.

WHY IT'S IMPORTANT:

Conceived as a follow-up to 1962's *The Day of the Triffids*, *Crack in the World* is in many ways a more polished film, lacking the Wyndham pedigree but boasting an intelligent, heartfelt performance by star Dana Andrews. Although often mistaken for a disaster epic, *Crack* adheres to the lab-centric sci-fi formula established in the '50s and realized with more ambitious production values a decade later. Outside of a few fx-laden field trips, our visionary heroes are mostly confined to their futuristic home base, allowing for more focused character development and spirited, plot-advancing technical jargon. Screenwriters White and Zimet deftly parallel the scientific/ideological differences of *Crack*'s leads with their personal choices, using the device of a romantic triangle to hold theme and plotline together. Even some potentially hokey symbolism (Sorensen can't give his wife a son, so he gives the world an extra moon) is cleverly integrated.

Although crisply directed by Andrew Marton, *Crack* owes much of its sci-fi punch to production designer Eugene Lourie, who fearlessly combines hanging miniatures and other forced perspective techniques with an avalanche of colorful optical effects. Also keeping the energy level up is John Douglas' masterful symphonic score.

Intelligent, compelling and quite spectacular given its budget limitations, *Crack in the World* was certainly welcome back in 1965, and remains a fine template for character-driven doomsday thrillers of any era.

INDEPENDENCE DAY 1996   145 2.35

Poster/photos: © 1996 20th Century Fox

The question of
whether or not
we are alone
in the universe
has been answered.

INDEPENDENCE DAY
Don't make plans for August.
www.id4.com

WHO MADE IT:

Twentieth Century Fox (U.S.). Director: Roland Emmerich. Writers/Producers: Dean Devlin, Roland Emmerich. Cinematography (color): Karl Walter Lindelaub. Music: David Arnold. Starring: Will Smith (Captain Steven Hiller), Bill Pullman (President Thomas J. Whitmore), Jeff Goldblum (David Levinson), Mary McDonnell (First Lady Marilyn Whitmore), Judd Hirsh (Julius Levinson), Robert Loggia (General Grey), Randy Quaid (Russell Casse), Margaret Colin (Constance Spano), Vivica A. Fox (Jasmine), Harvey Fierstein (Marty), Brent Spiner (Dr. Okun).

WHAT IT'S ABOUT:

Massive alien spaceships enter Earth's atmosphere and position themselves atop major cities. Although everyone from crop dusters to jet pilots wonder what will happen next, and the President of the United States tries to maintain some control of the situation, humanity's worst fears come true: the ships launch a devastating attack, slaughtering countless civilians in a deadly wave of flame, and leaving cities in ruins. Only the  discovery of a computer "virus" within the alien mothercraft enables two foolhardy and courageous humans to shut the space invaders down and put a halt to their monstrous global attack.

WHY IT'S IMPORTANT:

"Sorry, but we just don't believe 'War of the Worlds' is coming back," my late writing partner and I were told by most of the majors in 1990 when, fresh from our cult film *Pumpkinhead*, we pitched a grown-up, legally-optioned version of *Mars Attacks!* to producers. Just a few years later, in 1996, the two of us watched helplessly as Tim Burton's campy version of *Attacks!* hit screens, right after the relatively straight *Independence Day* was already breaking box office records. Sigh. If nothing else, Roland Emmerich's giddy homage to the spirit and commercial style of Irwin Allen disaster movies proved once and for all that "invasion from space" stories, produced with state-of-the-art special effects and impressive production values, have an enormous built-in audience. *ID4* wowed viewers just as much with its trailers as it did with the finished product, which some saw as a comedown: Images of the White House being obliterated, or scores of cars sent flying up the street by a wave of flame, gave viewers the kind of larger-than-life spectacle they'd been waiting years to see...*Star Wars* on Earth, with all the attendant pleasures of visual counterpointing (spaceship chase in the Grand Canyon? Hot diggity!). Soon-to-be sci-fi veteran Will Smith makes his movie debut in a role that places him somewhere between serious (as in *I Am Legend*) and comedic (*Men in Black*). There's low-voltage entertainment in the banter between his streetwise pilot and the semi-nerd strategist played by Jeff Goldbum, himself no stranger to the genre. Although Emmerich's tone is Toho-thin as usual and the Irwin Allen angle a tad too self-aware, the film does manage some clever twists, and the overall "chess game" scenario that Goldblum finally cracks is a shrewd, simple way of building suspense. In terms of actual effects, the director smartly employs every trick in the book, from state-of-the-art CGI to the old cannibalized plastic kits-approach to model building, harking back to *Star Wars* in 1977. Calculated and obvious, but bursting with spectacular, in some cases iconic visuals, *Independence Day* is a reminder to Hollywood that even superficial epics about subjects the public is interested in will make a fortune. This one sure did.

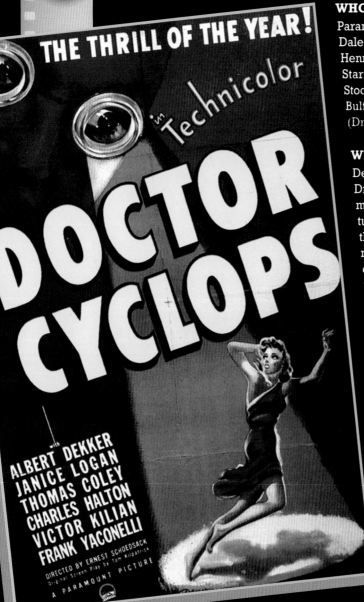

WHO MADE IT:

Paramount Pictures (U.S.) Director: Ernest B. Schoedsack. Producer: Dale Van Every. Writer: Tom Kilpatrick. Cinematography (Technicolor): Henry Sharp. Music: Gerald Carbonara, Albert Hay Malotte, Ernst Toch. Starring Albert Dekker (Dr. Alexander Thorkel), Thomas Coley (Bill Stockton), Janice Logan (Dr. Mary Robinson), Charles Halton (Dr. Rupert Bulfinch), Victor Kilian (Steve Baker), Frank Yaconelli (Pedro), Paul Fix (Dr. Mendoza)

WHAT IT'S ABOUT:

Deep in the Peruvian jungle, an accomplished but unhinged scientist, Dr. Thorkel, has perfected a device that can shrink living creatures to miniature size. Thorkel murders his associate, Dr. Mendoza, then turns his wrath – and shrinking process – on an investigating party that visits his camp and soon becomes suspicious. Soon, five miniaturized humans are braving the dangers of a suddenly enlarged world, fending off attacks from jungle animals, inclement weather, and the doctor's hungry black cat. After one of their number, Dr. Bulfinch, is ruthlessly murdered by Thorkel, the remaining victims resolve to battle their captor, smashing his spectacles and luring him into a deathtrap. Nicknamed Cyclops by his mini-adversaries, half-blinded Thorkel finally plunges to his well-deserved doom in a mine shaft. The little people return to their normal size within a matter of days.

WHY IT'S IMPORTANT:

If you're a director who specializes in over-the-top fantasy epics, how do you follow *King Kong*? *Dr. Cyclops* was Ernest B. Schoedsack's high-profile answer, a mad scientist melodrama in striking Technicolor that has more in common with pulpy cliffhangers than true science fiction. Regardless, Schoedsack serves up some pretty amazing visuals, pitting a quartet of miniaturized humans against one outsized peril after another. Chief among these is the titular monster himself, portrayed with scene-stealing relish by a bald and beady-eyed Albert Dekker. Like his mythological namesake, Cyclops is "blinded" and ultimately vanquished by the resourceful little interlopers he believes he has trapped.

Most pre-atomic age science fiction on the screen is a bit dicey, with reasonable speculation often taking a back seat to grandiose fantasy. *Dr. Cyclops* never quite transcends its carnival-level intentions, but at least makes considerable use of a major studio's facilities at a time when this kind of movie simply wasn't being made. Putting things in cultural perspective, it would be another twelve years before Paramount would embark on its next science fiction project (George Pal's *When Worlds Collide*). In the meantime, an escapist, pulp-inspired, handsomely produced Technicolor hybrid like *Cyclops* was eagerly welcomed by movie audiences starved for something a little different.

Best scenes: slain Dr. Mendoza's radiated face (see next page); off-screen victims trapped in the miniaturization chamber as Thorkel turns on the juice; little Dr. Bulfinch's horrific murder via cholorform; planning an armed counterattack.

Tidbit: The music heard in this film's climax was re-used in Preston Sturges' Hollywood-themed *Sullivan's Travels* to represent bombastic scoring for sordid movie melodramas.

ABOVE: Convinced that his mentor has become a madman, Dr. Mendoza (Paul Fix) has his worst fears confirmed when Dr. Thorkel ruthlessly slays him, reducing Mendoza's head to a glowing skull. RIGHT: Tapping into a virtually inexhaustible jungle power source, Thorkel winches up his cylinder for a little adjusting. The solid blacks, stark contrasts and dimensional qualities of three-strip Technicolor greatly enhance the atmosphere of this sequence.

LEFT: Dr. Bulfinch and his party check out Thorkel's ominous-looking miniaturizer. BELOW: Satana the cat corners her shrunken prey, who take refuge behind a cactus garden.

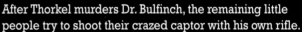

After Thorkel murders Dr. Bulfinch, the remaining little people try to shoot their crazed captor with his own rifle.

The "giant cactus" set was one of many constructed for *Dr. Cyclops*; the hissing cat was optically matted into the final scene.

WHO MADE IT:

Jack H. Harris Enterprises/University of Southern California (U.S.). Director: John Carpenter. Producers: John Carpenter, J. Stein Kaplan. Writers John Carpenter, Dan O'Bannon. Cinematography (Metrocolor): Douglas Knapp. Music: John Carpenter. Starring Brain Narelle (Lt. Doolittle), Cal Kuniholm (Boiler), Dre Pahich (Talby), Dan O'Bannon (Sgt. Pinback), Nick Castle (Alien; uncredited).

WHAT IT'S ABOUT:

Four astronauts battle loneliness and boredom aboard a small spaceship known as the Dark Star. Ship's mission? Destroy unstable planets in star systems soon to be colonized. Along the way, Dark Star's unofficial mascot, a circular-shaped alien, makes life tough for a frustrated Sgt. Pinback. But that's nothing compared to the threat posed by the ship's smart-ass smart bomb. When a computer glitch prevents it from detaching and dropping to its planetary target, the bomb threatens to detonate itself anyway, destroying Dark Star

in the process. Some quick-thinking (and advice from deceased, deep-frozen Commander Powell) delays the explosion, but soon Malibu-loving Lt. Doolittle is surfing his way to oblivion.

WHY IT'S IMPORTANT:

Originally produced as a USC student film, *Dark Star* is a delightful excursion into the bizarre, funny in a sad way (or is that sad in a funny way?) and gently irreverent, with enough pathos to keep the viewer involved. Working with minimum effects and sets put together with imagination and crossed fingers, Carpenter and scripter O'Bannon succeed where Douglas Trumbull failed with *Silent Running*, showcasing a bunch of bored astro-guys who are genuinely engaging and relatable. A twenty-year mission to blow up unstable planets has left these dudes understandably funked-out (they've only aged a few years, which is why they still resemble long-haired stoners), and the recent demise of Commander Powell has added to their growing unease. Fortunately, his deep-frozen corpse is still around to bestow much-needed wisdom from time to time. Yep, it's that kind of movie. In an outlandish set-piece that Carpenter has called "*Alien* in reverse," crewmate Pinback (Dan O'Bannon, who is very, very funny) tracks a playful extraterrestrial "mascot" all over the ship, nearly losing his life in an active elevator shaft. This alien is essentially a playful beach ball with the Creature from the Black Lagoon's talons, ultimately used to tickle Pinback mercilessly as he clings to life in that shaft. Equally perverse is the notorious, petulant "smart bomb," who engages in testy exchanges with the ship's soothing female-voiced computer (Cookie Knapp) and resourceful, desperate Lt. Doolittle, the latter's last-minute experiment in existential philosophy literally backfiring.

Fascinating as a cultural oddity in addition to being a cool movie, *Dark Star* anticipates George Lucas' excursions into space opera (hyperspeed jumping) and O'Bannon's own *Alien*, providing an ahead-of-time parody that functions beautifully as a loopy galactic adventure in its own right.

WHO MADE IT:

Fairview Productions/Tonylyn Productions Inc./Paramount Pictures (U.S.)
Directors: Irvin S. Yeaworth Jr., Russell Doughten (uncredited). Producers:
Jack H. Harris, Russell Doughten. Writers: Theodore Simonson & Kate Phillips
(Linaker), based on an idea by Irvine Millgate. Cinematography (Deluxe
Color): Thomas Spalding. Music: Ralph Carmichael. Starring Steve
McQueen (Steve Andrews), Aneta Corsaut (Jane Martin), Earl Rowe
(Lt. Dave), Olin Howlin (Old Man), Steven Chase (Dr. Hallen), John Benson
(Sgt. Jim Bert), George Karas (Officer Richie), Lee Payton (Kate the Nurse),
Elbert Smith (Henry Martin), Hugh Graham (Mr. Andrews).

WHAT IT'S ABOUT:

A strange mini-meteorite strikes the Earth, and from within it emerges a
weird, gelatinous alien creature. A pair of concerned teens take an old
man stricken by the entity to a local doctor, but soon this unfortunate vic-

tim, the doctor's nurse, and a
stunned Dr. Hallen himself are
engulfed by the ever-expand-
ing Blob. Although most of the
teenagers in town are dis-
trusted by local authorities,
earnest Steve Andrews finally
manages to convince everyone of the life-threatening
danger in their midst. The
Blob soon strikes more openly, invading a crowded movie theater
and finally trapping Steve and a few others in a nearby diner. Only
a freezing dose of CO_2 stops the aggressive alien in its jellyfish-like
tracks. It is then air-lifted and deposited deep in the Arctic, where,
in frozen form, it can no longer pose a threat to mankind.

WHY IT'S IMPORTANT:

Independently-made but scooped up by Jack Harris and peddled
to Paramount, *The Blob* is actually a lot better than its semi-satiric
title might suggest. Part monster-on-the-loose thriller, part *Rebel
Without a Cause*-like teen melodrama, it's mostly remembered
today as an early Steve McQueen vehicle, and for its catchy/
kitschy rock-and-roll title song, conceived in part by Burt Bacharach.
But this property seems to have transcended the movie that launched it. Which in a way is too
bad, because Irvin Yeaworth's little opus offers the unique pleasures of a feature film made outside the Hollywood mainstream, even if it hedges its bets with up-and-coming studio 'veteran' McQueen (he'd already had a small
but notable role in *Somebody Up There Likes Me*, opposite Paul Newman). There's an easy naturalism to the
teenage patter that is noticeably absent from mainstream flicks, even good ones like *Blackboard Jungle*.
Though still relatively young, McQueen demonstrates star quality with every nuance and subtle gesture; his
fearlessly earnest Dean-like performance is one of *The Blob*'s highlights. As for the movie's celebrated
special effects, they range from surprisingly clever to amazingly cheesy.

Harris would go on to handle Fairview's *4D Man* and
Dinosaurus! as pick-up releases for Universal; both contain
their share of offbeat pleasures. But for sheer audacity, small-
town style and pop cultural longevity, nothing tops the
original *Blob*. May it creep and leap forever!

WHO MADE IT:

Paramount Pictures (U.S.) Director: Byron Haskin. Producer: George Pal. Writers: Philip Yordan, Barre Lyndon, George Worthing Yates, from a book by Chesley Bonestell and Willy Ley. Cinematography (Technicolor): Lionel Lindon. Music: Van Cleave. Starring Walter Brooke (Gen. Samuel T. Merritt), Eric Fleming (Capt. Barney Merritt), Mickey Shaughnessy (Sgt. Mahoney), Phil Foster (Jackie Siegle), William Redfield (Roy Cooper), William Hopper (Dr. George Fenton), Benson Fong (Imoto), Ross Martin (Andre Fodor), Vito Scotti (Sanella), Rosemary Clooney (uncredited).

WHAT IT'S ABOUT:

Life aboard the Wheel, an orbiting space station commanded by General Merritt, can be hazardous and even monotonous for members of an elite exploratory team. It's the jumping off point for a Martian expedition to be headed by Merritt's son Barney, who has family-related issues with his father. The carefully-trained crew embarks on their hazardous journey, enduring various celestial dangers along the way... among them General Merritt's mental and moral disintegration. Convinced that God is against the expedition, he imperils it repeatedly, until he is accidentally killed by his own son. The explorers ultimately celebrate Christmas on Mars, overcome life-threatening obstacles, and take off for home.

WHY IT'S IMPORTANT:

A colorful combination of pseudo-documentary and Mars exploration flick, *Conquest of Space* was producer George Pal's uneven attempt to rework his highly successful *Destination Moon* formula. Unfortunately for the sci-fi specialist, box office lightning didn't strike twice, and *Conquest's* unexpected failure ended his long and profitable relationship with Paramount Studios (Pal would rebound half a decade later over at MGM, as producer/director of his greatest sci-fi film, *The Time Machine*).

Minus the horrific pleasures of smashing planets and invading Martian hordes, *Conquest* requires audiences to spend some down time on an orbiting space station and eventually take a fairly tepid journey to the red planet. Not surprisingly, colorful clichés of galactic travel are rolled out one-by-one, from meteorite storms to the obligatory crew member from Brooklyn, aboard for audience identification and comedy relief. Fortunately, director Byron Haskin's sense of dramatic composition is often inspired, generally distracting us from shaky matte lines and other technical imperfections. As with all George Pal films of this period, the three-strip Technicolor photography is luminous (Lionel Lindon will go on to shoot Mike Todd's *Around the World in 80 Days* one year later).

In terms of narrative, the challenges of living aboard a space station are novel and reasonably absorbing. But on the down side, a stock father-and-son conflict is unwisely bloated into a distasteful religious debate as the astronauts near their destination. It's as if something was required for third act suspense beyond the inevitable "we don't have enough fuel to leave" routine, so why not transform a perfectly adjusted scientist/explorer into a pistol-wielding fanatic who equates visiting Mars with a desecration of God's universe? Serviceable as melodrama, this kind of convenient conflict did little to enhance *Conquest's* critical reputation. Still, Pal's middling space opera is an entertaining period piece when viewed today, a flawed but welcome confection with reasonably noble intentions.

LEFT: Astronauts float toward the Wheel, an orbiting space station. ABOVE: *Conquest of Space* builds a reasonable father-son conflict (Walter Brooke in background, with Eric Fleming), then allows it to devolve into a bizarre 'religious zealot' subplot.

Astronaut Fodor (Ross Martin) is killed by an asteroid fragment, then is laid to rest with an evocative space burial that inspired a similar scene in *Star Trek II: The Wrath of Kahn*.

After some anxious moments, Captain Merritt and his crew manage to blast away from Mars.

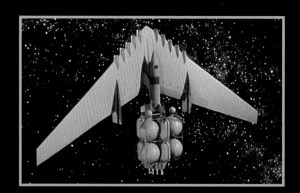

The impressive wing-like rocket prop, complete with external engines, currently resides in the collection of film historian Bob Burns.

93 THE GIANT BEHEMOTH 1959 ⟨80⟩ [1.66]

aka Behemoth the Sea Monster

THE BIGGEST THING SINCE CREATION!

The GIANT BEHEMOTH

starring GENE EVANS · ANDRE MORELL · JOHN TURNER · A DAVID DIAMOND PRODUCTION
Directed by EUGENE LOURIE · Screenplay by EUGENE LOURIE · JACK RABIN · IRVING BLOCK · LOUIS DE WITT
An ALLIED ARTISTS Picture

WHO MADE IT:

Allied Artists (U.S.)/Eros Films/Diamond Pictures Corp. (U.K.). Directors: Eugene Lourie, Douglas Hickox (uncredited). Producers: David Diamond, Ted Lloyd. Writers: Eugene Lourie and Daniel James, based on story by Robert Abel and Alan Adler. Visual effects: Willis O'Brien, Pete Peterson, Irving Block, Louis DeWitt, Jack Rabin. Cinematography (b/w): Desmond Davis, Ken Hodges. Music: Edwin Astley. Starring Gene Evans (Steve Karnes), Andre Morell (Prof. James Bickford), John Turner (John), Leigh Madison (Jean Trevethan), Jack MacGowran (Dr. Sampson), Maurice Kaufman (Mini Sub Officer), Henri Vidon (Tom Trevethan).

WHAT IT'S ABOUT:

Thousands of dead fish and mysterious deaths draw the attention of atomic experts Steve Karnes and James Bickford, dedicated investigators of oceanic contamination. Before long it's established that a radioactive prehistoric monster is at the heart of the crisis. Isolated incidents continue until the creature attacks London, sinking a ferry and contaminating pedestrians with radiation as it stalks through city streets. Eventually, Karnes manages to destroy the monster via submarine by shooting a radium-tipped torpedo into its mouth.

WHY IT'S IMPORTANT:

The middle entry in Eugene Lourie's beloved dinosaur trilogy (bookended by *The Beast from 20,000 Fathoms* and *Gorgo*), *The Giant Behemoth* has the flavor of an edgy British noir, with reliable leads Gene Evans and Andre Morell investigating ocean-based enigmas with Holmes and Watson-style authority. Despite some unavoidable similarities to his formula-establishing *Beast*, Lourie's second take on a resurrected prehistoric threat opts for atmosphere and procedural interrogation over spectacle. Part of the reason for this shift was the anemic fx budget, and never was this more apparent than during the monster's major attack on London. Shots are optically repeated and flopped to pad out the sequence and make it appear more spectacular, turning Willis O'Brien's painstaking work into a paste-and-cut potpourri. Even so, *Behemoth* showcases this critic's candidate for the single greatest stop-motion shot ever conceived for cinema. Starting with a long distance view, it follows the semi-silhouetted dinosaur as he walks from left-to-right, then stalks forward into close-up, obliterating high-tension towers while advancing; he finally marches up and over our viewpoint, kicking twisted girders toward the "camera." With full use made of perspective, depth, dramatic lighting and action, never has the magical potential of dimensional animation been on better display in a movie.

Unlike Lourie's other dinosaur dramas, *The Giant Behemoth* is something of an ecological polemic, with Evans and Morell the ever-vigilant protectors of an increasingly careless and disinterested mankind. In keeping with this agreeably frosty tone, a second radiated prehistoric monster is suggested before *B*'s final fade, more as an environmental warning than the set-up for a sequel. In truth, director Eugene Lourie would revisit an imperiled London with his next and most ambitious prehistoric story, but for an entirely different thematic purpose.

Tidbit: The poster art (pictured above) was rendered by Joe Smith, the same artist who would illustrate Lourie's *Gorgo* two years later.

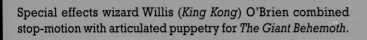

THE MAN FROM PLANET X 1951

The **WEIRDEST** visitor the Earth has ever seen!

The MAN FROM PLANET X

Sherrill Corwin presents
"The MAN from PLANET X" starring ROBERT CLARKE · MARGARET FIELD · WILLIAM SCHALLERT
Directed by Edgar G. Ulmer · Written and Produced by Aubrey Wisberg and Jack Pollexfen · Released thru United Artists

WHO MADE IT:

United Artists (U.S.). Director: Edgar G. Ulmer. Producers/Writers: Jack Pollexfen, Aubrey Wisberg. Cinematography (b/w): John L. Russell. Music: Charles Koff. Starring Robert Clarke (John Lawrence), Margaret Field (Enid Elliot), Raymond Bond (Prof. Elliot), William Schallert (Dr. Mears), Roy Engel (Tommy the Constable), David Ormont (Inspector Porter), Pat Goldin (The Man from Planet X; uncredited).

WHAT IT'S ABOUT:

Reporter John Lawrence travels to a remote Scottish village that will be quite close to a passing celestial body known as Planet X. Joining scientist Prof. Elliot and his daughter Enid, along with unscrupulous assistant Dr. Meers, Lawrence discovers an alien artifact on the moors, and eventually, a space being in a diving bell-like ship, who seems friendly enough at first. Profit-minded Meers tries to bend the visitor to his will, but winds up becoming his slave, like others from the village. Rescuing Enid and her father, Lawrence learns that a full-scale invasion will be launched when Planet X passes by. This is averted by a military attack against the invader.

WHY IT'S IMPORTANT:

At a time when the major studios were preparing relatively expensive, decidedly modern takes on science fiction themes, *The Man from Planet X* has the audacity to look backward for inspiration... specifically, to those fog-bound mysteries churned out assembly line-style in the 1940s. This film's obligatory bogeyman is no ghost or disguised killer, but a bubble-helmeted visitor from another world with something of a confused agenda. In terms of morality, scribe producers Pollexfen and Wisberg seem to want it both ways: Their "man" responds to positive human gestures with commendable trust and is clearly sinned against big-time by opportunistic criminal scientist Dr. Meers. Still, the little fellow does happen to be spearheading a full-scale invasion of our planet, so he's not exactly E.T.

Director Edgar G. Ulmer, famed for atmospheric compositions and operetta-like soundtracks, enjoyed a reputation in Hollywood for imbuing low-budget quickies with an aura

of dignity. Accordingly, *Planet X* makes extensive use of imposing sets from 1949's *Joan of Arc*, which effectively define the film's baroque flavor. Only the agreeably futuristic "diving bell" spaceship and its vanguard appendage suggest 1951; these objects are especially striking when contrasted with the quaint Scottish village and misty moors. Part victim, part alien menace, the Man himself registers well enough as a character, portrayed effectively by a quasi-Halloween mask made sinister through up-angle lighting. There was also some thought put into the fabrication of this visitor's howling, radio-wave-like "voice."

Standout scene: Enid (played by Margaret Field, Sally's mom) approaching the landed bell for the first time...and viewing its occupant through the porthole.

91

THE CRAWLING EYE 1958

 84 1.66

aka The Trollenberg Terror

Poster/photos: © 1959 DCA Releasing Corporation

The nightmare terror of the slithering eye that unleashed agonizing horror on a screaming world!

WARNING
If you've ever been hypnotized do not come alone.

A man dissolves... and out of the oozing mist comes the hungry eye, slave to the demon brain!

THE CRAWLING EYE

FORREST TUCKER · LAURENCE PAYNE · JENNIFER JAYNE
Directed by
ROBERT S. BAKER, MONTY BERMAN · QUENTIN LAWRENCE

Produced by

DCA release

the company that brought you "RODAN"

WHO MADE IT:

Tempean Films (U.K.)/DCA (U.S.). Director: Quentin Lawrence. Producers: Robert S. Baker, Monty Berman. Writers: Jimmy Sangster, from a story by Peter Key. Cinematography (b/w): Monty Berman. Music: Stanley Black. Starring Forrest Tucker (Alan Brooks), Laurence Payne (Phillip Truscott), Jennifer Jayne (Sarah Pilgrim), Janet Munro (Anne Pilgrim), Warren Mitchell (Prof. Crevett), Frederick Schiller (Mayor Klein), Andrew Faulds (Brett), Stuart Saunders (Dewhurst), Colin Douglas (Hans), Drek Sydney (Wilde).

WHAT IT'S ABOUT:

A series of gruesome accidents draws attention to Trollenberg mountain, where a mysterious radioactive cloud nests. U.N. investigator Alan Brooks looks into the situation, reuniting with scientist friend Prof. Crevett, who operates a futuristic laboratory on the mountain. When a visiting mind-reading performer begins experiencing bizarre visions, Brooks and Crevett begin to suspect that outer space creatures inhabit the cloud and are planning a worldwide invasion. These beings slay humans and use their reanimated corpses as spies and assassins. Finally, the invaders are fully revealed –  tentacled, one-eyed monstrosities – and everyone takes refuge in the mountain lab. An aerial attack of napalm wipes out the attacking monsters, freeing Trollenberg of its treacherous cloud at last.

WHY IT'S IMPORTANT:

Taking a cue from the Nigel Kneale school of fanciful speculation, *The Crawling Eye* combines mystery, horror and an outer space invasion, setting its unlikely scenario atop one of the tallest mountains in the world. Penned by noted Hammer scribe Jimmy Sangster, this feature incarnation of a popular BBC serial seems to revel in horrific acts of violence: we're off and bleeding with both a killing and a decapitation in *Eye*'s pre-credit sequence, and reanimated human corpses - stoic but sentient vessels for the invaders - menace our heroes throughout. Most memorable are the one-eyed, heavy-breathing Lovecraftian extraterrestrials that finally trundle into garish close-up come Act III. Keeping these hellacious brainiacs off-camera for most of the film proved a prudent game plan, director Quentin Lawrence holding interest throughout with exotic locations, focused puzzle-solving, some clever sci-fi theorizing, and a handful of genuinely scary suspense sequences. Star Forrest Tucker delivers another believable high-altitude performance, and Stanley Black's colorful music ranges from darkly evocative to rousingly militaristic. Producers Baker and Berman would next focus their atmospheric attention on *Jack the Ripper* (1960), again scripted by Jimmy Sangster with a score (at least in England) by Black.

Best scenes: Anne's unexpected vision of events in the cabin; discovery of beheaded Brett; Zombie-Dewhurst's inability to strike a match; his nocturnal murder mission; the fog-shrouded hotel doors collapsing, followed by the alien's startling appearance within the opening.

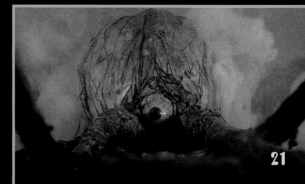

WHO MADE IT:

Security Pictures (U.K.)/Allied Artists (U. S.). Directors: Steve Sekely, Freddie Francis – uncredited. Producers: Philip Yordan, George Pitcher. Writer: Philip Yordan aka Bernard Gordon, from a novel by John Wyndham. Cinematography (Eastmancolor): Ted Moore. Music: Ron Goodwin, John Douglas. Starring Howard Keel (Howard Masen), Nicole Maurey (Christine Durrant), Janette Scott (Karen Goodwin), Kieron Moore (Tom Goodwin), Mervyn Johns (Mr. Coker), Ewan Roberts (Dr. Soames), Janina Faye (Susan), Geoffrey Matthgews (Luis de la Vega).

WHAT IT'S ABOUT:

After a meteorite shower blinds most of mankind, ambulatory plants from outer space begin to prey on stricken humans. Vision preserved because his eyes were bandaged during the celestial event, Bill Masen escapes London and tries to connect with other survivors before the triffids overrun Earth. Meanwhile, marine biologists Tom and Karen Goodman, trapped in an isolated island lighthouse, search for a way to kill the voracious monsters. Ultimately, they are cornered, and discover quite by accident that sea water dissolves the monster plants. Battered but not beaten, humanity survives.

WHY IT'S IMPORTANT:

After the international success of MGM's *Village of the Damned*, it was only a matter of time before author John Wyndham's second greatest sci-fi novel reached the big screen. Perhaps even more so than his *Midwich Cuckoos*, *The Day of the Triffids* is ideally suited to a movie adaptation, offering meteorite showers, a world stricken with blindness, and ambulatory, man-eating plants as visual attractions.

Totally by accident, Philip Yordan's reasonably ambitious take (color and widescreen) wound up providing two simultaneous plotlines: survivor Bill Masen's eventful trek across a decimated Europe in search of organized reconstruction, and a husband/wife pair of marine biologists fighting for life in an isolated lighthouse. Story #2 was added when story #1 came up short, both in terms of running time and a convincing climax (only part of the original "Pied Piper" finale remains in the finished film). Instead of triffids being led into the ocean and dissolving, the trapped lighthouse keepers douse them with sea water – a more economical and suspenseful way to achieve the same outcome.

If all this sounds a little like *War of the Worlds*, it should: Yordan cannily lifts both the religious motif and Wells' method of "clean" extermination from the George Pal classic (water doesn't harm triffids in the book), which covers similar story and thematic terrain. He even turns his title beasties into extraterrestrials, an almost obligatory touch Wyndham managed to avoid. But *Triffids* has its own unique flavors. The desperate, hastily-conceived "story 2" might've played as awkward and out of place, but here it's used to creative advantage. After all, this is a global crisis, and covering more than one set of characters in one location seems entirely logical, even ahead of its time. Moreover, the lighthouse interludes are especially well-crafted (a juiced Freddie Francis jumping in), so viewers never feel short-changed when the plot shifts back to them. Like many movies shot in inferior Eastmancolor, *Day of the Triffids* eventually began to fade, losing much of its original visual vibrancy. Thanks to the ongoing efforts of professional restorer Michael Hyatt, however, Sekely's fondly-remembered "Day" will soon shine brighter than ever before.

The film begins spectacularly with a multi-colored meteorite shower. Several matte paintings were created for this brief but memorable sequence.

Countless triffids are born in an enormous crater. The little monsters literally push themselves out of the soil.

Coker (Mervyn Johns) and Bill Masen (Howard Keel).

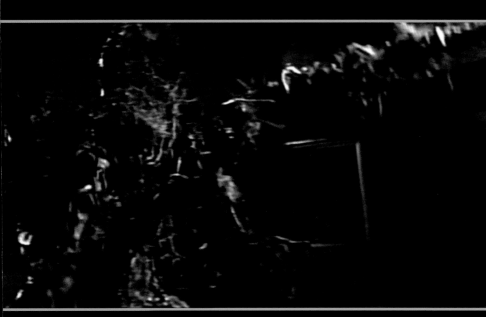

A triffid sneaks into the lighthouse, only to be slain by lance-wielding Goodman.

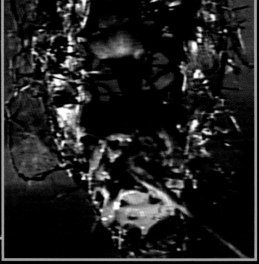

Masen tries to repel the triffids with fire and an electrically-charged fence.

Ultimately, it's ordinary sea water that saves humanity from extinction, dissolving the triffids in a frenzied bath of steam and slush. That's Kieron Moore as Goodman.

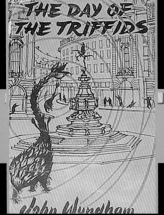

Triffids was based on a best-selling novel, which is significantly different in many ways. A new, 21st Century movie version is being prepared by director Sam Raimi.

SIXTIES SHOCK-O-RAMA

After an avalanche of black and white B-films in the 1950s, the "science fiction thriller" genre struck back a decade later with some startling innovations, such as widescreen and frequently garish color. Equally striking were the ultra-high concepts of relatively polished crowd pleasers like *The Day of the Triffids* ('62, OPPOSITE PAGE, featuring Janette Scott); and *X- The Man with the X-Ray Eyes* ('63, ABOVE), showcasing Oscar-winner Ray Milland (*The Lost Weekend*). INSERT: Dr. Xavier's X-Ray vision at work.

WHO MADE IT:

Alta Vista Productions/American International Pictures (U.S.). Director: Roger Corman. Producers: Roger Corman, James H. Nicholson, Samuel Z. Arkoff. Writers: Robert Dillon, Ray Russell, based on a story by Ray Russell. Cinematography (Pathe Color): Floyd Crosby. Music: Les Baxter. Starring Ray Milland (Dr. James Xavier), Diana Van der Vlis (Dr. Diane Fairfax), Harold J. Stone (Dr. Sam Brant), John Hoyt (Dr. Willard Benson), Don Rickles (Crane), Morris Ankrum (Mr. Bowhead), John Dierkes (Preacher), Dick Miller (Heckler), Jonathan Haze (Heckler).

WHAT IT'S ABOUT:

Experimenting on himself, Dr. James Xavier perfects a serum that enables him to see through solid objects. At odds with the medical community and even his friends, including Dr. Diane Fairfax, the driven scientist accidentally kills a colleague and becomes a wanted man. Still, the experiments continue, with Xavier becoming a slave to his fixation and a pawn of small-time bunko artist Crane. Hoping to secure large sums of money, he flees to Las Vegas with a reluctant Diane and uses his x-ray vision to make a killing. But the authorities close in, and Xavier, bruised and driven half-mad by the serum, confronts the real motive for his research...and kills himself.

WHY IT'S IMPORTANT:

Taking a break from his Poe adaptations, producer Roger Corman returned to science fiction with this tightly-scripted, thoughtful allegory, a fine showcase for Oscar-winning star Ray Milland. Personable but obsessed Dr. James Xavier is "closing in on the gods" with a chemical discovery that increases his visual perception astonishingly. This fixation guarantees *X*'s tragic denouement, smartly staged within a religious context. His need to "see all" is ultimately deemed blasphemous, resulting in a self-punishment of literally biblical proportions.

Corman's Poe regulars (cinematographer Floyd Crosby, art director Daniel Haller, composer Les Baxter) deliver a modern melodrama every bit as smart and stylish as their period horror confections, with multi-colored test tubes and beakers replacing red candlesticks and other ornate set decorations. Filtered POV shots are used for the x-ray vision sequences, and these eventually reach fever-pitch at a Las Vegas casino, as patrons become incandescent skeletons in Xavier's eyes. Two nifty sets of "final stage" contact lenses were developed for Milland, one with white pupils against black orbs, the second pair solid, glistening ebony.

Although not a first-tier classic, *X – the Man with the X-Ray Eyes* once again demonstrates Roger Corman's inherent class, colorful directorial style, and respect for intellectually challenging material. Whether Tim Burton's proposed remake will equal or surpass its inspiration remains to be seen, if you'll pardon the expression.

88 UNEARTHLY STRANGER 1963 (78) [1.66] ♂

TERRIFYING
WEIRD...MACABRE!
Unseen things out of
Time and Space!

**UNEARTHLY
STRANGER**

AN AMERICAN INTERNATIONAL PICTURE

Starring JOHN NEVILLE · GABRIELLA LICUDI · PHILIP STONE
Produced by ALBERT FENNELL · Directed by JOHN KRISH · Screenplay by REX CARLTON · A JULIAN WINTLE-LESLIE PARKYN PRODUCTION

WHO MADE IT:

Independent Artists/Anglo-Amalgamated (U.K.)/American International Pictures (U.S.). Director: John Krish. Producers: Albert Fennell, Leslie Parkyn, Julian Wintle. Writers: Rex Carlton, from a story by Jeffrey Stone. Cinematography (b/w): Reg Wyer. Music: Edward Williams. Starring John Neville (Dr. Mark Davidson), Philip Stone (Prof. John Lancaster), Gabriella Licudi (Julie Davidson), Patrick Newell (Clarke), Jean Marsh (Miss Ballard).

WHAT IT'S ABOUT:

Dr. Mark Davison begins to suspect that his wife is not human, probably a spy sent from another world to observe humans and possibly stop Davison's project, which involves star travel by sheer thought. Colleague John Lancaster is called in for an opinion, and he too observes things about Davison's wife Julie that seem to defy logic. Indeed, Julie truly is an alien, but a loving one with a conscience. Davison finally realizes that he is being targeted, but by another team member, Miss Ballard the secretary, who is also an extraterrestrial. She is finally destroyed by Davison and Lancaster; still, are there other camouflaged enemies in the world, ready to strike at us?

WHY IT'S IMPORTANT:

This is a strange movie. Shot in a handful of rooms and on a miniscule budget, *Unearthly Stranger* offers the *Body Snatchers*-like notion of a loved one being an extraterrestrial enemy, in this case the comely wife (Gabriella Licudi) of research scientist Mark Davidson (John Neville). But the film explores their relationship in a circuitous way, presenting some of Julie's low-key otherworldliness (she sleeps with her eyes open) before we even meet the character, or view her and her loving husband together in a relaxed domestic scene. The object of Davidson's advanced research is thoroughly bizarre to begin with: he hopes to visit other planets by simply "willing" the journey, a fanciful, somewhat preposterous notion that harkens back to pulp fantasies like *John Carter of Mars*. It's especially handy in a low-budget movie like this one, of course, since spaceships and other expensive hardware of the genre are not required. Director Krish tries to make up for this obvious deficiency with a hyper style of directing that amps up the urgency in already suspenseful sequences. A fascinating parallel to witchcraft mythology is the notion of tears scaring the flesh of evil beings, inspiring what is arguably the most compelling and memorable moment of *Stranger*. Even the cause of the sympathetic alien's tears, schoolchildren reacting with numbed terror upon seeing her and instinctively walking backward, makes for a disturbing scene. Best of all is the closing shot: after "bad girl" alien Jean Marsh bites the dust on a public street and leaves only empty clothes behind, a host of onlookers appear in a carefully composed and choreographed set-up, each well-chosen inquisitive face more disturbing than the last. Who among us is a friend, we wonder, who is an alien enemy?

Spare, but with the jolts and visual textures of a good nightmare, *Unearthly Stranger* explores familiar sci-fi thematic territory with a decidedly offbeat slant. Rarely seen today, it's a testament to what can be accomplished with a limited budget and a lot of moxie.

IT! THE TERROR FROM BEYOND SPACE 1958

WHO MADE IT:

United Artists (U.S.). Director: Edward L. Cahn. Producer: Robert E. Kent. Writer: Jerome Bixby. Cinematography (b/w): Kenneth Peach. Music: Paul Sawtell & Bert Shefter. Starring Marshall Thompson (Col. Carruthers), Shawn Smith (Ann Anderson), Kim Spalding (Col. Van Heusen), Ann Doran (Mary Royce), Dabbs Greer (Eric Royce), Paul Langton (Calder), Robert Bice (Purdue), Richard Benedict (Bob Finelli), Richard Hervey (Gino), Thom Carney (Kienholz), Ray Corrigan ("It").

WHAT IT'S ABOUT:

After the first expedition to Mars cracks up upon landing, a second ship is sent to pick up survivors. There is only one – Colonel Carruthers – and he is suspected of murdering his crewmates. Taking off for the return trip to Earth, no one notices a strange creature slipping aboard ship. But during the voyage home, this stowaway begins slaughtering crew members one-by-one, draining victims of all life fluid. Shipmates flee into the rocket's higher levels as the monster relentlessly pursues them, clawing his way upward through metal hatches. Bullets, gas bombs and even a bazooka fail to kill this bloodthirsty marauder, but he is finally suffocated when Carruthers hits on the idea of releasing all oxygen from the ship.

WHY IT'S IMPORTANT:

A treacherous alien planet... A rocketship returning to Earth... A bloodthirsty alien monster on board, slaughtering crew members one by one. It's an ingeniously simple premise for a sci-fi thriller, famously used in *Alien* but invented for this vest-pocket, surprisingly well-constructed B-movie. And even scripter Jerome Bixby can't help citing *The Thing from Another World* as a key influence, with desperate soldiers and scientists fighting for their lives against a seemingly invulnerable predator in a remote, claustrophobic environment.

Cahn wisely keeps his rubber-suited humanoid off-camera most of the time, settling for close ups of clawed hands and feet and the occasional full-body silhouette. This costume represents an upgrade for creature designer Paul Blaisdell, who had impressed Hollywood with beasties-on-a-budget for AIP quickies like *The She Creature* and *It Conquered the World*. His reptilian Martian suit is inhabited by former stuntman Ray (Crash) Corrigan, whose rather large and painfully visible chin was hastily transformed into an alien tongue by the resourceful on-set monster maker. Rounding out the serviceable cast are familiar character actors from this period, with lead Marshall Thompson appropriately dour as a space colonel wrongly accused of murdering his crewmates. Special credit should also be given to cinematographer Kenneth Peach and composers Paul Sawtell and Bert Shefter, who rework their emphatic score for *Kronos* (1957) to good effect.

Efficient and filmed with relative care, *It! The Terror from Beyond Space* takes a powerhouse premise and pretty much runs with it. The movie may not be blessed with Ridley Scott's eye for detail and textural beauty, but it's a harrowing, extremely entertaining nail-biter nonetheless.

Tidbit: Blaisdell's monster costume and the creature's distinctive heavy-breathing made a comeback of sorts in 1960's *Invisible Invaders*, also from United Artists.

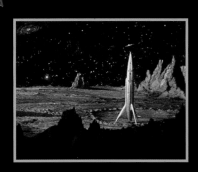

ABOVE: The second expedition to Mars is about to blast off for a return trip to Earth, suspected murderer Colonel Carruthers on board. This impressive matte painting was re-used in "The Invisible Enemy" episode of *The Outer Limits* (1964). RIGHT: Full view of "It." INSERT: Ominous shadows as "It" sneaks aboard the landed spaceship.

ABOVE, LEFT: Say goodbye to Bob Finelli (Richard Benedict). ABOVE: Spacemen use gas bombs on their bloodthirsty pursuer. LEFT, BOTTOM: They even try shooting him with a bazooka, never a good idea within a moving spaceship.

RIGHT: "It" makes scrap metal of another hatch as he claws his way up to the next level, seeking assorted human prey.

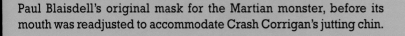

Paul Blaisdell's original mask for the Martian monster, before its mouth was readjusted to accommodate Crash Corrigan's jutting chin.

WHO MADE IT:

Genie Productions Inc./Emerson Film Enterprises (U.S.). Director: Wesley Barry. Producers: Wesley Barry, Edward J. Kay. Writer: Jay Simms. Cinematography (Eastmancolor): Hal Mohr. Music: Edward J. Kay. Makeup: Jack Pierce. Starring Don Megowan (Capt. Kenneth Cragis), Erica Elliot (Maxine Megan), Don Dolittle (Dr. Raven), George Milan (Acto, a clicker), Dudley Manlove (Lagan, a clicker), Frances McCann (Esme Cragis Milos), Malcolm Smith (Court), Richard Vath (Mark, a clicker), Reid Hammond (Hart), Pat Bradley (Dr. Moffitt).

WHAT IT'S ABOUT:

In a future contaminated by atomic radiation, human beings are an endangered species. To serve and ultimately replace them, relatively sophisticated, self-improving robots are incorporated into society. This prompts men to organize right-wing pressure groups to fight these intelligent machines, but the battle seems pointless. High in the Order of Flesh and Blood is outspoken Cragis, who learns, much to his initial horror, that he himself is the most advanced android ever devised, fully sentient and even capable of  procreation. It seems mankind will survive after all, but as a race of ultra-sophisticated androids.

WHY IT'S IMPORTANT:

Famous in cult circles as Andy Warhol's favorite science fiction movie, *Creation of the Humanoids* is barely a movie. With endless dialogue scenes and virtually no action, it plays more like an amateur stage production, even down to the mostly non-professional cast members. But Jay Simms' screenplay is unique and quite thought-provoking for its day, presenting robots as a stoic-faced minority group struggling against right-wing extremists, the last vestige of biological mankind decimated by atomic war. The clever racial slur "clickers" is used throughout, and questions of faith, physicality and essential human worth are addressed with an insight rarely found in a movie of this kind, let alone one that seems filmed in somebody's basement. Barrel-chested lead Don Megowan is a surprisingly effective spokesperson for humanity proper, evolving from narrow-minded bigot to progressive, emotion-feeling android during the course of events. And if Dr. Raven's whimsical reveal in the final moments is a tad cheeky – we're all robots, apparently, and just don't seem to realize it – most of *Humanoids'* scientific theorizing and philosophy is disarmingly logical, and quite welcome. Partial sets (the descending/ascending tubes) and costumes are leftovers from Universal's 1955 *This Island Earth*, and the greenish, pasty-faced robots with their metallic eyes were designed by veteran make-up wizard Jack (*Frankenstein*) Pierce. Like *Forbidden Planet*, Edward Kay's background music is electronic and atonal, as if it were composed by the "clickers" this movie ultimately celebrates.

THE MAN WHO FELL TO EARTH 1976 · 139 · 2.35 🎧

WHO MADE IT:

British Lion Film Corporation (U.K.)/Cinema 5 (U.S.). Director: Nicholas Roeg. Producers: Michael Deelay, Barry Spikings, Si Litvinoff, John Peverall. Writer: Paul Mayersberg, from the novel by Walter Tevis. Cinematography (color): Anthony B. Richmond. Music: John Phillips, Stomu Yamashta. Starring David Bowie (Thomas Jerome Newton), Rip Torn (Nathan Bryce), Candy Clark (Mary-Lou), Buck Henry (Oliver Farnsworth), Bernie Casey (Peters), Jackson D. Kane (Professor Canutti), Rick Riccardo (Trevor), Tony Mascia (Arthur), Linda Hutton (Elaine).

WHAT IT'S ABOUT:

An extraterrestrial arrives on Earth, takes the name of Thomas Newton and proceeds to amass millions through various business enterprises. Why? To build a spacecraft and rescue his imperiled family from their planetary drought. Although he comes close to achieving his goal, Newton is ultimately thwarted over the years by various factors, including efforts by the government to study him. He establishes close, enriching personal relationship with a few Earthly natives, trusting innocent Mary Lou among them. But in the end Newton is a beaten man, his unfinished ship destroyed, his hopes and dreams of reuniting with loved ones lost in a growing fog of alcoholism and disillusionment.

WHY IT'S IMPORTANT:

Going against the grain of traditional sci-fi movies but perfectly in tune with mid-'70s' sensibilities, Nicholas Roeg's *The Man Who Fell to Earth* is a bittersweet odyssey that makes full use of star David Bowie's inherent other-worldliness. As a clairvoyant alien on a life-or-death mission to save his family from a planetary drought, "Thomas Jerome Newton" unceremoniously arrives on our world and proceeds to make full use of capitalist America's logical advantages, like amassing fortunes through a series of commercial patents (his advanced science and technology coming in handy). As he builds a spaceship, Newton crosses paths and befriends a handful of agreeable humans, including business manager Farnsworth (Buck Henry), disillusioned, womanizing scientist Nathan Bryce (Rip Torn), and, most poignantly, a simple girl named Mary-Lou (Candy Clark). Heartbreaking memories of his eternally-waiting alien family slip in and out of Newton's psyche, even as the dark side of Earthly existence begins to manifest itself, threatening his all-important, increasingly elusive objective. Government forces eventually descend upon this gentle visitor, turning his already-compromised life into a living hell. Only the strained fellowship of Bryce and the innocent trust and passion of Mary-Lou give him a few fleeting moments of solace.

Relentlessly somber and often self-consciously poetic, Roeg's *Man* is nevertheless a compelling study of heartfelt hope gone awry, a cruel evaluation of sentient life that apparently applies to all planetary civilizations (a thoroughly deflated Newton confirms to Bryce that if the situation had been reversed, his own people would have been just as brutal to an alien visitor). Well that's what Newton says, anyway; his own gentle, considerate, ultimately Christlike actions suggest otherwise. About to be swallowed up by the comic strip pleasures of *Star Wars*, *Man Who Fell to Earth* still resonates as the last gasp of socially relevant, agreeably adult sci-fi downers produced in the wake of Kubrick's *2001*.

David Bowie
The man who fell to Earth

WHO MADE IT:

Dino de Laurentiis/Universal Studios (U.S.). Director: David Lynch. Producers: Dino de Laurentiis, Raffaella de Laurentiis, Jose Lopez Rodero. Writer: David Lynch, based on the novel by Frank Herbert. Cinematography (Technicolor): Freddie Francis. Music: Toto. Costume Design: Bob Ringwood. Starring Kyle McLahlan (Paul Atreides), Sting (Feyd Rautha), Jurgen Prochnow (Duke Leto Atreides), Sean Young (Chani), Jose Ferrer (Padishah Emperor Shaddam IV), Sian Phillips (Reverend Mother Gaius Helen Mohian), Francesca Annis (Lady Jessica), Brad Dourif (Piter De Vries), Richard Jordan (Duncan Idaho), Patrick Stewart (Gurney Halleck), Max Von Sydow (Doctor Kynes), Virginia Madsen (Princess Irulan), Kenneth McMillan (Baron Harkonnen).

WHAT IT'S ABOUT:

In a distant galaxy of the far future, two rival familes, the noble Atreides and the reprehensible Harkonnens, fight for control of planetary operations mining a vital drug known as Melange, or Spice, which is used by Guild Navigators to travel through space. After Duke Leto Atreides is assassinated by his evil opposite number, the Duke's endangered wife and son flee to the worm-infested desert of planet Arrakis and are befriended by various natives, called Fremen. Exposure to Melange endows young Paul Atreides with remarkable powers, including the ability to see into the future. Soon, fulfilling an ancient prophecy, he leads the giant worm-riding Freman in a spectacular assault on Arrakis' corrupt Emperor and his kill-crazy partners, the Harkonnens. Living legend Atredies prevails, and rain falls upon this world for the first time.

WHY IT'S IMPORTANT:

Many of my friends are angry that I've included this film among the Top 100, so disappointed were they with David Lynch's high profile crack at Frank Herbert's sprawling, celebrated science fiction opus. In truth, this ambitious interpretation should have spanned more than one film, as Herbert's dense mega-verse contains a plethora of sophisticated concepts and themes that barely resonate when presented to a bewildered audience in thumbnail form. Finally, Lynch even resorts to one of Hollywood's oldest storytelling tricks, thought-revealing voice-overs, as exotic, offbeat characters grapple with an assortment of escalating enigmas. In a film where people also happen to communicate psychically, this can be a problem. In all fairness, producer Dino de Laurentiis certainly spared no expense, providing *Dune* with awe-inspiring production values and (generally speaking) convincing special effects. The worms would certainly be handled with CGI technology today (much as they were in a '90s TV mini-series), but the energetic puppetry used here works just fine, and the final raid on the Emperor's palace, with countless optical effects and miniatures doing their job, is both thrilling and novel. As for the cast, Lynch assembles a small army of solid performers, with handsome Kyle MacLachlan front-and-center as *Dune*'s young, confident outcast prince, a leader with a most significant destiny. He is ably supported by Jurgen Prochnow as his proud, ill-fated father, Sian Phillips as the volatile Reverend Mother, Dean Stockwell as Doctor Yueh (the guilt-ridden Judas of this parable), Kenneth McMillan as ultra-gross, bloated Baron Harkonnen, and a pre-*Star Trek* Patrick Stewart portraying MacLachlan's intensely loyal, no-nonsense combat instructor. And that's just a sampling. With his stupendous *Lord of the Rings* trilogy of movies, Peter Jackson proved that dense, arcane material can indeed be dramatized with class and clarity, given enough running time. Lynch's film strives for a similar, large-canvas poetic sensibility, but winds up irritating its core audience with an overly complex, somewhat disjointed plot structure. All this said, *Dune* does manage to capture the astonishing scope of its extravagant subject, and the movie functions as a reasonable primer for anyone interested in reading the book. Another plus: Toto's awesome background music, supporting a memorable four-note main theme semi-borrowed from Ronald Stein's *Haunted Palace* score (1963).

The Royal Atreides (Kyle McLahlan, Jurgen Prochnow, Francesca Annis) must leave their native waterworld.

LEFT: Emperor Shaddam (Jose Ferrer) reports to his Guild Navigator. RIGHT: Baron Harkonnen (Kenneth McMillian).

RIGHT: "We have Worm Sign!" These massive behemoths of the Arrakis desert dominate *Dune*. Director David Lynch, famed for offbeat classics like *The Elephant Man* and *Blue Velvet*, was greatly displeased with his own movie. On the other hand, author Frank Herbert found much to enjoy in this lavish adaptation.

LEFT (A): Alia (Alicia Witt) revels in Paul Atreides' victory. LEFT (B): "I *will* kill him!" shouts hate-crazed Feyd Rautha (Sting). Atreides must face a final challenge from his vicious alter-ego.

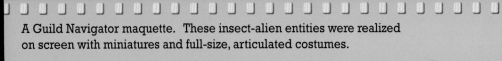

A Guild Navigator maquette. These insect-alien entities were realized on screen with miniatures and full-size, articulated costumes.

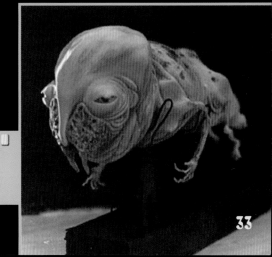

83

RED PLANET MARS 1952

WHO MADE IT:

United Artists (U.S.). Director: Harry Horner. Producers: Anthony Veiller, Donald Hyde. Writers: John L. Balderston and Anthony Veiller, based on a play by Balderston and John Hoare. Cinematography (b/w): Joseph Biroc. Music: Mahlon Merrick. Starring Peter Graves (Chris Cronyn), Andrea King (Linda Cronyn), Herbert Berghof (Franz Calder), Walter Sande (Admiral Bill Carey), Marvin Miller (Arjenian), Willis Bouchey (President), Morris Ankrum (Secretary of Defense Sparks), Orley Lindgren (Stewart Cronyn), Bayard Veiller (Roger Cronyn).

WHAT IT'S ABOUT:

The Cronyns, a husband-and-wife team of California scientists, make radio contact with planet Mars using a valve developed by a Nazi war criminal. Details of the advanced Martian culture have a devastating effect on Earth's politics and industry, and oddly inspiring religious messages from the red planet soon lead to the end of totalitarianism in Russia. Unfortunately for the Cronyns, the original valve inventor reappears and tells them that he faked all the galactic messages from a remote transmitting cabin. But a final, true message from Mars comes through at that very moment...

WHY IT'S IMPORTANT:

This movie is a fascinating anachronism. Despised by many because of its conservative religious dogma and red scare tactics, it also breaks interesting ground as the only '50s sci-fi melodrama to deal with the social and political impact of alien contact. Writer Balderston is determined to give his story a personal, even folksy ambience, very much in the style of William Wellman's "God's on the radio" social drama, *The Next Voice You Hear...* Scientists Chris and Lynda Cronyn are a happily married American couple complete with two kids and a Nazi-invented radio valve that enables them to transmit and receive messages from Mars. Before long, residents of the red planet are astounding everyone with their remarkable cultural and scientific advances, unintentionally giving us Earthlings the greatest inferiority complex of all time. Most 1950s sci-fi movies depict monstrous alien warships blasting cities to smithereens. *Red Planet Mars* saves some of its biggest salvos for despairing security chiefs, selfish union bosses and profit-minded Americans in general. Finally, with the introduction of those Christmas card-like religious messages in Act III, faith conquers faithlessness ("God Speaks from Mars"), causing totalitarian nations to tremble and fall before a reawakened populace.

Balderston balderdash, right? Absolutely. Then again... For every offensive pro-religion or flag-waving moment, *Mars* whips up an equally daring and imaginative social/scientific theory to conjure with. Jesus Christ a Martian? That's something we expect to hear in a semi-subversive Quatermass screenplay, not an early '50s conservative polemic. On balance, *Red Planet Mars* uses political and religious propaganda to fuel a fundamentally thought-provoking scenario that's worth checking out, if only to sneer at. Take your chances, and try to bring an open mind along.

2010: THE YEAR WE MAKE CONTACT 1984

116 2.20

WHO MADE IT:

Metro-Goldwyn-Mayer (U.S.). Director: Peter Hyams. Producers: Peter Hyams, Neil A. Machlis, Jonathan Z. Zimbert. Writer: Peter Hyams, based on the novel by Arthur C. Clarke. Cinematography (Metrocolor): Peter Hymans. Music: David Shire. Starring Roy Scheider (Dr. Heywood Floyd), John Lithgow (Dr. Walter Curnow), Helen Mirren (Tanya Kirbuk), Bob Balaban (Dr. Chandra), Keir Dullea (Dave Bowman), Douglas Rain (HAL 9000), Madolyn Smith (Caroline Floyd), James McEachin (Victor Milson).

WHAT IT'S ABOUT:

What became of Dr. Heywood Floyd's hush-hush mission to Jupiter in 2001? Astronaut David Bowman is officially classified as deceased, but is this really the case? These and other questions are asked by an uneasy alliance of American and Russian personnel on a journey to the spinning, still-orbiting spacecraft, with Floyd himself on this all-important mission. As the threat of war between the U.S. and the Soviet Union looms on Earth, Floyd and his colleagues from both countries must put aside suspicions and work on the enigma in their midst, which involves Jupiter's evolving moon and the mysterious alien monolith. The return of HAL-9000 and David Bowman figure into a metaphysical occurrence that will forever change life on Earth.

WHY IT'S IMPORTANT:

Forget about topping Kubrick's 2001; how does one even follow it? Peter Hyams came up with a subtly ingenious solution: follow Arthur C. Clarke's 2001 instead, and even bring author Clarke along for the creative ride. This sequel rightly casts Dr. Heywood Floyd as its distantly guilty protagonist, the man who launched 2001's Jupiter mission, played by William (Gorgo) Sylvester in Kubrick's film, and Roy Scheider here. More a scientist than a bureaucrat, Floyd is ideal as the decent, no-nonsense investigator of a phenomenon that keeps getting more interesting the longer he and his scientific colleagues stick around. Although the U.S.-Russia doomsday scenario would soon lose all potency on screen after the collapse of the Soviet government (unthinkable just a few years before), it does dovetail with some moments from Kubrick's film, and is perfectly serviceable as a suspense device. Humanity is always on the brink of catastrophic warfare and self-annihilation, even if the names of countries involved happen to change. Perhaps the most significant accomplishment of 2010 is the redemption of HAL-9000, who apparently "went crazy" and murdered most of the Discovery crew back in 2001. Arthur Clarke makes it very clear that HAL was ordered to lie by the White House, and his honest-by-design circuits couldn't handle this inherent immorality, so he "interpreted their orders as best he could." Guess 2001's HAL was right after all – it was "human error" that led to all the tech screw-ups/killings, not something deliberately malevolent on HAL's part. Another interesting element of continuity is the return of Keir Dullea as astronaut Frank Bowman, the man who grew old, then young again, in an austere, alien-controlled environment. Bowman and HAL are reunited in a charming scene at tale's end, as both disembodied entities face the cosmic unknown together, once again as friends. Smartly keeping the monolith as enigmatic as ever, even while adding some intriguing meat to extremely cherished bones, 2010: The Year We Make Contact is a commendable, handsome-made continuation of Arthur C. Clarke's vision. It's also a refreshing example of a sci-fi movie that doesn't require comic book-style action to maintain the viewer's interest.

35

81

JOURNEY TO THE FAR SIDE OF THE SUN 1969 (101) 1.85 ♂

aka Doppelganger

When in Southern California visit Universal Studios

MAN HAS CONQUERED THE MOON WITH THE EPIC APOLLO 11 FLIGHT! NOW TAKE ANOTHER MOMENTOUS JOURNEY!

YOU will meet yourself face-to-face...when Earth meets its duplicate in outer space!

"JOURNEY TO THE FAR SIDE OF THE SUN"

starring ROY THINNES · IAN HENDRY · LYNN LORING · PATRICK WYMARK · LONI von FRIEDL · HERBERT LOM

Screenplay by GERRY and SYLVIA ANDERSON and DONALD JAMES / Directed by ROBERT PARRISH / Produced by GERRY and SYLVIA ANDERSON A UNIVERSAL PICTURES LTD. PICTURE in TECHNICOLOR®

G Suggested for GENERAL audiences

WHO MADE IT:

J. Arthur Rank Film Distributors (U.K.)/Universal Pictures (U.S.). Director: Robert Parrish. Producers: Gerry & Sylvia Anderson, Ernest Holding. Writers: Gerry & Sylvia Anderson, Donald James. Cinematography (Technicolor): John Read. Music: Barry Gray. Starring Roy Thinnes (Colonel Glenn Ross), Ian Hendry (John Kane), Patrick Wymark (Jason Webb), Lynn Loring (Sharon Ross), Loni von Friedl (Lisa Hartmann), Franco De Rosa (Paulo Landi), George Sewell (Mark Neuman), Ed Bishop (David Poulson), Herbert Lom (Doctor Hassler).

WHAT IT'S ABOUT:

The discovery of a new planet in Earth's orbit prompts a hasty expedition. But when astronaut Glenn Ross lands on this world, he discovers that he's back on Earth, with everyone believing he aborted the mission. Before very long, Ross deduces that he is on the new planet after all, which happens to be an exact duplicate of Earth. An effort is made to return him to his rightful planet, but scientific mishaps result in the destruction of his spaceship and the base from which it was launched.

WHY IT'S IMPORTANT:

Long before science fiction movies became action flicks with exotic gimmicks, fantastic voyages and imaginative journeys of discovery pretty much characterized the genre's better moments. *Journey to the Far Side of the Sun* is a fine example of speculative fantasy in the late '60s, using the notion of a twin Earth to expose some interesting realities about our individual natures. One wishes the screenplay by Gerry & Sylvia Anderson delved even deeper into its troubled characters. But with unfaithful wives, reckless administrators and allegedly sterile astronauts as plot points, one should give credit where credit is due. *Journey* is post-*2001*, after all, and all major space-themed movies are automatically required to be relentlessly grown-up and enigmatic (*Star Wars* will change all this a decade later).

Star Roy Thinnes, perhaps best known as saucer-chaser David Vincent from TV's *The Invaders*, is persuasive as a nice-guy astronaut catapulted into an inexplicable conundrum; equally believable is Patrick Wymark as his bullish, no-nonsense project administrator, a role very much in the Quatermass-Donlevy tradition. With Universal backing this British-made space drama, studio production values are more than serviceable. Of course, no one will ever mistake an Anderson fx fest for Stanley Kubrick's approach to this genre, but the lovingly-crafted tinker-toy spacecraft are generally satisfying, and it's always fun to watch miniature sets blowing up.

X THE UNKNOWN 1956

Poster/photos: © 1956 Exclusive Films

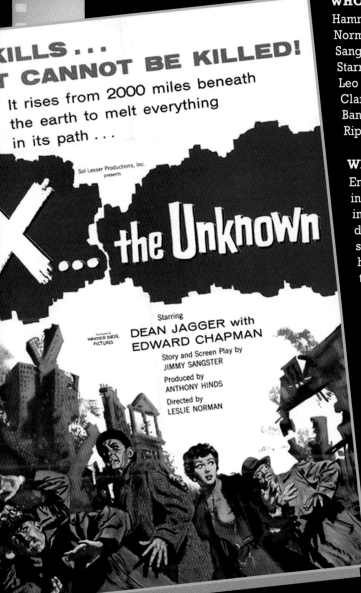

WHO MADE IT:

Hammer Films/Exclusive Films (U.K.)/Warner Bros. (U.S.). Director: Leslie Norman. Producers: Michael Carreras, Anthony Hinds. Writer: Jimmy Sangster. Cinematography (b/w): Gerald Gibbs. Music: James Bernard. Starring Dean Jagger (Dr. Adam Royston), Edward Chapman (John Elliott), Leo McKern (Inspector McGill), Anthony Newley ('Spider' Webb), Jameson Clark (Jack Harding), William Lucas (Peter Elliott), Peter Hammond (Lt. Bannerman), Marianne Brauns (Zena), Ian MacNaughton (Haggis), Michael Ripper (Sgt. Harry Grimsdyke), John Harvey (Major Cartwright).

WHAT IT'S ABOUT:

Enormous cracks appear in a Scottish field, prompting various authorities, including noted scientist Dr. Adam Royston, to investigate. Before long, bizarre, horrific deaths are reported in the vicinity; it seems some strange force that feeds on pure energy has emerged from the fissure and is now threatening to engulf a nearby atomic plant, along with a village filled with terrified locals. This creeping, sentient sludge knocks out communications and grows to alarming proportions as scientists and military men search desperately for a means of neutralizing it. Only an unusual effort by Dr. Royston manages to end the world-threatening crisis.

WHY IT'S IMPORTANT:

Offering a premise that borders on sheer insanity (radioactive mud with an intelligence), *X the Unknown* is a methodical, no-nonsense science class of a movie that deserves credit for the courage of its thoroughly bizarre convictions. Basically, director Les Norman was filming a Quatermass story (*The Creeping Unknown*, *Enemy from Space*) without Quatermass; in the professor's stead is smoothly persuasive Dr. Adam Royston, played with just the right amount of agreeable detachment by Oscar-winning American Dean Jagger. It's this actor's daunting task to make all the high-sounding and outlandishly preposterous theorizing somehow palatable, a job ultra-civilized Jagger pulls off impressively. In many ways, he's the opposite of bullish, charmless Prof. Quatermass, as interpreted in Guest's films by Brian Donlevy. Then there's the radioactive "monster" itself, very much inspired by Nigel Kneale's specific take on alien life: amorphous, sentient, deadly to all humans. At first, we only know of this thing's existence because of various gruesome casualties (deformed fingers and flesh melting off a skull are shock moments not easily forgotten). An entire scene is dedicated to Royston's grand theory, delivered with straightforward earnestness that undercuts inevitable qualms from sane listeners. Soon we all get to see what the good doctor is actually talking about: an implacable blob-like ooze sliming its way through Scottish fields and imperiling a small village. As is generally the case with Kneale scenarios, the hero scientist just happens to have a dandy new invention that saves the day, in this case a sophisticated force field that neutralizes atomic explosions (say what?). In any event, the monster mud is finally stopped in its messy "tracks." Like the sci-fi movies that inspired it, *X* benefits from night-for-night photography, freezing temperatures (breath vapor everywhere), and the "working class" British ambience that seems to categorize Guest's documentary-like procedural noirs. It's a style that has aged quite well, supported very nicely indeed by Jagger's fearless performance. Although derivative and super-talky, *X the Unknown* satisfies.

ROCKETSHIP X-M 1950

77 | 1.37

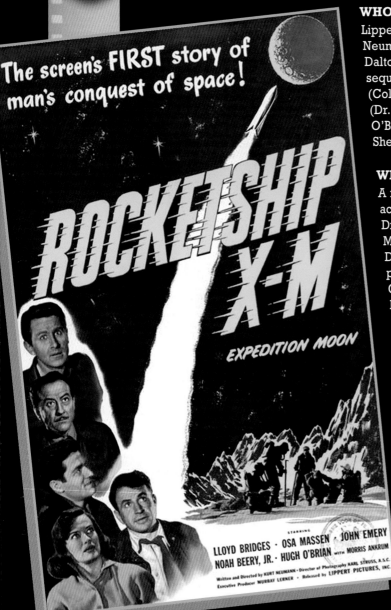

The screen's FIRST story of man's conquest of space!

ROCKETSHIP X-M

EXPEDITION MOON

STARRING
LLOYD BRIDGES · OSA MASSEN · JOHN EMERY
NOAH BEERY, JR. · HUGH O'BRIAN with MORRIS ANKRUM

Written and Directed by KURT NEUMANN · Director of Photography KARL STRUSS, A.S.C.
Executive Producer MURRAY LERNER · Released by LIPPERT PICTURES, INC.

WHO MADE IT:

Lippert Pictures (U.S.). Director: Kurt Neumann. Producers: Kurt Neumann, Murray Lerner. Writers: Kurt Neumann, Orville Hampton, Dalton Trumbo (uncredited). Cinematography (b/w with tinted sequences): Karl Struss. Music: Ferde Grofe. Starring Lloyd Bridges (Col. Floyd Graham), Osa Massen (Dr. Lisa Van Horn), John Emery (Dr. Karl Eckstrom), Noah Beery Jr. (Major William Corrigan), Hugh O'Brian (Harry Chamberlain), Morris Ankrum (Dr. Ralph Fleming), Sherry Moreland (Martian Girl).

WHAT IT'S ABOUT:

A rocketship crew sets out to land on the moon, but an unexpected accident in space propels them to Mars instead. On the red planet, Dr. Karl Eckstrom and his team discover the remains of an advanced Martian civilization, destroyed ages ago by nuclear war. Descendents of survivors live on as blinded and scarred mutants, primitive beings with a passion to kill. Only crew members Floyd Graham and Lisa Van Horn manage to escape the bloodbath and blast away safely in their spaceship, but an absence of fuel causes them to crash-land on earth. Undaunted by this tragedy, project administrator Dr. Ralph Fleming vows to continue with space exploration.

WHY IT'S IMPORTANT:

Forget competition between America and the Soviets... the real space race was between George Pal's *Destination Moon* and Kurt Neumann's decidedly less ambitious *Rocketship X-M (Expedition Moon)*, the two movies that officially launched Hollywood's sudden love affair with futuristic subjects in the 1950s. Neumann's flick blasted off the launching pad first, complete with limited fx and tinted sequences to represent red planet Mars. Excuse me, Mars? Yep. Unable to compete with Pal's considerable production advantages, Neumann and company gamely substitute wild imagination for scientific plausibility. *Destination Moon* has the flavor of a sober documentary, while *Rocketship X-M* provides breathless viewers with an annihilated Martian city, bloodthirsty mutants, and a tragic attempt to return home. These are two very different movies, both starting off with the same fundamental premise.

Rocketship nearly gave us dinosaurs, as well. Instead, Neumann wisely expanded the "tragic death of the Martians" subplot, which lends his little adventure some sophistication and pathos. Dealing with these discoveries are five stalwart explorers, unencumbered by *Destination Moon*'s bulky spacesuits (lighter protection is acceptable for Martian field trips). Somehow, actor Lloyd Bridges managed to avoid sci-fi for most of his lengthy career (TV's *Sea Hunt* star was offered *Star Trek*'s lead in '66, but declined). For relatable laughs, *X-M* serves up a lovable Texan (Noah Berry) instead of the traditional Brooklynite. And finally, Neumann includes a component that Pal's team couldn't possibly top: Osa Massen as Dr. Lisa Van Horne, the first '50s female into space and, in certain ways, the forerunner of Sigourney Weaver's Ellen Ripley.

Distinguished by its downbeat discoveries and tragic ending, *Rocketship X-M* is an unexpected oddity posing as a commercial confection. It's almost as if solemn, message-addicted Stanley Kramer were making a sci-fi picture (he eventually will, nine years later).

TOP: The ship just before its fateful launch into space. RIGHT: Expedition leader Dr. Eckstrom (John Emery) briefs reporters as his four fellow crew members look on. That's Dr. Fleming (Morris Ankrum) with his back to us.

Is a woman's place in space? Graham (Lloyd Bridges) has his doubts. But that doesn't stop him from falling in love with Lisa (Osa Massen).

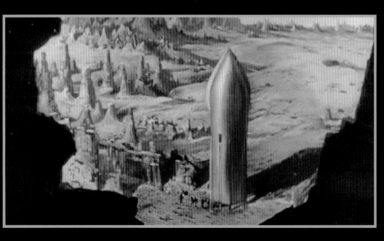

The discovery of a destroyed Martian civilization is a high point of *Rocketship XM*. Descendents of surviving mutations are blind and scarred by atomic radiation.

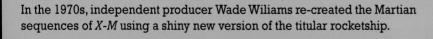

In the 1970s, independent producer Wade Wiliams re-created the Martian sequences of *X-M* using a shiny new version of the titular rocketship.

78 BACK TO THE FUTURE 1985 ✓ ⏲116 [1.37] 🎧

WHO MADE IT:

Amblin/Universal Studios (U.S.). Director: Robert Zemeckis. Producers: Kathleen Kennedy, Frank Marshall, Steven Spielberg, Neil Canton, Bob Gale. Writers: Robert Zemeckis & Bob Gale. Cinematography (Technicolor): Dean Cundey. Starring Michael J. Fox (Marty McFly), Christopher Lloyd (Dr. Emmett Brown), Lea Thompson (Lorraine Baines), Crispin Glover (George McFly), Thomas F. Wilson (Biff Tannen), Claudia Wells (Jennifer Parker), Marc McClure (Dave McFly), Wendie Jo Sperber (Linda McFly), George DiCenzo (Sam Baines), J.J.Cohen (Skinhead), Casey Siemaszko (3-D), Billy Zane (Match), Harry Waters Jr. (Marvin Berry).

WHAT IT'S ABOUT:

Driving the DeLorean time machine invented by eccentric pal Doc Brown, teenager Marty McFly suddenly finds himself back in the 1950s. He accidentally gets in the way of a chance meeting between his parents, both teenagers themselves at this point, and ultimately realizes that if he doesn't find a way to bring them together, he will simply cease to exist. Poor Marty has his hands full warding off the amorous advances of his eventual mother while trying to make his father less of a nerd and therefore more appealing. He finally succeeds and time-warps out of the 1950s, having created a much better life for himself and his family in the here-and-now.

WHY IT'S IMPORTANT:

As the '80s rolled along, Steven Spielberg was happily re-visiting all thematic and conceptual aspects of the genre he loved most, science fiction and fantasy. Time travel hadn't been tapped by either himself or buddy George Lucas yet, so *Back to the Future*, helmed by Robert (*Who Framed Roger Rabbit?*) Zmeckis, became Mr. S's vehicle for family-style temporal adventure. Not surprisingly, it embraces feel-good whimsy and pseudo-sitcom sensibilities (TV comedy star Michael J. Fox replaced original lead Eric Stoltz, whose acting style proved too deep and realistic for the breezy tone required here). Adding to the perverse atmosphere is *Taxi* regular Christopher Lloyd as local wacko scientist Doc Brown, inventor of the plutonium-powered, time-traveling Delorean that gets young Marty McFly (Fox) into a mess of trouble.

It's the nature of that trouble that gives *Back to the Future* its resonance: Marty accidentally prevents his parents from meeting, which threatens to negate his own existence if he doesn't set things straight. The notion of Marty's teenage mom being turned on by her own son was titillating for audiences, and both Michael Fox and Lea Thompson manage to pull off these funny scenes without getting too creepy. But far more interesting is the notion of being able to "fix" your parents' inherent personal problems, which will not only make them happier and more successful, but will also provide a better life for yourself, ultimately. It's a "high concept" notion so darned clever it practically borders on genius.

Combining elements of *It's a Wonderful Life* and *The Twilight Zone*, *Back to the Future* scores as a charmingly conceived sci-fi confection, a pleasant surprise at the time of release. Two far less charming and less successful sequels were produced almost immediately by Spielberg and company, proving that some stories work best when they aren't pointlessly extended.

Local mad scientist Emmett Brown (Christopher Lloyd) and teen friend Marty McFly (Michael J. Fox) take Brown's DeLorean Time Machine for a road test...with predictably bizarre complications.

LEFT: Like Dr. Brainard from Disney's *Flubber* movies, Doc Brown is an eccentric genius who complicates the lives of those in his orbit with outrageous, over-the-top inventions. Actor Lloyd graduated from TV sitcoms to big screen sci-fi movies (he also played the grim-faced Klingon murderer of Captain Kirk's son in *Star Trek 3*). Although time travel stories are commonplace in films and television, *Back to the Future* found an ingratiating new way to make the concept personal, while never losing sight of its Disney-style whimsy.

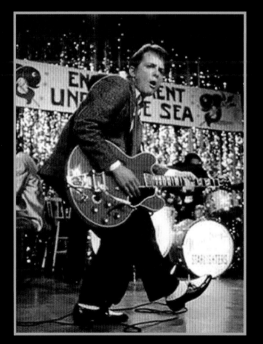

ABOVE: A key part of *Back to the Future*'s appeal is time traveler Marty's desperate efforts to forge a romantic relationship between his parents (Crispin Glover, Lea Thompson), who are teenagers in the '50s.

LEFT: Frustrated rocker Marty outdoes himself at the big 1950s dance, only to discover that his brand of music is a tad too advanced for Eisenhower-era teens.

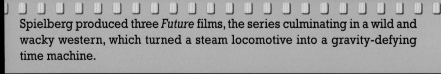

Spielberg produced three *Future* films, the series culminating in a wild and wacky western, which turned a steam locomotive into a gravity-defying time machine.

A WORLD BEYOND IMAGINATION!

ADVENTURE BEYOND BELIEF!

WHO MADE IT:

Columbia Pictures (U.K./U.S.). Director: Cy Enfield. Producer: Charles H. Schneer. Writers: John Prebble & Daniel Ullman, Crane Wilbur, from a novel by Jules Verne. Special Visual Effects: Ray Harryhausen. Cinematography (Eastmancolor): Wilkie Cooper. Music: Bernard Herrmann. Starring Michael Craig (Captain Cyrus Harding), Joan Greenwood (Lady Mary Fairchild), Michael Callan (Herbert Brown), Gary Merrill (Gideon Spilitt), Herbert Lom (Captain Nemo), Beth Rogan (Elena Fairchild), Percy Herbert (Sgt. Pencroft), Dan Jackson (Neb Nugent).

WHAT IT'S ABOUT:

Union soldiers escaping from prison steal a hot-air balloon and are buffeted by a horrendous storm. They land on an uncharted island populated by strange foliage and enormous monsters, the handiwork of infamous Captain Nemo. Experimenting with ways of increasing man's food supply, the renegade scientist finally reveals himself to his castaway "guests" when the unstable island faces volcanic destruction. Although these unlikely allies manage to raise a sunken pirate ship as a means of escape, Nemo becomes trapped within his Nautilus submarine, and perishes.

WHY IT'S IMPORTANT:

Mysterious Island functions as a solid sequel to Disney's 1954 *20,000 Leagues Under the Sea*, although the two films are not officially connected. In some ways, Cy Enfield's muscular outdoor adventure is even smoother than Fleischer's widescreen opus; it's more cinematic, characters have greater range, and Harryhausen's celebrated effects are breathtaking without being intrusive. Although essentially a survival melodrama, *Mysterious* is ultimately Captain Nemo's show and personal soapbox: it's his "for the betterment of mankind" mutations that characterize the island, essentially a giant petri dish for experiments that have something in common with Prof. Deemer's goals in 1955's *Tarantula*. Nemo's distain for military violence contrasts with a war being fought "to set men free," setting up the subtle but effective ideological duel between himself and Captain Harding (Michael Craig). Distinguished Herbert Lom is perfect as the great Sea Lion in Winter, still dedicated to his world-changing ideals, but humbled a bit by time and ongoing disappointment. Meanwhile, on the technical end, re-creating Nemo's super-submarine Nautilus posed some unique problems for Harryhausen. Everyone (including Ray) wanted a return to Disney's very specific look, inside and out, which had become iconic as a result of *20,000 Leagues*. What they settled on was a most efficient compromise; the inoperative Nautilus doesn't flaunt its Disney-inspired flavors, and remains docked in a colorful grotto for all of its screen time.

A solid, well-crafted adventure-fantasy told with style and sweat, *Mysterious Island* is arguably the best movie Harryhausen and company ever made. For once, characterization and cinematic values are not sacrificed on the altar of stop motion set-pieces, and the striking fx cease often enough for a truly enjoyable story to emerge. As always, composer Bernard Herrmann elevates the proceedings with a magnificent symphonic score, his third for a Harryhausen film.

Trivia tidbit: Columbia had previously visited Verne's *Mysterious Island* in a 1950s serial that bore little resemblance to this 1961 effort, or to Verne's novel, for that matter.

ABOVE, LEFT: After escaping a Confederate prison via balloon, Union soldiers face monstrous mutations on Captain Nemo's unstable volcanic island. RIGHT: Herbert Lom as Nemo. Originally, James Mason was asked to reprise his famous Disney take on the character. BELOW: Nemo leads the castaways to his grotto-docked Nautilus.

Bernard Herrmann composed a variation of "Flight of the Bumble Bee" for *Island*'s giant honeycomb sequence.

Famed for his animation effects, Ray Harryhausen is a master of movie miniatures in general, including the hot-air balloon showcased in Act I.

HARRYHAUSEN GLAMOR: BETH ROGAN

Or, the girl we'd most like to be sealed inside a giant beehive with. A young English model/actress with only a handful of films to her credit, Beth Rogan nevertheless made a lasting impression as Lady Elena Fairchild, stranded aristocrat-turned-scantily costumed island sprite. Although she'd be eclipsed by an iconic Raquel Welch just a few years later (Harryhausen's own *One Million Years B.C.*, 1966), the lovely Rogan's dolphin-smooth legs and ample bosom sent many a baby boomer's temperature rising. BELOW: Pursued by one of Captain Nemo's pet projects, an enormous bee, Elena and Herbert (Michael Callan) take refuge inside the creature's hive.

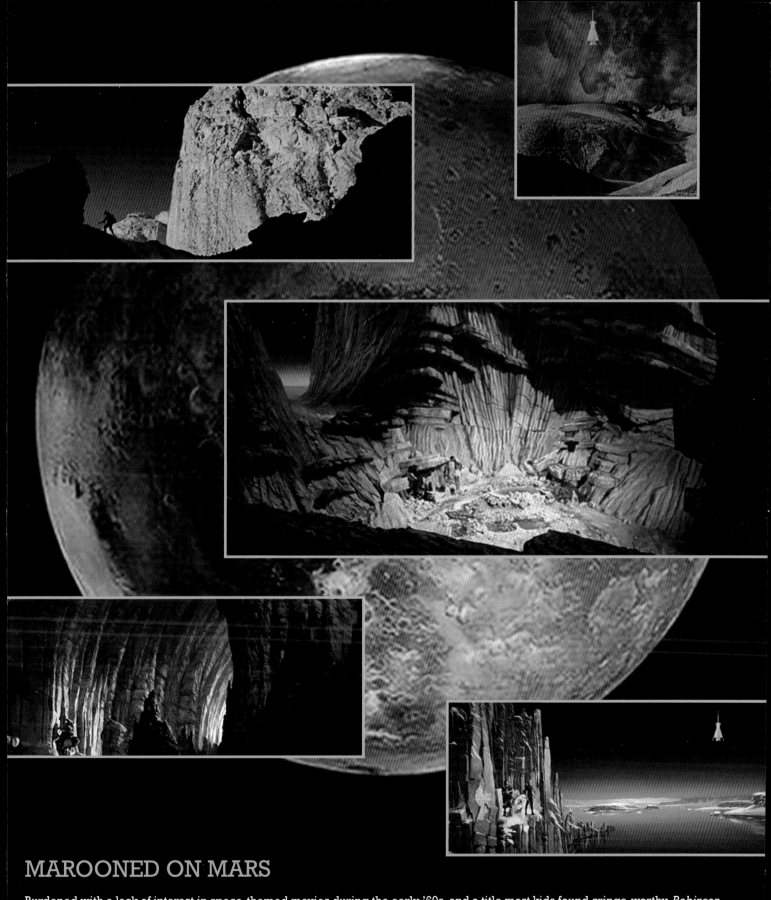

MAROONED ON MARS

Burdened with a lack of interest in space-themed movies during the early '60s, and a title most kids found cringe-worthy, *Robinson Crusoe on Mars* failed to find an audience in its day. But after decades of TV showings, this agreeable George Pal-influenced oddity has become something of a second-tier sci-fi classic. With just a fraction of today's special effects budget, director Byron Haskin and his team did a masterful job passing off Hollywood sound stages, matte paintings and actual desert locations for seething Martian landscapes. Above images chronicle an astronaut's forced landing on the red planet, his explorations, a temporary oasis, tunnel-walking under the celebrated canals, and his final rescue at the polar ice cap.

76 · ROBINSON CRUSOE ON MARS 1964 · (110) · 2.35

WHO MADE IT:

Paramount Pictures (U.S.). Director: Byron Haskin. Producers: Aubrey Schenck, Edwin F. Zabel. Writers: Ib Melchoir, John C. Higgins, based on a novel by Daniel Defoe. Cinematography (Technicolor): Winton C. Hoch. Music: Van Cleave. Starring Paul Mantee (Commander Christopher 'Kit' Draper), Victor Lundin (Friday), Adam West (Col. Dan McReady), The Wooley Monkey (Mona).

WHAT IT'S ABOUT:

His astronaut buddy killed in a crash landing, Commander 'Kit' Draper finds himself marooned on Mars. He uses his training and considerable ingenuity to survive on the inhospitable sphere, his only companion a wooly monkey. Eventually, Draper encounters alien miners from another galaxy, who use fantastic starships and slave workers to achieve their plundering goals. The astronaut rescues

and befriends Friday, an escaped slave, and the two of them manage to elude capture and endure various climactic hardships before a rescue ship from Earth finally arrives.

WHY IT'S IMPORTANT:

Back in 1955, Paramount produced a semi-realistic movie about mankind's "final frontier," called it *Conquest of Space*, hired Byron Haskin to direct and Van Cleave to write the celestial music score. It failed big time, resulting in the exile of sci-fi producer George Pal. Almost a decade later, Paramount decides to take a second crack at a semi-realistic movie about planetary landings, and calls it (wince) *Robinson Crusoe on Mars*. The studio hires Byron Haskin to direct and Van Cleave to write the celestial music score. And although Pal is nowhere near the Paramount premises at this point, the molds for his *War of the Worlds* spaceships still are, so they're promptly pressed into use again with some entertaining differences. Guess what? This movie flops just as badly. Welcome to Hollywood, kids! (Next stop for Paramount and space opera: TV's *Star Trek* in '66).

Rugged Paul Mantee is totally convincing in the demanding lead role of stranded astronaut Draper, a decent, resourceful guy who simply wants to get home. But *Mars* has a few bizarre surprises up its technological sleeve. After almost an hour of semi-documentary NASA-esque procedurals, the movie makes an abrupt shift into weird science territory, dishing up fantastic harvesting starships that seem to move at warp speed, a race of mysterious alien miners, and human-like slaves held in check by glowing wrist cuffs. At film's end, however, a more sober tone returns, and both spaceman and alien sidekick Friday (not to mention scene-stealer Mona the monkey) are picked up by Earthly rescuers.

Filmed at Death Valley National Park, with rocky vistas enhanced by optically-added crimson skies, *Robinson Crusoe on Mars* is a good movie that actually improves with age. Although it did little to enhance sci-fi's reputation at the box office in '64, it has since achieved cult status and continues to attract new fans.

THX-1138 1971

86 2.35

WHO MADE IT:

Warner Bros. (U.S.). Director: George Lucas. Writers: George Lucas, Walter Murch. Producers: Francis Ford Coppola, Edward Folger, Lawrence Strurhahn. Cinematography (Technicolor): Albert Kihn, David Myers. Music: Lalo Schifrin. Starring Robert Duvall (THX), Donald Pleasence (SEN), Don Pedro Colley (SRT), Maggie McOmie (LUH), Ian Wolfe (PTO), Marshall Efron (TWA), Sid Haig (NCH), John Pearce (DWY), Gary Alan Marsh (CAM).

WHAT IT'S ABOUT:

In a dehumanized 25th Century, the population lives underground in a constantly monitored environment, with residents drugged and conditioned to a limited, easily controllable existence. Factory worker THX-1138 runs afoul of the law when he falls in love with roommate LUH 3417 and makes her pregnant. Battling stoic robot police and finally escaping from imprisonment, renegade THX is joined by an illegal programmer and an upbeat hologram. Finally, his determination undiluted, THX manages to elude his metallic pursuers and climbs to the surface, facing a blazing, welcoming sun.

WHY IT'S IMPORTANT:

Star Wars fans might be surprised at the astonishing level of cinematic sophistication on display in *THX-1138*, George Lucas' relentlessly adult feature incarnation of his well-received student film. Produced by friend and admirer Francis Ford Coppola, the movie horrified Warners execs when it was initially screened; they couldn't follow the convoluted and at times indecipherable plot, viewing this apparent failing as a commercial deathblow (they were right about that). At a time when American cinema was changing from studio-system confection to independent-style, European-influenced art house efforts made by the "film school" generation, techno-driven *THX* consistently challenges viewers, and sometimes that challenge becomes a bit much. Even so, for a sci-fi movie made in 1970, it remains profoundly ahead of its time.

Robert Duvall is terrific as the fly in tomorrow's ointment. His character dares to defy 25th Century convention by refusing to take drugs (used to control the population) and having sex with his roommate LUH, which results in an illegal pregnancy. He manages to escape from confinement and, with the aid of an illegal programmer (played to perfection by Donald Pleasence) and an amiable hologram (Don Pedro Colley), defies this underground "peeping tom" society and ultimately escapes from it. Several critics have considered *THX*'s grim indictment of techno-dominance as something of a sequel to Kubrick's *2001*, but that would be shortchanging Lucas' fearless, always-on-display originality. *THX-1138* has its own unique vibe, an agreeably challenging, frequently oft-putting ambience totally in keeping with its depressing subject matter.

Best scenes: the love-making between THX and LUH; punishment by staff-wielding robot police; the final chase and escape.

The Future is here.
THX 1138

Warner Bros. presents THX 1138 · An American Zoetrope Production · Starring Robert Duvall and Donald Pleasence · with Don Pedro Colley, Maggie McOmie and Ian Wolfe · Technicolor® · Techniscope® · Executive Producer, Francis Ford Coppola · Screenplay by George Lucas and Walter Murch · Story by George Lucas · Directed by George Lucas · Music by Lalo Schifrin · Produced by Lawrence Sturhahn · Warner bros. Kinney company GP

74 THE ROAD WARRIOR 1981

94 | 2.20

aka Mad Max II

In the future, cities will become deserts, roads will become battlefields and the hope of mankind will appear as a stranger.

THE ROAD WARRIOR

"THE ROAD WARRIOR" A KENNEDY MILLER PRODUCTION
Starring MEL GIBSON Music by BRIAN MAY
Written by TERRY HAYES, GEORGE MILLER with BRIAN HANNANT
Produced by BYRON KENNEDY Directed by GEORGE MILLER

WHO MADE IT:

Warner Bros. (U.S.). Director: George Miller. Producer: Byron Kennedy. Writers: Terry Hayes, George Miller, Brian Hannant. Cinematography (b/w/color): Dean Semler. Music: Brian May. Starring Mel Gibson (Mad Max Rockatansky), Bruce Spence (The Gyro Captain), Michael Preston (Pappagallo), Max Phipps (The Toadie), Vernon Wells (Wez), Kjell Nilsson (The Humungus), Emil Minty (The Feral Kid), Virginia Hey (Warrior Woman), William Zappa (Zetta), Arkie Whitely (Captain's Girl), Steve J. Spears (Mechanic), Syd Heylen (Curmudgeon).

WHAT IT'S ABOUT:

In the aftermath of a future ravaged by nuclear war, rag-tag humans fight for survival on the road, with gasoline being the prize possession. Max is a man who lost his wife and a piece of his humanity during this conflict; now he is a nomadic, almost mythic figure, traveling the wastes and occasionally interacting with other desperate survivors. He makes a deal for gas with members of a small group fighting to preserve their community from sadistic marauders, but his selfish ways ultimately backfire. After some serious soul searching, Max becomes this group's remarkable lead driver, defeating their enemies and helping to set in motion the return of civilization. He remains an almost legendary hero to those who remember the event.

WHY IT'S IMPORTANT:

The early '80s was an exciting period for sci-fi/fantasy movie fans; several blockbusters by Steven Spielberg and George Lucas had transformed the genre, mating it with high-powered "rollercoaster" special effects and an action movie/video game sensibility that persists to this day, for better or worse. A couple of directors followed groundbreakers Steven and George into this crowd-pleasing zone, most notably Ridley Scott and James Cameron. But also making a name for himself was Australian helmer George Miller; few people saw the original *Mad Max*, but its sequel, *The Road Warrior*, was a significant Warner Bros. release meant to capitalize on the public's fascination with "fast, with all the trimmings" fantasy films. "If you thought the high-speed chase in *Raiders* was something, wait'll you see what this picture offers!" was pretty much the reason why most people bought a ticket for *Blade Runner* (eventual superstar/social pariah Mel Gibson was an unknown at this point). What they got was a surprisingly textural, occasionally poetic vision of a ruined future and the rag-tag survivors who inhabit it. Granted, the road/chase sequences are thrilling, offering heart-stopping edits, furious "how did they do that?" camerawork and exhilarating point of view shots from the perspective of speeding vehicles. But it's the film's bookend device that lingers in the mind, narrated (we eventually learn) by the grown-up Feral Child we meet at the encampment. Somehow, a vibrant youngster growing up in this monstrous, violent and lawless world resonates with subtle tragedy, adding dimension and Cameron-style textural weight to what might otherwise be the latest David Carradine/Roger Corman *Death Race* flick.

Consistently imaginative and ultra-exciting, *Road Warrior* purged the wholesome Disney element from its creative mix, while maintaining the serial-inspired wipes and bouncy military themes of George Lucas' *Star Wars* movies. It's almost as if director Miller was saying, "Hey, I can make one of these, but without that extra spoonful of sugar." He ultimately did, and we moviegoers enjoyed the grittier flavor.

WHO MADE IT:

United Artists (U.S.). Director: Philip Kaufman. Producer: Robert H. Solo. Writer: W.D. Richter, based on the novel "The Body Snatchers" by Jack Finney. Cinematography (Technicolor): Michael Chapman. Music: Denny Zeitlin. Starring Donald Sutherland (Matthew Bennell), Brooke Adams (Elizabeth Driscoll), Jeff Goldblum (Jack Bellicec), Veronica Cartwright (Nancy Bellicec), Leonard Nimoy (Dr. David Kibner), Art Hindle (Dr. Howell, DDS), Lelia Goldoni (Katherine Hendley), Kevin McCarthy (Dr. Miles J. Bennell), Don Siegel (Taxi Driver), Stan Ritchie (Stan).

WHAT IT'S ABOUT:

Strange spores from another world take root in San Francisco's rich earth. Before long humans find that their bodies are being duplicated by this alien life form, which can imitate everything but emotions. At first, people feel alienated from their secretly reborn loved ones, but soon more and more residents are "taken over." Heath inspector Miles Bennell is persuaded by employee Elizabeth Driscoll that something malevolent is taking place, but local psychiatric guru Dr. Kibner chalks the whole thing up to anxiety and the  breakdown of family values. Soon, Miles and Elizabeth are literally on the run, winning some victories for ever-loving humanity, but ultimately losing the war for their souls.

WHY IT'S IMPORTANT:

Philip Kaufman's remake of Don Siegel's 1956 classic is a compelling, intelligently-crafted suspenser, easily establishing a very specific creative identity of its own while acknowledging and honoring the original film throughout. Set in San Francisco, this new study of alienation and the precious importance of human emotion offers a terrific ensemble: reliable genre vets Donald Sutherland, Jeff Goldblum, Veronica Cartwright and even Leonard Nimoy do full justice to Kaufman's take on Finney's seminal tale. We live through the horror of losing someone to replication along with distraught, mystified and ultimately terror-stricken Brooke Adams, not-so-secretly coveted by Health Inspector boss and loyal guy-pal Sutherland. Together they try to fathom this monstrous mystery and struggle to survive what amounts to an insidious, all but invisible global invasion. Without breaking *Body Snatchers'* relentless forward motion, Kaufman deftly explores the escalating, semi-surreal paranoia of his protagonists, using visual devices (close-ups of running feet, hand-held photography) and sophisticated sound techniques to convey the increasingly alien world that surrounds them. And *Snatchers'* special make-up work doesn't stink, either. Although primarily a suspense thriller, the movie recognizes its "horror/sci-fi" obligations, providing some truly spectacular physical effects sequences of the bogus alien bodies taking form, starting with the blooming of their outsized flower petals. Producer Robert Solo even springs for a self-contained outer space sequence played under the opening titles, as viewers take part in a solar-windswept journey from the pod's home planet to our unsuspecting blue marble. A fine example of doing something exactly right on a limited budget, Kaufman's *Invasion* hits home with an imaginatively-staged exploration of human paranoia, while at the same time winking at classic film buffs who happen to know the 1956 original (even Kevin McCarthy gets a second chance to be hysterical).

RODAN 1957

72 · 1.37 ·

aka Radon, Rodan the Flying Monster

Poster/photos: © 1956 Toho Co., Ltd.

WHO MADE IT:

Toho (Japan)/DCA (U.S.). Director: Ishiro Honda. Producers: Tomoyuki Tanaka, Frank King, Maurice King. Writers: Takeshi Kimura, Takeo Murata, Ken Kuronuma, David Duncan. Cinematography (Eastmancolor/Technicolor): Isamu Ashida. Music: Akira Ifukube. Starring Kenji Sawara aka Sahara (Shigeru), Yumi Shirakawa (Kiyo), Akihiko Hirata (Professor Kashiwagi), Akio Kobori (Police Chief Nishimura), Minosuke Yamada (Chief Osaki), Yoshifumi Tajima (Izeki).

WHAT IT'S ABOUT:

Miners are slain by monstrous giant insects who eventually threaten the population at large. But these creatures are insignificant when compared to the enormous prehistoric flying reptiles who also emerge from the center of the Earth. Soon Japan is buzzed by the airborne giants, and major cities fall victim to their devastating attacks. Taking refuge in a volcanic mountainside, both Rodan and his mate are finally slain in an explosion of fire and lava after authorities use rockets to force the volcano to erupt.

WHY IT'S IMPORTANT:

There are Japanese monster movies, and then there is the original *Godzilla* (1954) and *Rodan* (1956). These two expertly-crafted sci-fi noirs have so little in common with the campfests that followed in the '60s and '70s that to mention them in the same breath seems almost blasphemous. *Rodan* accomplished the rare feat of following *Godzilla* with a film just as powerful and memorable in its own way. One of the very few '50s noirs to use blazing Technicolor effectively (*Slightly Scarlet* and *Niagara* also come to mind), *Rodan* soaks up every micro-particle of atmosphere from its clammy, sewer-flooded mine tunnels, infesting them with monster caterpillars and other unpleasant distractions. Rodan's egg-hatching, depicted in a feverdream flashback, plays like a quick trip to Hell ("...most sickening sight"...). And once the flying monsters are out in the open, even in broad daylight, textured attack sequences and city burnings are given the same stark, uncompromising treatment. Pacing is even faster in the American King Bros. version, anticipating the rapid-fire editing flourishes of their next major monster movie, *Gorgo*. Killing off the Rodans with a volcanic eruption is another clever move, bringing the prolonged existence of these majestic creatures full-circle. Making brilliant use of a miniature, lava-spewing mountain, it's at once cinematically thrilling and unashamedly poetic.

Rodan was released stateside in 1957, which turned out to be a very big year for flying monsters at the movies. *The Deadly Mantis* was spreading its hummingbird-like wings over at Universal, while the space-sired *Giant Claw* (a beaky buzzard) was gaudily nesting on Manhattan landmarks over at Columbia. Not surprisingly, Ishiro Honda's innovative, meticulously-crafted *Rodan* soared above them all.

For the record, the Japanese edition of this film runs slightly longer, and has a minimal music score, which was replaced with familiar stock cues for English-language release. There are additional fx shots of both the giant caterpillars and the flying monsters, which were probably cut because wires and cables were plainly visible.

Tidbit: Stock footage from *Rodan*, including shots of the flying monster itself, turned up in later sci-fi movies, including Columbia's *Valley of the Dragons* (1961).

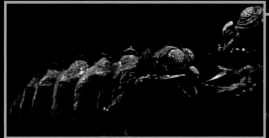

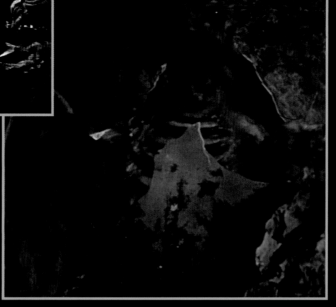

TOP: A pair of outsized caterpillars (or "Meganurons") battle to the death. These frightening underground sequences were clearly inspired by the giant ant attacks from Warner Bros.' *Them!* (1954). Eventually the resuscitated Rodan winds up feeding on these killer bugs, giving startled viewers a clear sense of the reptile's size.

LEFT: Birth of a monster... The infant Rodan hatches from its giant egg deep below ground. Notice the difference in design between baby beast and full-fledged adult. BELOW: Kenji Sawara (Sahara) as Shigeru, fear-frenzied witness to the nightmarish event.

Rodan and his mate succumb to the fire and fury of an erupted volcano in the film's spectacular, strangely compelling conclusion. An attempt is made to parallel the love story between Shigeru and Kiyo with the inseparable Rodans, "strongest, swiftest creatures who ever lived."

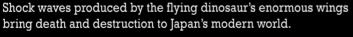

Shock waves produced by the flying dinosaur's enormous wings bring death and destruction to Japan's modern world.

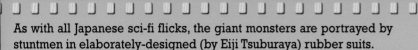

As with all Japanese sci-fi flicks, the giant monsters are portrayed by stuntmen in elaborately-designed (by Eiji Tsuburaya) rubber suits.

Novel time-travel adventure with brawny heroes and busty future babes...

71

WORLD WITHOUT END 1956 80 2.55

CINEMASCOPE'S
FIRST SCIENCE-
FICTION THRILLER
HURLS YOU INTO
THE YEAR 2508!

WHO MADE IT:

Allied Artists (U.S.). Director: Edward Bernds. Producer: Richard Heermance. Writer: Edward Bernds. Cinematography (Technicolor): Ellsworth Fredericks. Music: Leith Stevens. Starring Hugh Marlowe (John Borden), Nancy Gates (Garnet), Nelson Leigh (Dr. Eldon Galbraithe), Rod Taylor (Herbert Ellis), Shawn Smith aka Shirley Patterson (Elaine), Lisa Montell (Deena), Christopher Dark (Henry 'Hank' Jaffe), Booth Coleman (Mories), Everett Glass (Timmek), Stanley Fraser (Elda).

WHAT IT'S ABOUT:

A team of space explorers break the time barrier and crash-land on Earth of the distant future. Soon they learn that a devastating nuclear war caused humanity to divide itself: stone age-like mutations now prowl the landscape, while advanced humans live below the Earth's surface in a protected environment. The explorers insist that mankind reassert itself and reclaim the Earth's surface, but this creates division among their cautious hosts. After a vicious frame-up is exposed, everyone works together in a common effort to defeat the savages and re-start human civilization.

WHY IT'S IMPORTANT:

Time travel was rare in 1950s sci-fi movies. A commendable entry in this genre is Edward Bernds' mostly-forgotten and underrated *World Without End*, which sends an iconic spaceship (seen in a few films already) on a reasonably captivating, time barrier-smashing adventure into the unknown. One really can't blame Bernds and company for shamelessly borrowing H.G. Wells' vision of a future divided into two cultures: one gentle and peace-loving (for the most part), the other bestial, like some mutated version of primitive man. The stalwart space explorers reek a bit of dated machismo, which may color this film for some viewers. But these four stranded travelers are in truth separate individuals, some with tragic back stories. And one can certainly forgive the entertaining presence of broad-shouldered Rod Taylor, who'd soon be taking an official trip to a Wellsian future with producer George Pal.

In addition to the pleasures of various characters, from sexy Vargas-style babes to skulking villains (Booth Coleman in a showy role), this movie looks damn good in Technicolor, its elongated CinemaScope frame soaking up every last luminous detail. We are reminded of Pal's well-produced films, even down to the Leith Stevens score that ranks among his most hum-worthy. Not exactly a classic but always worth a gander, *World Without End* remains an energetic attempt to explore some new (for '56) sci-fi ideas, and plainly deserves credit for doing so.

Best scenes: the spaceship whipped by a savage time warp; the first mutant attack, discovering the terrible truth at a cemetery; big reveal of the futuristic corridor; building a bazooka; preparing for a bright future on the surface of Earth (epilog).

Tidbit: Director Edward Bernds would return to widescreen sci-fi with *Queen of Outer Space* (1958), a Zsa Zsa Gabor vehicle that utilizes stock footage and props from *World Without End*.

Additional tidbit: Booth Coleman, who plays the wiley Mories, eventually wound up playing the equally crafty Dr. Zaius in the short-lived *Planet of the Apes* TV series.

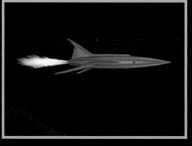

The opening scenes of *World Without End* introduce us to Dr. Galbraithe's rocketship crew, which includes Herbert Ellis (Rod Taylor) and John Borden (Hugh Marlowe). Christopher Dark as Hank Jaffe is privy to the film's most emotionally-wrenching dialogue ("My wife and children died... ages ago.")

Galbraith and his crew discover that non-mutated humans are living a meager existence within futuristic tunnels.

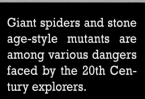

Giant spiders and stone age-style mutants are among various dangers faced by the 20th Century explorers.

A re-creation of the *World Without End* rocketship model, originally created for 1951's *Flight to Mars*.

WHO MADE IT:

Universal-International (U.S.). Director: Jack Arnold. Producer: William Alland. Writers: Harry Essex, Arthur A. Ross, Maurice Zimm. Cinematography (b/w): William E. Snyder. Music: Hans J. Salter, Herman Stein, Henry Mancini (all uncredited). Special makeup: Bud Westmore, Chris Mueller, Jack Kevan, Millicent Patrick. Starring Richard Carlson (Dr. David Reed), Julia Adams (Kay Lawrence), Richard Denning (Dr. Mark Williams), Antonio Moreno (Carl Maia), Nestor Paiva (Lucas), Whit Bissell (Dr. Edwin Thompson), Bernie Gozier (Zako), Henry Escalante (Chico), Ricou Browning (Underwater Creature – uncredited), Ben Chapman (Land Creature – uncredited).

WHAT IT'S ABOUT:

In an Amazon lagoon, a scaly, amphibious Gill Man is captivated by the girl on a scientific expedition. Scientists David Reed and Mark Williams try to capture this unique life-form, but they have different agendas: Reed seeks to increase scientific knowledge, Williams wants glory at any price. Polluting the lagoon with rotonone does indeed lead to the monster's capture, but he soon escapes and claims more lives, Williams among these victims. Although Reed is successful in removing a log placed across the lagoon as a barrier, Kay is abducted by the Creature and brought to his subterranean grotto. It takes several bullets to slow the Gill Man down during her rescue, but Reed allows him to escape into the murky depths of the Black Lagoon.

WHY IT'S IMPORTANT:

Unlike Universal's pre-war gothics, *Creature from the Black Lagoon* is firmly rooted in the hyper-rational, atomically-aware 1950s. If a Devonian man-fish truly does exist, then he should be captured and studied, thereby paving the way for a "new world of the future." When Richard Carlson aka Dr. David Reed says stuff like this with science class authority, we hang on every well-delivered word.

Almost inevitably, producer Alland and his scenarists borrow heavily from the plotline and thematics of *King Kong*, with Kong's unforgettable city attack saved for a potential second *Creature* feature. The beauty and beast motif has a frustrated Kay (Julia Adams) sandwiched between her distracted male admirers, all the while recoiling from a genuine suitor who happens to have a penis-shaped cranium. Much has been written about the sexual symbolism of this movie in general, and a certain swimming sequence in particular. Yes, it does indeed resemble a "stylized representation of sexual intercourse" when the Gill Man glides gracefully beneath Adams' inviting body (her stunt double, actually). Cool imagery, but this movie has some other worthwhile fish to fry, if you'll pardon the expression. There are potent themes of white science versus black, along with safety for others (David) facing off against reckless ambition (Mark). And dropping cigarette butts in the lagoon while polluting it with an unstable chemical sends shivers up contemporary spines in a way surely never intended by the filmmakers.

Scientifically, there is far less likelihood of an aquatic humanoid than, say, a Yeti. But if such a missing link should exist, it would probably resemble what Jack Kevan and his team of Bud Westmore-approved designers conjured up. Supported by a stylish, well-directed and finally appreciated sci-fi thriller, the age-resistant Gill Man will probably be scaring/delighting monster movie audiences for eons to come.

ABOVE: Creation, complete with a Big Bang in 3D, results in a newly-born Earth, as presented by Universal's fx department. BELOW: Scientists get a gander at the fossil claw that inspires their expedition. Director Jack Arnold imbues his monster movie with subtle symbolism, mostly on display in the Gill Man-Kay swimming duet.

The nighttime attack on Dr. Maia's camp is one of the film's best-remembered set-pieces.

Bud Westmore and Jack Kevan apply some finishing touches to the Gill Man head. The iconic monster was designed by studio artist Millicent Patrick.

THE SCREEN'S GREATEST GARGOYLE

Even in this hi-tech age of Aliens and Predators, most Hollywood make-up artists choose 1954's Creature from the Black Lagoon as the greatest full-body monster character ever conceived. ABOVE, RIGHT: the less-detailed "underwater" costume worn by swimmer Ricou Browning. OPPOSITE PAGE: the photogenic "land suit" inhabited by a much taller Ben Chapman, seen here abducting co-star Julie Adams. OP. PAGE INSERT: Fully-outfitted Browning is prepared for test shooting at Universal.

WHO MADE IT:

Ameran Films/Columbia Pictures (U.K./U.S.). Director: Nathan Juran. Producer: Charles H. Schneer. Writers: Nigel Kneale, Jan Read , based on the story by H.G. Wells. Cinematography (Lunacolor): Wilkie Cooper, Harry Gillam. Music: Laurie Johnson. Starring Edward Judd (Arnold Bedford), Martha Hyer (Katherine 'Kate' Callender), Lionel Jeffries (Joseph Cavor), Miles Malleson (Dymchurch Registrar), Norman Bird (Stuart), Betty McDowall (Margaret Hoy), Peter Finch (Bailiff's Man – uncredited).

WHAT IT'S ABOUT:

A U.N. exploratory expedition on the moon leads to the discovery of Victorian-era artifacts, left behind by a man still living. On Earth, aged Arnold Bedford explains to reporters how he, girlfriend Kate, and next-door scientist neighbor Dr. Cavor made an unorthodox trip to the moon almost a century earlier. Applying anti-gravity Cavorite to the panels of a small sphere, they fashioned a workable spaceship and landed on the lunar surface. But within the moon existed a race of advanced, insect-like creatures, who viewed Earthly knowledge of space travel as a threat. Arnold and Kate manage to escape and return to Earth, while Cavor remains with the germ-vulnerable moon beings – and, while nursing a cold, eventually wipes out their entire civilization.

WHY IT'S IMPORTANT:

Like all of Harryhausen's Columbia films from this period, *First Men in the Moon* is a well-crafted, stylishly presented take on a fanciful classic. The choice of scenarist Nigel Kneale to co-write the screenplay was a canny one; Britain's premiere science fiction writer, he is oddly suited to this tale of insect humanoids and the threat these lunar inhabitants pose to unsuspecting Earthly visitors. Lionel Jeffries gives one of his typically over-the-top performances (Cavor's played straight in Wells' book), but his nervous fussiness grows on the viewer, becoming charming and ultimately sympathetic, as he pleads humanity's shaky case before the implacable High Lunar. Stalwart Edward Judd was already an old hand at sci-fi by 1964, and Martha Hyer, still a major Hollywood star, probably figured that *Journey to the Center of the Earth* didn't hurt Arlene Dahl's reputation, so what the hell.

Not surprisingly, Ray Harryhausen's animation effects are stupendous, and featured for the first time in full CinemaScope. The giant caterpillar (or "lunar calf") appears to have been designed for widescreen, and the paneled sphere hurtling through space is a miraculous recreation of Wells' concept. Perhaps most unnerving are the stop-motion Selenites, particularly the Grand Lunar, with his bloated cranium and mellifluous voice.

Smart, stylish and a great deal of fun, *First Men in the Moon* is the last truly memorable Harryhausen flick. The times they were a changin' circa mid-'60s, *Planet of the Apes* and *2001* were just a few years off, and the master of dynamation would eventually return to tried-and-true fantasy subjects (dinosaurs on the loose, Arabian/mythological monsters) for the remainder of his spectacular career. But as a colorful farewell to the once-flourishing Wells/Verne movie genre, it doesn't get much better than this commendable take on *First Men*.

Tidbit: It was composer Bernard Herrmann who recommended that colleague Laurie Johnson (*Dr. Strangelove, I Aim at the Stars*) score the film when Herrmann himself was unavailable.

The film's bookend structure, with Victorian artifacts inexplicably discovered on the moon by a current U.N. expedition, is pure Nigel Kneale. *First Men* is the last of the period-style sci-fi movies (1954-64), ending a trend that allowed major studios to explore the genre with the same respect and production values given to "normal" motion pictures.

An aging Bedford (Edward Judd) recalls his fantastic lunar trip, made with scientist Cavor and girlfriend Kate.

The Selenites consider Earthly knowledge of space travel a threat to their civilization.

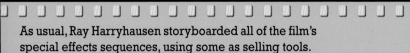

As usual, Ray Harryhausen storyboarded all of the film's special effects sequences, using some as selling tools.

59

68 THIS ISLAND EARTH 1955

87 2.00

THE SUPREME EXCITEMENT OF OUR TIME!

IN COLOR BY TECHNICOLOR

THIS ISLAND EARTH

2½ YEARS IN THE MAKING!

starring JEFF MORROW · FAITH DOMERGUE · REX REASON with LANCE FULLER · RUSSELL JOHNSON

DIRECTED BY JOSEPH NEWMAN · SCREENPLAY BY FRANKLIN COEN AND EDWARD G. O'CALLAGHAN · PRODUCED BY WILLIAM ALLAND · A UNIVERSAL-INTERNATIONAL PICTURE

WHO MADE IT:

Universal-International (U.S.). Director: Joseph M. Newman. Producer: William Alland. Writers: Edward G. O'Callaghan, Franklin Coen, based on the story "The Alien Machine" by Raymond F. Jones. Cinematography (Technicolor): Clifford Stine. Music: Herman Stein, Hans J. Salter, Henry Mancini (all uncredited). Starring Jeff Morrow (Exeter), Rex Reason (Dr. Cal Meacham), Faith Domergue (Dr. Ruth Adams), Lance Fuller (Brack), Russell Johnson (Steve Carlson), Douglas Spencer (The Monitor), Richard Deacon (Saucer Pilot – uncredited), Regis Parton (Mutant – uncredited).

WHAT IT'S ABOUT:

Nuclear scientist Cal Meacham is tested by a mysterious group that sends him equally mysterious plans for a futuristic communications device. Cal builds the machine, and is soon accepted into a secret fraternity of scientists gathered together by Exeter. In truth, this high-domed gentleman is an alien from the planet Metaluna, ordered to abduct physicists and make use of their knowledge to save his endangered home world. Meacham and colleague Ruth Adams are whisked away via flying saucer and brought to Metaluna, which is now losing its war with neighboring planet Zaghon. But it's too late to help, and, after some tense moments with irate leaders and menacing mutants, the Earth people are fortunate enough to be returned home by Exeter, who crashes his saucer, and himself, into the ocean.

WHY IT'S IMPORTANT:

Although it would be eclipsed by Metro's *Forbidden Planet* a mere year later, *This Island Earth* enjoys its own comfortable reputation as a diverting, even intriguing space opera with absolutely beautiful studio production values. Like its short story inspiration, the movie begins with a mystery worthy of an exotic spy tale: just who are these melancholy geniuses with enlarged/indented foreheads and wavy white hair? Why are scientists of Cal Meacham's "aptitude" being tested, and for what unstated purpose? Eventually these issues and others are earnestly addressed by sympathetic Metalunian Exeter (Jeff Morrow), a character somewhat inspired by Michael Rennie's Klaatu from *The Day the Earth Stood Still*. Ordered to infiltrate human society, he's a sucker for Earth culture (Mozart, anyone?) and has developed some serious misgivings about his scientist-gathering mission. Nevertheless, by the middle of Act II, he's off and flying into deep space, abducted nuclear physicists in tow.

The visit to Metaluna is brief, but memorably filled with mass-destruction, arrogant leaders getting theirs, and lobster-clawed mutant monstrosities running amok. The planet's dramatic incineration, viewed from a safe distance, allows Exeter to bid farewell with an appropriately poetic epitaph. He'll have a few more earnestly poignant observations ("I'm afraid my wounds can never be healed") before crashing his saucer into the sea in an extended, especially effective aerial shot worthy of *The Longest Day*.

Ironically, most movie audiences of 1955 seemed to prefer black-and-white invasion shockers to colorful (and far more expensive) galactic excursions, so very few sci-fi films with this level of ambition were tried again until a decade later. But as an Eisenhower-era glimpse of the universe, literally glowing with visual imagination, *This Island Earth* remains an iconic essential.

Tidbit: Co-stars Jeff Morrow and Rex Reason would re-team a year later for Universal's *The Creature Walks Among Us*.

An outer space travelogue in luminous Technicolor, *This Island Earth* was Universal's most ambitious science fiction project of the 1950s. With a relatively generous budget, producer William Alland took on the considerable challenge of depicting a futuristic planet under siege, at war with another advanced alien civilization. This meant complex miniature work and optical composites in just about every space-related shot were required.

ABOVE: an Interociter at work.
RIGHT INSERT: dodging a meteor.

Jeff Morrow (Exeter) and Rex Reason (Cal Meacham)

On war-torn Metaluna, viewers get a big whiff of the arrogant Monitor, "supreme head of our government," and have an even juicier time with the crab-clawed, bulbous-brained Mutant. Bred as slave workers, these towering insectoids enjoy only limited screen time, but were memorable enough to become instant sci-fi icons.

Cast members relax on the saucer set. That's future Mel Cooley Richard Deacon as Ship's Commander, way in the back.

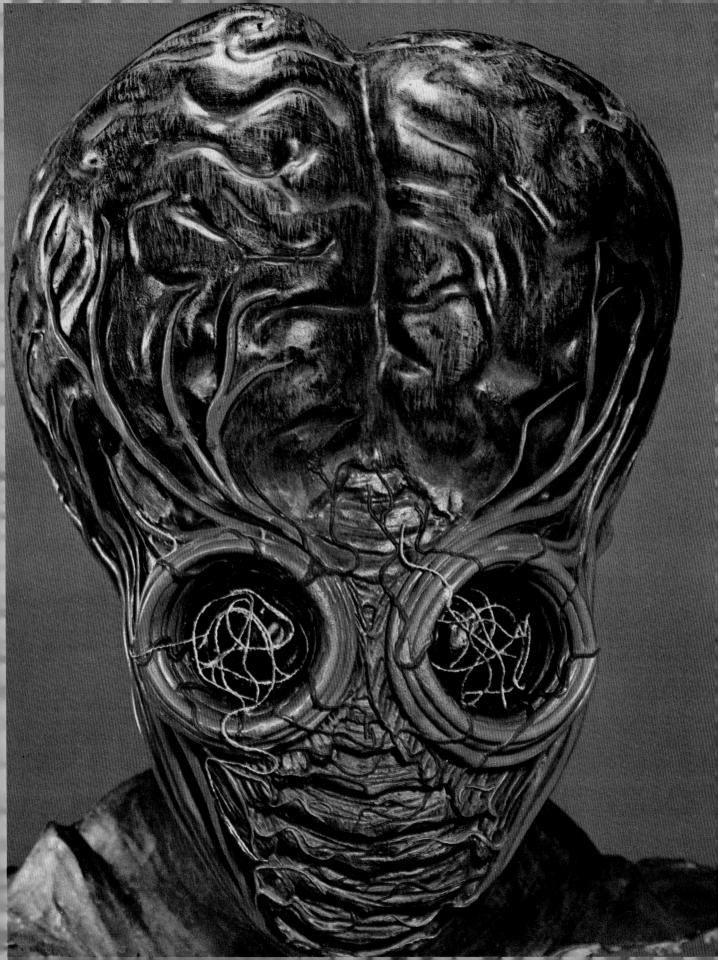

DECADE OF THE BEMs

…Bug-Eyed Monsters, to be precise. Some of the most audacious movie aliens ever conceived were born in the 1950s. Seeking a new kind of relationship is the titular terror from Paramount's *I Married a Monster from Outer Space*, fearlessly designed by Charles (*War of the Worlds*) Gemora. OPPOSITE PAGE: *This Island Earth*'s big-brained Metaluna Mutant, one of the most iconic extraterrestrials from the Eisenhower era. This headpiece was specifically designed for only two shots in the movie, each of them smoky close-ups; the creature's segmented mouth was refitted with a more sophisticated version that throbbed (INSERT, BOTTOM), thanks to air compression from off-screen operators.

In the mid-1960s, enterprising mask manufacturer Don Post acquired this original *This Island Earth* movie mold from Universal, and has been providing lucky collectors with first generation latex pulls ever since. The Mutant featured in all long shots of the film (see page 61) sports an even larger cranium.

Love and the not-so-single alien, with great rubber monsters...

67 **I MARRIED A MONSTER FROM OUTER SPACE** 1958 1.85

Poster/photos © 1958 Paramount Pictures

WHO MADE IT:

Paramount Pictures (U.S.). Director/Producer: Gene Fowler Jr. Writer: Louis Vittes. Cinematography (b/w): Haskell B. Boggs. Music: Paramount Stock Library. Starring Tom Tryon (Bill Farrell), Gloria Talbot (Marge Bradley Farrell), Peter Baldwin (Officer Hank Swanson), Robert Ivers (Harry Phillips), Chuck Wassil (Ted Hanks), Valerie Allen (Hooker), Ty Hungerford aka Hardin (Mac Brody), Ken Lynch (Dr. Wayne), Maxie Rosenbloom (Max Grady), John Eldredge (Police Captain Collins), Alan Dexter (Sam Benson), James Anderson (Weldon), Jean Carson (Helen Rhodes).

WHAT IT'S ABOUT:

Marge Bradley marries sweetheart Bill Farrell, unaware that Farrell is actually a shape-shifting alien that caught and replaced her fiancée sometime earlier. Soon, other members of the community are substituted with aliens, part of a full-scale invasion effort. Marge becomes suspicious, follows Bill into the night, and watches him enter a landed spaceship. Most disbelieve her fantastic stories. Meanwhile, the alien disguised as Bill begins to feel the power of human emotions, including love, even as a last-minute band of  believers attacks the spaceship and its monstrous crew members. Ultimately, Bill and the other captive humans are rescued, and the fleeing aliens must look elsewhere for a planet to inhabit.

WHY IT'S IMPORTANT:

Part *Invasion of the Body Snatchers*, part *It Came from Outer Space*, this minor studio offering has earned some notable critical praise over the years. "Don't be fooled by the title," warned TV Guide's capsule review back in the '70s. "This one's a neat yarn..." And, truth to tell, it is. Alien shape-shifters were hardly new to post-war movie audiences, but the marriage angle was dramatically different, even unexpectedly salacious when viewed with a naughty wink.

Director/Producer Gene Fowler Jr. wisely builds this offbeat tale of intergalactic deception and personal reawakening around the growing suspicions of newlywed Marge Bradley Farrell (Gloria Talbot). It's a fairly unnerving *Rosemary's Baby*-style plot trajectory, with few of the locals believing distraught, inevitably paranoid Madge. Fowler wisely explores both sides in this strange study of marriage, providing the "masquerading alien" with a semi-plausible, borderline tragic arc. Once exposed to Earthly emotions, Bill's double begins to understand the true meaning of love... and marriage. *Monster* is indeed lucky to have rugged but sexually-ambivalent Tom Tryon as the bewildered e.t., torn between his natural, detached impulses and unexpected feelings of human compassion.

66

E.T. THE EXTRA-TERRESTRIAL 1982 √ (115) [1.85] ♂

WHO MADE IT:

Amblin Entertainment/Universal Pictures(U.S.). Director: Steven Spielberg. Producers: Kathleen Kennedy, Melissa Mathison, Steven Spielberg. Writer: Melissa Mathison. Cinematography (color): Allen Daviau. Music: John Williams. Starring Dee Wallace (Mary), Henry Thomas (Elliott), Peter Coyote (Keys), Robert MacNaughton (Michael), Drew Barrymore (Gertie), K.C. Martel (Greg), C. Thomas Howell (Tyler), Erika Eleniak (Pretty Girl).

WHAT IT'S ABOUT:

A diminutive extraterrestrial is stranded on Earth when his people are forced to take off in their spaceship. Pursued by Earthly authorities, E.T. is drawn to the lights of suburbia and makes his way to a small family's backyard. He ultimately befriends a lonely little boy named Elliott. At first, the child treats him like a beloved pet, but before long Elliott begins to realize the significance of his new friend, and helps him escape from relentless U.S. government scientists. Responding to a desperately-rigged communications device, E.T.'s people finally return and pick him up, but not before the grateful alien gives his little earthly benefactor a heartfelt hug.

WHY IT'S IMPORTANT:

Inspired in large part by the golden aura of Disney family fare, *E.T.* provides its celebrated director with an opportunity to thoroughly embrace and ultimately define "feel good" sci-fi, blurring the distinction between futuristic parable and heart-tugging fairy tale. It was also a clever way of resurrecting the long-dormant "boy and his dog" genre (e.g., *Lassie Come Home*) in a more sophisticated, cinematically flamboyant package. The kind of homespun warmth Mr. Spielberg dabbled with in *Close Encounters* he completely mines here. Although Dee (*The Howling*) Wallace is top-billed as a mostly oblivious mom, the movie really belongs to E.T. designer Carlo Rambaldi and the trio of wide-eyed child actors who interact with this awkward, leathery, anything-but-cute alien botanist. Most of the film's humorous set-pieces may play as semi-cloying or sitcom-like for 21st Century viewers, but back in an era of relative innocence, audiences found themselves totally enamored, rejecting the dark, bleak pleasures of Ridley Scott's *Blade Runner* that very same summer in favor of Spielberg's far more endearing ride. Today, the films have pretty much reversed themselves in popularity. But *E.T.* still resonates, even with surly cynics, mostly because it is magnificently crafted by a first-tier filmmaker clearly in love with his inoffensive subject. When E.T. levitates himself, little Elliott, and all of those bike-riding kids out of harm's way, and they go peddling across the sky and past the moon, nothing less than movie magic is achieved, no matter when this story is experienced or by whom. Not surprisingly, composer John Williams rises to the occasion with yet another highly hummable and heartfelt score, this one practically gushing with childlike wonder. From the Xmas-tree like spaceship in the forest to E.T.'s backlit, emotional farewell, this film catches fireflies in a bottle... and seems more than happy to share them with us.

65

Poster/photos: © 1987 20th Century Fox

WHO MADE IT:

20th Century Fox/Lawrence Gordon Productions/Silver Pictures (U.S.). Director: John McTiernan. Producers: Joel Silver, Lawrence Gordon, John Davis, Jim Thomas, John Vallone, Laurence Pereira. Writers: Jim Thomas & John Thomas. Cinematography (color): Donald McAlpine. Music: Alan Silvestri. Predator Design: Stan Winston. Starring Arnold Schwarzenegger (Dutch), Carl Weathers (Dillon), Elpidia Carrillo (Anna), Bill Duke (Mac), Jesse Ventura (Blain), Sonny Landham (Billy), Richard Chaves (Poncho), R.G. Armstrong (General Phillips), Shane Black (Hawkins), Kevin Peter Hall (The Predator/Helicopter Pilot).

WHAT IT'S ABOUT:

A group of tough commandos is sent into the Central American jungle on a rescue mission. But during the course of this endeavor, they find themselves stalked by a mysterious, invisible alien creature, who hunts and slays them one by one. Ultimately, only the group leader, Dutch, is left to confront the his enormously powerful and technologically superior extraterrestrial adversary.

WHY IT'S IMPORTANT:

After Arnold Schwarzenegger's unexpected success as *The Terminator*, he was immediately cast in another action-packed science fiction movie, this one produced by a major studio. When I first read the screenplay for *Hunter* in 1985, I assumed Schwarzenegger would be playing the titular character, who, like his infamous T-1000, was ruthless, unstoppable and full of nasty high-tech surprises. As things turned out, *Hunter* evolved into *Predator*, and Mr. S settled into the brawny but decidedly human role of Dutch, cigar-chomping leader of a rag-tag team of macho commandoes. Sent on a *Rambo*-like mission in the jungles of Central America, they find themselves attacked by a monstrous alien creature, a sophisticated hunter from another galaxy with the convenient ability to render himself transparent. Kevin Peter Hall, the towering sasquatch of *Harry and the Hendersons*, fills Stan Winston's state-of-the-art monster suit most impressively.

By design, *Predator* embraces the exaggerated flavors of a war-themed comic book. Director John McTiernan's most audacious and distinctive move is to begin the film (apart from a brief prologue that owes something to Carpenter's *The Thing*) as a straight jungle-set war movie, continue in that vein for the first 40 minutes or so, then switch to sci-fi action thriller for the remaining running time. This approach has a curious emotional effect on viewers, who have allowed themselves to participate in a specific movie reality, only to be jarred (in a good way) into a decidedly different sensibility. Robert Rodriguez's *From Dusk Till Dawn* also goes this tricky route.

Once the creature stuff kicks in, a thoroughly engaging and suspenseful variation on *The Most Dangerous Game* unfolds, as Dutch's expendables (Carl Weathers and Jesse Ventura among them) are slaughtered with methodical precision by the vicious, trophy-collecting extraterrestrial. *Predator*'s script inevitably saves the best for last, as brawny Dutch must somehow rise to the occasion and hold his own against this inhuman, technologically-advanced giant. Their climactic one-on-one scenes have a primal power about them, with Predator's sneaky talent for imitating human voices serving as an ironic counterpoint to melodramatic events.

No one will ever mistake *Predator* for an exceptional science fiction film; but it is a terrific popcorn movie, one of Schwarzenegger's most satisfying vehicles and another opportunity for Stan Winston to dazzle viewers with an awesome, ultimately iconic creation.

ABOVE: Dillon (Carl Weathers, Apollo Creed from the *Rocky* films) bonds with buddy Dutch (Arnold Schwarzenegger) at the film's outset. BELOW (A): Dutch's mega-soldiers have their deadly work cut out for them. Elpidia Carrillo (Anna) is the only female in the cast, and is wisely given *Predator*'s most evocative and lengthy speech ("...the demon who makes trophies of man.") BELOW (B): The unseen enemy blasts away. RIGHT: The Predator (Kevin Peter Hall) in a glorious publicity photo.

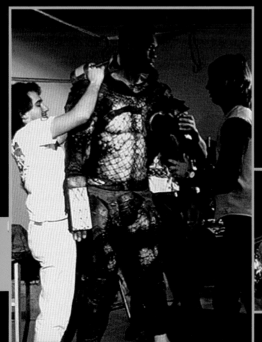

In an interesting touch, the Predator checks out his number one opponent, wondering how so effective a warrior can be a mere human being. Originally, the alien was designed with satyr-like legs, but this concept limited extravagant physical movement and had to be scrapped (Winston would revisit the idea for the far less ambulatory *Pumpkinhead* a year later).

The Predator (Hall) is suited-up. Transparent figure fx were accomplished with CG replacement techniques.

aka The Abominable Snowman of the Himalayas

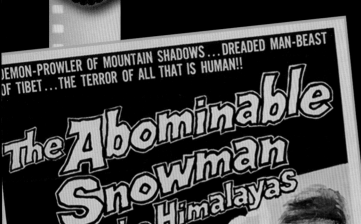

WHO MADE IT:

Hammer Films (U.K.)/20th Century-Fox (U.S.). Director: Val Guest.
Producers: Aubrey Baring, Michael Carreras, Anthony Nelson Keys.
Writer: Nigel Kneale, based on his BBC television serial.
Cinematography (b/w): Arthur Grant. Music: Humphrey Searle.
Forrest Tucker (Tom Friend), Peter Cushing (Dr. John Rollason),
Maureen Connell (Helen Rollason), Richard Wattis (Peter Fox), Robert
Brown (Ed Shelley), Michael Brill (Andrew McNee), Arnold Marle (Lhama).

WHAT IT'S ABOUT:

Doing research in the Himalayas, botanist John Rollason reluctantly
joins an expedition searching for the legendary Yeti, much against
the wishes of a local Lhama. Although expedition partners Tom
Friend and Ed Shelley are brash, possibly untrustworthy fortune
seekers, Rollason has faith in
the scientific value of their
quest. After enduring bad
weather and bandits, the
seekers finally find their
elusive, unearthly quarry.
The Yeti appear to be an
advanced race with curious

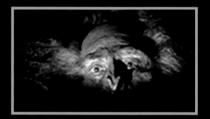

mental powers. One is shot and killed, but telepathic mind tricks
finally drive Friend insane, and soon only Rollason is left to look
upon their living, noble faces.

WHY IT'S IMPORTANT:

There were only a handful of "Yeti" movies made during the
1950s. Poverty-row thrillers like *Man Beast*, *Snow Creature* and
Japan's *Half Human* offered only mild diversion and promptly
faded into obscurity. On the other end of the spectrum is
Hammer's 1957 *The Abominable Snowman (of the Himalayas)*,
scripted by sf veteran Nigel Kneale. As is typical with the
author, evocative sci-fi concepts elevate an adventuresome
storyline into something with far more resonance. This is no
wild animal hunt: the Yeti are portrayed as noble entities with
a profound sense of their role in the world's social evolution, now and
after humanity inevitably self-destructs. Embracing this theme, the film's mini-expedition provides
a palatable microcosm of our tumultuous species: leaders Tom Friend and Ed Shelly are brash opportunists, hoping to catch a
Yeti for circus-style exhibition; unstable Andrew McNee has been haunted by the creatures ever since he saw one years earlier; and
Peter Cushing as Dr. Rollason represents mankind at its most progressive and admirable, hoping to expand scientific knowledge for the
good of all. It's hardy surprising that Rollason is the only person to survive
this snowy trek, although his memory of what transpired is wiped clean by the
Yeti's psychic powers.

Director Val Guest fearlessly keeps his titular snowman "under wraps" until an
evocative close-up at the end of the film. Although we glimpse the enormous
body of a fallen Yeti, it is the snowman's face - ancient and wise, almost Godlike
- that leaves the strongest impression when it finally appears. Also worthy of
praise is the film's widescreen black-and-white photography by Arthur Grant
and Humphrey Searle's music score, which makes impressive use of gongs,
horns and other unusual percussion instruments to suggest the exotic locale.

Canny homage to comic book superheroes enlivened by satire and violence...

ROBOCOP 1988

PART MAN,
PART MACHINE,
ALL COP.

RoboCop
THE FUTURE OF LAW ENFORCEMENT

A Jon Davison PRODUCTION A Paul Verhoeven FILM Peter Weller Nancy Allen Robocop Daniel O'Herlihy
Ronny Cox Kurtwood Smith Miguel Ferrer MUSIC BY Basil Poledouris DIRECTOR OF PHOTOGRAPHY Jost Vacano
FILM EDITOR Frank J. Urioste ROBOCOP DESIGNED BY Rob Bottin EXECUTIVE PRODUCER Jon Davison
WRITTEN BY Edward Neumeier & Michael Miner PRODUCED BY Arne Schmidt DIRECTED BY Paul Verhoeven
An ORION PICTURES Release
R RESTRICTED

WHO MADE IT:

Orion Pictures Corporation (U.S.). Director: Paul Verhoeven. Producers: Jon Davison, Arne Schmidt, Stephen Lim, Edward Neumeier, Phil Tippett. Writers: Edward Neumeier & Michael Miner. Cinematography (color): Sol Negrin, Jost Vacano. Music: Basil Poledouris. Special Makeup Effects: Rob Bottin. Starring Peter Weller (Officer Alex Murphy/RoboCop), Nancy Allen (Officer Anne Lewis), Dan O'Herlihy (The Old Man), Ronny Cox (Dick Jones), Kurtwood Smith (Clarence J. Boddicker), Miguel Ferrer (Bob Morton).

WHAT IT'S ABOUT:

In a dangerous, corporate-controlled future Detroit, robots are being developed as crime prevention tools. When a courageous officer named

Murphy is killed in the line of duty, he is resurrected as a hybrid machine man known as RoboCop, part of an experimental program. This metallic hero turns out to be more effective as an anti-crime weapon than the hulking, heavily-armored ED-209 robots currently being prepped. But Murphy is plagued by memories of his human past, and must reconcile these two realities while bringing crazed killer Clarence Boddiker to justice. Along the way he is challenged by corrupt corporate forces in his midst, some of whom are partnered with underworld kingpins.

WHY IT'S IMPORTANT:

Most fans groaned when they heard the title of this movie – robot policemen had been plentiful in TV movies and series in the '70s, usually partnered with disgruntled, old school human partners. But the sneers turned to cheers after this perversely entertaining combination of comic book ultra-violence and surprisingly sharp satire appeared. *RoboCop* began as sci-fi producer Jon Davison's homage to superhero comics, fearlessly showcasing the pop-tragic story of gunned-down officer Murphy (a smartly cast Peter Weir), who is amazingly reborn as a metallic avenger. In keeping with the "super heroes with super problems" motif that drove the early '60s Marvel movement, this solemn mandroid frequently endures painful memories of his former, fully-human life. Once a loving husband and dad, now officially deceased, he must somehow balance both realities and thwart the sicko criminal schemes of his own sadistic "murderer" (bald baddie Kurtwood Smith, who threatens to steal this popcorn show from several potential scene robbers).

RoboCop's wry social skewering and slightly unreal tone allows for colorful, artfully crafted set-pieces of extreme carnage (paging ED-209!) that would be distasteful under other circumstances. This irreverent comic book tone is succinctly established with skit-like TV news breaks that provide a fuller view of the story's tainted future, enabling everything in this spirited cartoon of an action flick, from histrionics to musical score, to be played full-out. Never again was this canny balance achieved, with numerous sequels and even a short-lived TV series failing to capture the special magic of director Paul Verhoeven's sharp, black comical foray.

ULIE CHRISTIE · OSCAR WERNER

AFLAME
WITH THE
EXCITEMENT
AND
EMOTIONS
OF
TOMORROW!

FAHRENHEIT 451

TECHNICOLOR®

CO-STARRING
CYRIL CUSACK
ANTON DIFFRING · JEREMY SPENSER · ALEX SCOTT

Directed by

FRANÇOIS TRUFFAUT

Screenplay by FRANCOIS TRUFFAUT and JEAN-LOUIS RICHARD
Based on the novel by RAY BRADBURY
Produced by LEWIS M. ALLEN
AN ENTERPRISE VINEYARD FILM PRODUCTION

A UNIVERSAL RELEASE

WHO MADE IT:

UPF (France)/Universal Pictures (U.S.). Director: Francois Truffaut. Producers: Michael Lewis M. Allen, Miriam Brickman. Writers: Francois Truffaut, Jean-Louis Richard, based on the novel by Ray Bradbury. Cinematography (Technicolor): Nicholas Roeg. Music: Bernard Herrmann. Starring Oskar Werner (Guy Montag), Julie Christie (Clarisse/Linda Montag), Cyril Cusack (The Captain), Anton Differing (Fabian), Bee Duffell (Book Woman), Alex Scott (Book Person).

WHAT IT'S ABOUT:

At some point in the future, society burns pre-existing books on a regular basis, with firemen patrolling antiseptic neighborhoods in search of hidden volumes. One of these officers, Montag, befriends a

pretty but unorthodox young neighbor, Clarisse, who happens to resemble his wife. This free spirit opens Montag's eyes to the joys of book-reading, and soon he's smuggling stolen editions into his home for nocturnal consumption. Horrified, his wife Linda reports him to the authorities. Instead of burning books on a final call,

Montag turns his flamethrower against oppressive enemies and becomes a fugitive. Ultimately, he finds his way to a makeshift society trying to preserve mankind's endangered cultural heritage by memorizing books before they are destroyed. Patiently waiting for the current "dark age" to pass, these Book People become humanity's noble caretakers, with Montag and his beautiful ex-neighbor Clarisse, now among them.

WHY IT'S IMPORTANT:

It's hard to fathom why mid-'60s critics found such fault with Truffaut's adaptation of this seminal Bradbury story, although I suspect it may have something to do with social politics (the French "new wave" was in decline at this juncture). Regardless, *Fahrenheit 451* captures the author's unique blend of science and poetry better than any other movie inspired by his stories, and there have been a few. Of course, even in book form, *451*'s premise requires some serious suspension of disbelief: no modern society can truly function without the written word, rendering this entire exercise in social melodrama semi-metaphorical. And just for the record, how can a re-enlightened Montag read books with such fervor when he's never been taught to read at all, words being nonexistent in his repressed culture? But none of this illogic matters, either in the book or in Truffaut's fine incarnation of it. Although star Oskar Werner (Montag) was an obnoxious blowhard during production and irritated everyone, his sensitive, intelligent performance on film is letter-perfect. Matching him deftly is straight-from-her-Oscar win Julie Christie, showcased in a double role (brilliant idea) as the bland wife/radical babe next door. With Hitchcock favorite Bernard Herrmann

scoring the picture, a heavy romantic layering counterpoints the "distant strangeness" music and his relentless, on-the-road military theme, associated with speeding fire engines. Standout sequences: the librarian choosing to die in a swirling inferno with her printed volumes is a moment not easily forgotten. Equally indelible are the film's final scenes with the placid Book People, enhanced oh-so-miraculously by a cleansing snowfall, one of those lucky breaks a director thanks Providence for. A difficult nut to crack cinematically, *Fahrenheit 451* remains unique and alive with worthy observations at every turn. Time to take a belated and well-deserved bow, Monsieur Truffaut.

61 SECONDS 1966

-100- 1.85

WHO MADE IT:

Paramount Pictures (U.S.). Director: John Frankenheimer. Producers: John Frankenheimer, Edward Lewis. Writer: Lewis John Carlino, based on a novel by David Ely. Cinematography (b/w): James Wong Howe. Music: Jerry Goldsmith. Starring Rock Hudson (Antiochus 'Tony' Wilson), Salome Jens (Nora Marcus), John Randolph (Arthur Hamilton), Will Geer (Old Man), Jeff Corey (Mr. Ruby), Richard Anderson (Dr. Innes), Murray Hamilton (Charlie).

WHAT IT'S ABOUT:

A successful middle-aged banker named Arthur Hamilton receives mysterious phone calls from Charlie, an old friend who was believed to be dead. Through this curious contact, Hamilton meets up with a clandestine business firm that makes him a most startling offer: these people will fake his death and create an entirely new look and life for him. After some soul-searching, Hamilton agrees, and soon undergoes extensive physical reconstruction and months of psychotherapy. He finally emerges as handsome young artist Tony Wilson, living in Malibu with a manservant who belongs to the firm, present to assist him with his adjustment. But Hamilton becomes increasingly despondent, and before long it becomes tragically clear that his new identity won't hold. The firm's next course of action is a grim and final one.

WHY IT'S IMPORTANT:

Director John Frankenheimer re-defined the parameters of science fiction in the '60s, mixing the form with political cynicism and social commentary. Neither *The Manchurian Candidate* nor *Seven Days in May* really qualify as sf, but *Seconds* does, showcasing a patently fantastic surgical process that puts a person's "soul" into a different human body. The director thrusts his aggressive, faux-European style of filmmaking at viewers from frame one, as grim, unsuspecting John Randolph is cryptically approached by a shadowy stranger in Grand Central Station. The rest of the film continues in this hyper manner, with distorted lenses and outré angles reminding us that the harrowing world of *Seconds* is distorted, disturbing and potentially deadly. It's also an interesting case of over-directing, or jam-on-jam; when a strange story is filmed strangely, viewers become somewhat detached and overwhelmed, clearly not what Frankenheimer intended. As a result, the French actually booed the film in its initial Cannes screening. But critics saved some earnest applause for star Rock Hudson, the other side of Randolph's body-swapping equation. Generally a lightweight presence on screen, he had hoped John Frankenheimer's "meaningful" project would give him added credibility as a actor. It didn't, but no one in Hollywood blamed Hudson. Perhaps his earnest performance as a man under the strain of being something he's not dovetailed with his now-famous personal life, which was managed (and, in many ways, manufactured) by the studio system, of which he was a key player.

Other sci-fi stories have effectively dealt with the tragic futility of soul-transplanting, most memorably "The Trade-Ins" episode of Rod Serling's *Twilight Zone* TV series. Frankenheimer and company press their considerable talents to tell this cautionary tale with more edge than usual, and the entire production (including the wonderful location shooting) is unquestionably first-rate. Still, less is generally more with such an intimate, offbeat subject. *Seconds* certainly has its moments, but it's the least successful of the director's much-analyzed '60s social trilogy.

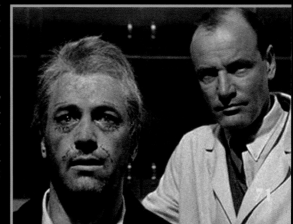

WHO MADE IT:

Warner Bros. (U.S.). Director: Eugene Lourie. Producers: Jack Dietz, Hal E. Chester, Bernard W. Burton. Writers: Fred Freiberger, Lou Morheim, Robert Smith, Eugene Lourie, based on the story "The Fog Horn" by Ray Bradbury. Animation Effects: Ray Harryhausen. Cinematography (b/w): John L. Russell. Music: David Buttolph. Starring Paul Christian aka Paul Hubschmid (Prof. Tom Nesbitt), Paula Raymond (Lee Hunter), Cecil Kellaway (Prof. Elson), Kenneth Tobey (Col. Jack Evans), Donald Woods (Capt. Phil Jackson), Lee Van Cleef (Corp. Stone), Steve Brodie (Sgt. Loomis), Ross Elliott (George Richie), Jack Pennick (Jacob Bowman), Frank Ferguson (Dr. Morton), King Donovan (Dr. Ingersoll).

WHAT IT'S ABOUT:

In the Arctic, a nuclear bomb test frees a prehistoric monster from its icy tomb. This enormous dinosaur is observed by injured physicist Tom Nesbitt, but no one believes his story. Meanwhile, the marauding creature wreaks havoc at sea, and eventually destroys a lighthouse. Paleontology professor Elson investigates in a diving bell, but is swallowed whole by the Rhedosaurus. Government and local authorities finally mobilize, but it's too late to stop the rampaging monster from attacking New York City. Finally bloodied and trapped in the amusement park area of Manhattan Beach, the Beast is killed when Nesbitt orders the firing of a radioactive isotope into its gaping wound.

WHY IT'S IMPORTANT:

Impressed by the super-successful re-release of *King Kong* in 1952, independent producers Jack Dietz and Hal Chester decided to hatch a monster epic of their own, though with decidedly less capital. Fortunately, they were able to secure the services of an eager Ray Harryhausen, animator Willis (*Kong*) O'Brien's successor, to create the picture's all-important special effects. Equally fortunate was the choice of director: Eugene Lourie was a world-acclaimed craftsman with a penchant for solving offbeat production problems. Legendary sci-fi author Ray Bradbury figures into the picture as well, his short story providing the impetus for *Beast's* plotline.

Monsters unleashed by nuclear explosions became a staple during the '50s, usually featuring the same atomic/hydrogen bomb stock footage in their narrated prologues. Although imitated like crazy, Lourie's film is the first to fully explore this timely premise and resulting plot formula. Instead of a giant raging gorilla wreaking havoc, Lourie drafts a Mesozoic reptile for the privilege of trashing New York, borrowing a notion first explored in O'Brien' silent masterpiece, *The Lost World*. This makes the bellowing, lizard-like Rhedasaurus Hollywood's first prehistoric monster of the 1950s. And what a monster he is! Harryhausen's genius is on full display in each and every animation set-piece, most notably the evocative lighthouse attack, slyly informed by Bradbury's poetic words. Tracking the dinosaur are earnest, reasonably believable Paul Christian and his love interest Paula Raymond, a beautiful contract player on loan from MGM. Impish Cecil Kellaway establishes the lovable father-figure archetype, while Kenneth (*The Thing*) Tobey is afforded another opportunity for low-key military toughness. Shooting on location in Manhattan is a significant plus, as is David Buttolph's exciting music score, built around an incessantly repeated four-note signature theme.

Not a single penny of its modest budget wasted, *The Beast from 20,000 Fathoms* is an enjoyable, carefully-prepared entertainment that showcases both Lourie's intuitive creative skills and Harryhausen's jaw-dropping special effects. Although many dinosaur-on-the-loose thrillers would follow, few would equal the level of freshness and competence on display here.

BELOW: Prof. Tom Nesbitt (Paul Christian) is having trouble convincing Frank Ferguson, Kenneth Tobey and King Donovan that he saw a prehistoric monster in the Arctic. RIGHT: the famous lighthouse attack.

The Beast destroys ships at sea (LEFT) before finding its way to Manhattan proper (BELOW), bringing death and carnage to the Big Apple. Military forces get into the picture (TOP, LEFT), but it's a radioactive isotope fired under the supervision of Dr. Nesbitt that finally vanquishes this monstrous relic from prehistoric times.

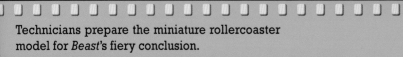

Technicians prepare the miniature rollercoaster model for *Beast*'s fiery conclusion.

SANE SCIENTISTS WITH MAD PROJECTS

Mankind's plunge into atomic uncertainty had a bizarre effect on nature during the 1950s, at least at the movies. *The Beast from 20,000 Fathoms* ('53, ABOVE) was resurrected by a nuclear bomb test in the Arctic, providing a memorable showcase for both fx creator Ray Harryhausen and director Eugene Lourie. INSERT: Al (David) Hedison as the title mutation of *The Fly*. OPPOSITE PAGE: One careless, tragic mistake shatters teleporter Andre Delambre (Hedison)'s idyllic romantic life with devoted better-half Helene (Patricia Owens).

Elegant romantic tragedy with an unforgettable "sick" ending...

THE FLY 1958

94 2.35

WHO MADE IT:

20th Century-Fox (U.S.). Director/Producer: Kurt Neumann. Writer: James Clavell, based on a story by George Langelaan. Cinematography (Deluxe Color): Karl Struss. Music: Paul Sawtell. Creature Makeup: Ben Nye. Starring Al aka David Hedison (Andre Delambre), Patricia Owens (Helene Delambre), Vincent Price (Francois Delambre), Herbert Marshall (Inspector Charas), Kathleen Freeman (Emma), Charles Herbert (Philipe Delambre).

WHAT IT'S ABOUT:

Young wife Helene Delambre informs the police that she's just killed her husband; indeed, the man's head and arm have been crushed in an industrial hydraulic press. Eventually she tells the authorities all about the bizarre tragedy that has shattered her life. Husband Andre Delambre was a brilliant scientist working in secret on a tele-portation process. Although he successfully transmitted inanimate objects, a common fly was accidentally trapped in his disintegration chamber when Andre tried the process on himself. Transformed into a half human, half insect creature, the desperate scientist enlisted the aid of his horrified wife in finding his scrambled fly counterpart, but was unsuccessful. Ultimately, Helene was forced to assist Andre in the ghastly act of destroying himself. The remaining, still-alive mutation, a tiny fly with Delambre's rapidly-aging human head, soon becomes trapped in a spider web before a stunned investigator ends his wretched existence.

WHY IT'S IMPORTANT:

At a time when big-budget prestige movies were flopping, *The Fly* made an unexpected splash, reminding 20th Century Fox that well-crafted science fiction can indeed be profitable. One generally doesn't associate the genre with husband-and-wife interplay, let alone highly romantic love stories. But *The Fly* provides both, and uses a flashback structure to boot (a luxury not granted *The Incredible Shrinking Ma*n). The film breaks new ground in other areas, as well. 1958 was a turning point for fantastic cinema, as sci-fi procedurals were giving way to richly-colored gothic horror reboots from Hammer and eventually AIP. Kurt Neumann's CinemaScope thriller seems to be on the cusp of this transition, clearly rooted in '50s technology but just as comfortable in the colorful shadows of the bold new gothics.

Fine as Hedison is as the handsome, brilliant but unlucky Andre Delambre, it is Patricia Owens' emotion-choked performance that ultimately dominates. She has to carry the movie for most of its running time, be convincing in a highly unbelievable scenario, and represent the viewing audience as she pieces together this horrific puzzle. Reduced to supporting players, vets Vincent Price and Herbert Marshall lend star presence and a certain respectability throughout. As for special make-up, Ben Nye fashions a gas mask-like headpiece that fits snugly over Hedison, along with a grotesque clawed hand. Most disturbing of all, perhaps, is the horror make-up for Andre in his mini-fly state, trapped within that giant web and waiting to be devoured. Aged prematurely by an insect's lifespan, eyes swollen and straining in horror at the oncoming spider, it is the stuff late '50s nightmares are made of.

The Fly earned one direct sequel (*Return of the Fly*) and a curious re-working (*The Curse of the Fly*) before the property was successfully re-visited by David Cronenberg in 1986. Although penned in the '50s, George Langelaan's original tale of twisted bodies and shattered relationships continues to hold interest, made more relevant, perhaps, by sharper scripts and even gorier, state-of-the-art horror fx.

LEFT: Francois Delambre (Vincent Price) receives some horrific news from sister-in-law Helene: she's killed her husband using a hydraulic press (BELOW). Andre Delambre was conducting experiments in matter transmission; pet cat Dandelo was lost in such a test, and a solid plate was reconstituted in "flopped" mode.

Helene (Patricia Owens) tries valiantly to stand by her genetically mixed-up husband, Andre (Al "David" Hedison). The revelation of his insectoid talon is bad enough; but that monstrous, inhuman face is simply too much to bear. The iconic image of horrified Helene's multiple screaming faces represents Andre's fly-like POV.

Fox makeup artist Ben Nye transforms a patient Al Hedison into the Fly.

58 MINORITY REPORT 2002 145 2.35

TOM CRUISE

MINORITY REPORT

A STEVEN SPIELBERG FILM

WHO MADE IT:

20th Century Fox/DreamWorks SKG (U.S.). Director: Steven Spielberg. Producers: Ronald Shusett, Gary Goldman, Jan de Bont, Bonnie Curtis, Gerald R. Molen, Walter F. Parkes. Writers: Scott Frank, Jon Cohen, based on a short story by Philip K. Dick. Cinematography (color): Janusz Kaminski. Music: John Williams. Starring Tom Cruise (Chief John Anderton), Max von Sydow (Director Lamar Burgess), Steve Harris (Jad), Neal McDonough (Fletcher), Patrick Kilpatrick (Knott), Jessica Capshaw (Evanna), Richard Coca (Pre-Crime Cop), Keith Campbell (Pre-Crime Cop), James Henderson (Office Worker).

WHAT IT'S ABOUT:

Year: 2054. An elite Washington D.C. law enforcing squad called "Precrime" uses three genetically-altered humans to see into the future and predict murders before they happen. Squad leader John Anderton, still recovering from the kidnapping of his young son, faces an aggressive Federal challenge to this operation, as well as the shock of seeing himself commiting a murder in the future. Set-up by someone close to him, he soon finds himself a desperate fugitive, pursued by his Precrime unit. Only the location of a tell-all "minority report" can clear Anderton and expose the inherent fallibility of this experimental short cut to law enforcement.

WHY IT'S IMPORTANT:

One of Steven Spielberg's decidedly "mature" sci-fi thrillers, *Minority Report* sets up a marvelously imaginative concept that enables an equally wonderful moral paradox to unfold: Are murderers guilty of being murderers if science can pre-realize their crimes and rescue the victims before the heinous act is committed? Upping the ante as only a good thriller can, what if an ace policeman (Tom Cruise) who uses "precog" data to nail these culprits suddenly observes himself committing a future murder? Does he turn himself in? Does he defy his own moral integrity and leave this killing to chance? Or does he assume he's been set-up by a clever enemy, which just happens to be the truth in this case? In many ways, *Minority Report* is a sci-fi spin on those old "crystal ball" pulp mysteries, with spiritualists foretelling murder and often pre-seeing themselves as either victim or killer. For Phillip K. Dick's cautionary tale, the resident psychics are three highly-evolved "precogs" who are never, ever wrong in their damning observations...or are they? That inevitable question leads to the existence of a well-hidden "minority report," which apparently provides proof that these supposedly sacrosanct visions don't always match. This devastates Cruise's conscientious law enforcer/tracker, who realizes that he may have apprehended or even terminated "innocent" culprits.

Spielberg directs this twisty mystery with his usual verve, doling out showy special effects only when required (the "spider" sequence is a filmmaking standout, more because of the director's use of a cutaway set than CGI). But ultimately, too many subplots begin to sap the concept's inherent power and emotional impact. Dick's precog story is a movie onto itself – Spielberg even ends this tale with the psychic trio, finally enjoying a "normal" life instead of remaining slave workers for society. Clearly, the related issues of "How can I prevent myself from becoming a murderer?" and "We need proof that Precrime is not infallible" are more than enough to sustain an extremely inventive, multi-faceted adventure which offers some salient insights about moral compromise and personal intregrity.

57 ROLLERBALL 1975

Poster/photos: © 1975 United Artists

WHO MADE IT:

United Artists (U.S.). Director: Norman Jewison. Producers: Norman Jewison, Patrick J. Palmer. Writer: William Harrison. Cinematography (Technicolor): Douglas Slocombe. Music: Andre Previn. Starring James Caan (Jonathan E.), John Houseman (Bartholomew), Maud Adams (Ella), John Beck (Moonpie), Moses Gunn (Cletus), Pamela Hensley (Mackie), Barbara Trentham (Daphne), John Normington (Executive), Robert Ito (Strategy Coach), Ralph Richardson (Librarian).

WHAT IT'S ABOUT:

In a depressingly bleak civilization of the future, capitalism in its most virulent form has taken over the world, following years of unstable, uncertain "corporate wars." An elite group of business managers keep the public placated with an exciting, ultra-violent spectator sport called Rollerball, which combines the worst attributes of football, roller derby, and the Roman coliseum. Rising from these games is legendary champion Johnny E., who disrupts the status quo by refusing to retire after a long and successful career. He soon becomes a threat to the rigid managers, who ultimately target him for defeat in the arena. Coming to grips with what's truly important, Johnny E. must call upon his finest skills to fend off these calculated efforts to destroy him.

WHY IT'S IMPORTANT:

The period after Kubrick's *2001* and before Lucas' *Star Wars* produced some notable science fiction movies, most of them dark, adult, and more than a little cynical. Norman Jewison's *Rollerball* is among the best of these discomforting projections. It depicts a thoroughly corrupt but deceptively comfortable future as some vague form of super-capitalism now holds the world together. And how are society's potentially unruly masses kept pacified? Through that diabolical deception known as rollerball, an internationally-adored killer-sport that enables spectators and participants alike to unleash their most aggressive and anti-social emotions. One champion (James Caan) defies convention by refusing to retire from the game, sending shock waves through this society's by-the-book management chairmen (epitomized by a glowering John Houseman) who certainly don't want individuals "growing stronger" through a vicious sport designed to keep the masses dispirited. Or something like that. In the end, Caan's unlikely hero spits in the company's eye and wins a final, all-important rollerball game besides. Freeze frame. But hey, this isn't *Rocky*. As with *Fiddler on the Roof* and *Jesus Christ Superstar*, director Jewison coaxes complex performances from his wonderful cast, with even a "living symbol of corporate badness" like Houseman rendered human enough for some subtle reflection. Still, there's a fundamental flaw in the inherent logic of *Rollerball* as a universal tonic. Using a bloodsport to placate the masses is one of history's oldest tricks. But not realizing that individual stars or heroes must inevitably rise from such media-supported super-popularity seems a bit naive, given the parallel in real life. In short, rollerball defeats its original purpose and actually encourages individuality and rebellion, clearly negating whatever "keep those masses in low self-esteem" value Houseman and Jewison clearly think it has. Best scene: shooting living trees for sport and setting them aflame. It's a wonderful portrait of a placid, picture-perfect society that is nevertheless totally corrupt and guilty as sin.

56 JOURNEY TO THE CENTER OF THE EARTH 1959 (132) 2.35

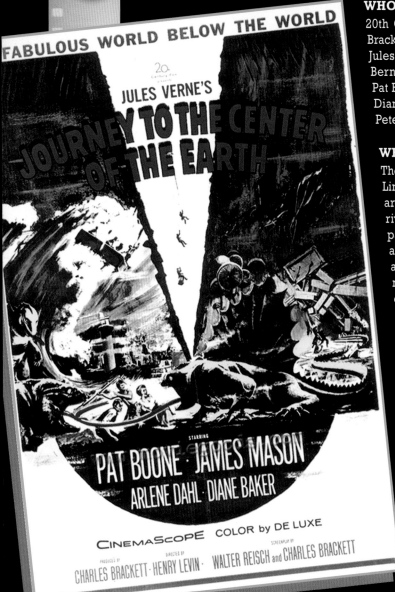

WHO MADE IT:

20th Century-Fox (U.S.). Director: Henry Levin. Producer: Charles Brackett. Writers: Charles Brackett, Walter Reisch, based on the novel by Jules Verne. Cinematography (DeLuxe Color): Leo Tover. Music: Bernard Herrmann. Starring James Mason (Sir Oliver Lindenbrook), Pat Boone (Alexander 'Alec' McKuen), Arlene Dahl (Carla Goteborg), Diane Baker (Jenny Lindenbrook), Thayer David (Count Saknusem), Peter Ronson (Hans Belker), Alan Napier (Dean).

WHAT IT'S ABOUT:

The discovery of an ancient artifact leads slightly eccentric Professor Lindenbrook and his assistant Alec McKuen to Iceland, where they are soon joined by Carla Goteberg, beautiful wife of a deceased rival, and a local worker named Hans. Bravely, these four follow the path of a previous explorer, enter a volcanic crater, and engage in an amazing expedition beneath the Earth's surface. Along the way they are imperiled by tremors, a horde of hungry dinosaurs and the murderous schemes of Count Saknusem, descendent of the original explorer. Lindenbrook and his resilient party do indeed reach the center of the Earth; they also stumble upon the remains of sunken Atlantis, and finally return to the surface world via a live volcano and a sturdy heathen altarstone.

WHY IT'S IMPORTANT:

Remembering the success Disney had with their CinemaScope epic *20,000 Leagues Under the Sea*, and hardly oblivious to Mike Todd's record-shattering *Around the World in 80 Days*, 20th Century-Fox felt fairly comfortable green-lighting another Jules Verne perennial. For additional assurance, the studio hired *Leagues* star James Mason, although the showy lead role of Prof. Lindenbrook was originally written for Clifton Webb (Webb died before production began). Arlene Dahl plays opposite Mason in a charming battle-of-the-sexes romance, a kind of Tracy-Hepburn comedy enlivened by prehistoric monsters, and one of *Journey*'s greatest strengths is the palpable charm of this relationship. It's no surprise hearing Mason delivering amusing criticisms of females a la Henry Higgins; but Dahl matches him point for point, and this is clearly the gorgeous actresses' finest moment in a starring vehicle. Perfectly welcome on the journey is an earnest, unobtrusive Pat Boone, and that always reliable larger-than-life presence Thayer David as *Journey*'s resident villain. Producer/co-writer Charles Brackett spares no expense for this lavish, first-class family adventure, from underground caverns to attacking dinosaurs and even the lost city of Atlantis, perhaps inspiring George Pal to make his version of that fable a year and a half later. Nixing stop motion for customized lizards, director Henry Levin delivers the best example of this now-antiquated/immoral fx approach ever put on film. Tellingly, when Irwin Allen tried the same technique a year later with his update of *The Lost World*, the magic was totally gone, and his "dinosaurs" looked ridiculous.

Since Bernard Herrmann was still a regular Fox composer in 1959, it made perfect sense to match him up with flamboyant period fantasy. Herrmann responds with the same assurance and majesty he exhibited eight years earlier for a Fox sci-fi film of stature, *The Day the Earth Stood Still*. His score is simply unforgettable, particularly the dramatic use of organ and harp ("There is our gateway!").

Brisk, colorful and always engaging, *Journey to the Center of the Earth* benefits from charming performers and grade A production values, along with the general smartness of Billy Wilder's ex-collaborator as producer/writer.

ABOVE: It's a gift from student Alec McKuen (Pat Boone) that inspires Prof. Lindenbrook's (James Mason) expedition. LEFT: A gateway is provided for the professor and his party.

Lindenbrook's team faces a plethora of challenges, including a runaway boulder (paging Indiana Jones), hungry dinosaurs, an underground ocean, even the remains of sunken Atlantis. Also providing wonderment and beauty is a spectacular crystal formation (RIGHT).

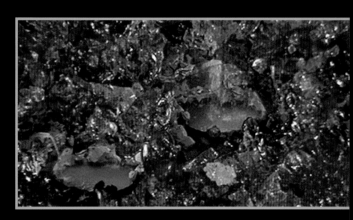

This colorful painting, depicting various Verne story icons, was created for *Journey*'s trailer.

WHO MADE IT:

British Lion (U.K.)/Universal-International (U.S.). Director: Val Guest. Producers: Val Guest, F. Sherwin Green. Writers: Wolf Mankowitz & Val Guest. Cinematography (b/w with color tint sequences): Harry Waxman. Music: Stanley Black (uncredited). Special Effects: Les Bowie. Starring Edward Judd (Peter Stenning), Janet Munro (Jeannie Craig), Leo McKern (Bill Maguire), Michael Goodlife ('Jacko'), Bernard Braden (News Editor), Reginald Beckwith (Harry), Gene Anderson (May), Arthur Christiansen (Editor), Edward Underdown (Sanderson).

WHAT IT'S ABOUT:

Massive nuclear bomb tests conducted by the superpowers at exactly the same hour alter the Earth's rotation, sending it in a new, deadly orbit, toward the sun. Down on his luck journalist Peter Stenning, fighting off alcoholism and bitterness over his failed marriage, begins putting the pieces of this incredible story together, with some impromptu help from government worker Jeannie Craig, his new contact and love interest. Soon the horrible effects of this disaster become all too clear: weather changes, freak storms and blanketing fog are only the beginning. With time running out, world authorities unite (finally) and work together in common cause. Will a desperate plan to realign Earth's rotation through the use of thermonuclear bombs succeed? Or are we doomed to burn in a Hell of our own making?

WHY IT'S IMPORTANT:

Hot on the atomic heels of Stanley Kramer's *On the Beach*, *The Day the Earth Caught Fire* is a grittier, more realistic depiction of impending global doom, replacing star power with unblinking documentary-style filmmaking. That said, director Val Guest recognizes an obligation to provide some horrific spectacle for special effects-craving viewers, offering CinemaScope vistas that are appropriately apocalyptic (freak fogs blanketing London, the Thames bone dry, etc.). For added flavor, frames are eventually tinted amber-red the closer our world moves to its solar destroyer. But the real power of this movie lies in its unflinching frankness and decidedly adult perspective. As bitter, divorced journalist Peter Stenning, Edward Judd is completely convincing, going from boozer to redeemed and responsible pro as conditions around the planet worsen. Janet Munro is pert and sexy as his government contact turned lover, and Leo McKern practically steals the show as cynical columnist Bill Maguire, Stenning's best friend and constant sounding board. Director Guest smartly fills his newspaper bullpen with civilians along with actors, starting with Arthur Christiansen as the paper's no-nonsense but compassionate editor.

A criticism of Kramer's film is that everything is too tidy; humanity accepts its death sentence with quiet dignity and profound humility. Not so here... There are riots, disrespect for government decisions, gouged prices for supplies, and the regretful ugliness that would accompany such a catastrophic event. Val Guest's dialogue is sharp and biting, and the overall "screw you" tone seems far closer to reality than *On the Beach*'s romantically melancholy ambience. Still, love is all that is left for sweat-glistening homo sapiens as doomsday closes in, with man-on-the-scene Stenning having earned some tender solace after finding his better lights and slaying various personal demons. The open ending suggests that we humans still have time to correct the monumental errors of our ways.

Well-received critically and commercially, *The Day the Earth Caught Fire* remains one of the best end-of-the-world thrillers ever made, a solid statement about the dangers of our nuclear age told with conviction, intelligence and edgy style.

Heat-challenged journalist Peter Stenning (Edward Judd) prepares to report on humanity's future in *Day*'s amber-tinted opening, before flashbacks provide the story proper.

A blanketing mist, freak storms, and dry-as-dust former waterways provide Guest's film with some spectacular special effect vistas.

TOP: Helping to establish an air of authenticity is the casting of Arthur Christiansen, seen here with his newspaper staff. BELOW: Stenning, Jeannie (Janet Munro), and Bill Maguire (Leo McKern) face the end of the world in May's pub.

This is the way the world ends, not with a whimper, but with a wild party in Chelsea.

Another definition of "hot": perspiring co-star Janet Munro in a brief nude scene that was ultimately snipped.

83

Grim and grandiose, a shattering parable and first-tier monster flick...

GODZILLA, KING OF THE MONSTERS 1956 ⟨80⟩ [1.33] 𝔉

aka Gojira, Godzilla

INCREDIBLE, UNSTOPPABLE TITAN OF TERROR!

GODZILLA It's Alive!

KING OF THE MONSTERS!

CIVILIZATION CRUMBLES as its death rays blast a city of 6 million from the face of the earth!

MIGHTIEST MONSTER! MIGHTIEST MELODRAMA of them all!

RAYMOND BURR

WHO MADE IT:

Toho (Japan)/Embassy Pictures and TransWorld Releasing Corp. (U.S.). Director: Ishiro Honda. Producers: Tomoyuki Tanaka, Joseph E. Levine, Terry Turner, Richard Kay, Edward B Barison, Harry Rybnick. Writers: Ishiro Honda, Takeo Murata, Shigeru Kayama, Al C. Ward. Cinematography (b/w): Masao Tamai. Music: Akira Ifukube. SFX: Eiji Tsuburaya. Editor U.S. version: Terry O. Morse. Starring Raymond Burr (Steve Martin), Takashi Shimura (Dr. Yamane), Akira Takarada (Ogata), Momoko Kochi (Emiko Yamane), Akihiko Hirata (Dr. Serizawa), Ryosaku Takasugi, Haruo Nakajima, Katsumi Tezuka (Godzilla).

WHAT IT'S ABOUT:

Injured reporter Steve Martin recalls the terrifying and unbelievable events of a recent stopover in Tokyo. It was a series of unexplained ship disasters that first led authorities and scientists to investigate. Much to everyone's horror, it was soon established that the cause of these tragedies was an enormous prehistoric monster, known to local islanders as Godzilla. Resurrected by hydrogen bomb testing, Godzilla then attacked the Japanese mainland, reducing Tokyo to a graveyard with his devastating radioactive breath. Mankind's only hope is a deadly weapon, the oxygen destroyer, recently invented by guilt-plagued scientist Dr. Serizawa. Working with his romantic rival, Ogata, Serizawa finally sets the device in place beneath the sea and activates it. Before long, monstrous Godzilla is reduced to a stream of oceanic atoms.

WHY IT'S IMPORTANT:

Long before he became a camp superstar, Godzilla was the subject of a surprisingly sober and sophisticated Japanese sci-fi thriller with political resonance. Inspired in large part by both *King Kong* and *The Beast from 20,000 Fathoms*, *Gojira* (1954) re-imagines the 'giant monster' genre as a dark allegory and social warning. In place of stop-motion animation is one of the oldest fx techniques in the book, the man in a rubber monster suit. Still, like the movie it supports, this costume is meticulously designed, and the miniature cityscape Godzilla trudges through is an equally amazing work of art.

After *Gojira* was acquired for U.S. release, entirely new scenes featuring Raymond Burr as a reporter visiting Japan were skillfully integrated into the body of Ishiro Honda's picture. What emerges is a parallel, streamlined hybrid for American audiences, with character-driven sequences and politically-charged moments either cut or shortened substantially. These U.S. edits were amazingly smooth and picked up the pace for mainstream viewers; fans curious about the Japanese original would have to wait twenty years for art house revivals.

From its grim "mass graveyard" opening to the final shot of a tranquil ocean, *King of the Monsters* commands our attention, Burr's presence and narration helping to sell some of the wilder aspects of Honda's scenario. There is genuine mystery and dread in the early ship disaster and Ohto Island sequences. Tokyo's eventual devastation is compelling if improbable spectacle, a triumph of analog special effects, music and mood lighting. In many ways, this apocalyptic docu-noir has the somber, adult quality of Kurosawa's early b/w classics, and the great director himself is an outspoken fan of Japanese "kaiju" (monster movies).

Audacious in its theme and content, *Godzilla, King of the Monsters* loses some of *Gojira*'s political edge in translation, but retains the unique, shattering impact of Honda's dark vision. Indeed, with tragic hospital scenes and rows of schoolchildren singing numbly for a life-saving miracle, it may be the saddest sci-fi film of the '50s.

TOP: Iconic panning shot of devastated Tokyo begins the American cut's wraparound sequence; it's presented in Act III of *Gojira*. Scenes of U.S. actor Raymond Burr were incorporated into the Japanese film, which featured Takashi Shimura, Momoko Kochi, Akira Takarada, and Akihiko Hirata as Dr. Serizawa.

Godzilla's dramatic first appearance on a remote island leads to his apocalyptic attack on Tokyo.

LEFT: "Mushroom cloud" head design. RIGHT: FX supervisor Eija Tsuburaya on the 1954 movie set.

53

THE MATRIX 1999

136   2.35

WHO MADE IT:

Roadshow Entertainment (Australia)/Warner Bros. (U.S.). Directors/Writers: Andy & Lana Wachowski. Producers: Joel Silver, Bruce Berman, Erwin Stoff, Barrie M. Osborne, Andrew Mason, the Wachowskis. Cinematography (color): Bill Pope. Music: Don Davis. Starring Keanu Reeves (Neo), Laurence Fishburne (Morpheous), Carrie-Anne Moss (Trinity), Hugo Weaving (Agent Smith), Gloria Foster (Oracle), Joe Pantoliano (Cypher), Marcus Chong (Tank).

WHAT IT'S ABOUT:

An unsuspecting computer hacker known as Neo is besieged by mysterious rebels who confront him with some astonishing truths: his day-to-day "reality" is a sham, humans are being used as energy sources by advanced machines of the future, and only Neo has the power to defeat these controllers and win freedom for his species.

WHY IT'S IMPORTANT:

It's probably significant that *The Matrix* made its appearance in 1999, the same year George Lucas unleashed his high-profile return to the *Star Wars* saga. Plucky *SW* changed the world for wide-eyed kids in '77 following the twin traumas of Viet Nam and Watergate, but two decades later, with the advent of the Internet and a new, bleaker awareness of human imperfection, the world had become a far more cynical and unhappy place. Lucas' cartoon-like homage to old cliffhangers seemed strangely irrelevant when compared to this shiny, edgy, oh-so-sophisticated-in-its-philosophy plunge into comparatively soulless digi-adventure. At its core, *The Matrix* is a complex reworking of James Cameron's "war with the machines" scenario. Much-mocked actor Keanu Reeves is completely believable as a software engineer/computer hacker who comes to realize that his concept of reality is more than a little limited. Following a thrilling, now-iconic action-adventure set-up, "Neo" is soon caught between rival factions, unsure of what is real and what he might be dreaming. In spite of the ultra-hip digital sheen, this is classic, suspenseful filmmaking with a welcome whiff of Frankenheimer, allowing strong ideas to resonate without special effects doing the job for them. What follows, of course, is a spectacular, completely made-up universe that nearly defies description, as Neo is introduced to the shattered "real world" by enigmatic host Morpheus (Laurence Fishburne) and his colorful hovercraft crew. Tapping into the "prophecy fulfilled" theme, noble Neo is destined to be the precious liberator of humanity, which now lives "in a computer-generated dream world created to keep us under control," Morpheus explains. People have literally become power sources for an omnipresent artificial intelligence that thrives on their heat-generating electrical impulses. Ultimately, our bewildered hero must return to the made-up world of the Matrix to combat a host of super-powerful computer programs in human form, with the future of mankind's freedom hanging in the balance. Although its use of CGI is splendid, *The Matrix* is more than just state-of-the-art eyewash; it provides a surprisingly sophisticated philosophy of life and more unbridled imagination than any five movies of its kind. It also introduces striking visual concepts and set-pieces (slowing, then speeding up action) that became standard devices in countless ultra-cool action films that followed in its wake. Ironically, the audience that proclaimed *Matrix* the second coming turned against its equally well-produced sequels with a passion that only a nerd living in his parent's basement can muster. Even so, the cultural and technical significance of this initial Wachowski brothers groundbreaker cannot be underestimated. Indeed, the real *Phantom Menace* of 1999 (at least from director George Lucas' perspective) was this unexpected gem of a science fiction adventure, which spoke directly to a receptive new generation just as surely as his own movie did back in the '70s.

Carrie-Ann Moss as sleek, high-flying Trinity redefined the superheroine look.

LEFT: Battery People, born and raised in the Matrix. ABOVE, RIGHT: Heroic Neo (Keanu Reeves) discovers that he has amazing powers which enable him, along with ally Trinity, to fight humanoid computer programs (Hugo Weaving as Agent Smith). BELOW: Morpheous (Laurence Fishburne) in a tense moment.

BELOW: Before Doc Ock became a movie villain, the Sentinels awed viewers with CGI tentacles.

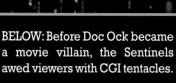

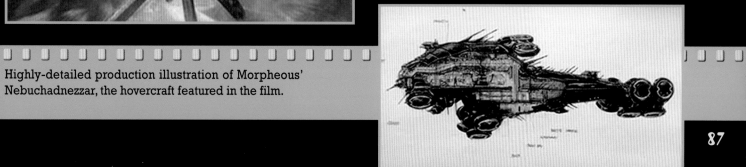

Highly-detailed production illustration of Morpheous' Nebuchadnezzar, the hovercraft featured in the film.

WHO MADE IT:

Metro-Goldwyn-Mayer (U.S.). Director: Byron Haskin. Producer: George Pal. Writer: John Gay, based on a novel by Frank M. Robinson. Cinematography (Metrocolor): Ellsworth Fredericks. Music: Miklos Rozsa. Starring George Hamilton (Prof. Jim Tanner), Suzanne Pleshette (Prof. Margery Lansing), Richard Carlson (Prof. Van Zandt), Yvonne De Carlo (Mrs. Sally Hallson), Earl Holliman (Scotty), Gary Merrill (Mark Corlane), Arthur O'Connell (Prof. Henry Hallson), Nehemiah Persoff (Prof. Carl Melnicker), Aldo Ray (Bruce), Michael Rennie (Arthur Nordlund/Adam Hart), Ken Murray (Grover), Celia Lovsky (Mrs. Hallson), Vaughn Taylor (Mr. Hallson), Lawrence Montaigne (Briggs).

WHAT IT'S ABOUT:

An impromptu experiment at a government scientific research center reveals the existence of a person with incredibly advanced telepathic powers. Soon members of this elite team are gruesomely murdered, one by one, convincing Dr. Jim Tanner than the mysterious psychic - known as Adam Hart - wants all knowledge of his existence erased. After surviving various mental assassination attempts, including a nearly fatal ride on an out-of-control merry-go-round, Tanner realizes that he himself is gifted with extraordinary  powers, that it was he who revealed this fact during that initial experiment without realizing it. In a dramatic confrontation with arrogant, self-confident Hart, Tanner turns the tables and destroys him.

WHY IT'S IMPORTANT:

When movies began to change in the late '60s, it was a tad difficult for homespun producer George Pal to change with them. Like Walt Disney, he was accustomed to providing more-or-less wholesome entertainment for family consumption, not R-rated adult fare or edgy social commentary. *The Power*, based on a reasonably adult sci-fi novel, is a good example of traditional mainstream filmmakers caught in that fascinating transition. Director Byron Haskin, ignoring the strides of *2001* (1968) and acting as if he were helming a two-part *Outer Limits*, tries to balance self-conscious salaciousness (the new Hollywood freedom) with a rather intriguing tale of an advanced psychic mutation capable of, in the words of co-star Michael Rennie, "preternatural and transcendental phenomena." Haskin envelopes us in a modern, reality-bending murder mystery, as beset research scientist Jim Tanner (sleek and streamlined George Hamilton, surprisingly well cast) eludes murder at every turn before discovering his own infinite source of "power." Along the way, there are all-night parties and love-making sessions mixed with genuinely brilliant terror set-pieces, such as Tanner's wild ride on an out-of-control carousel, the best sequence of its kind since Hitchcock's *Strangers on a Train*. Supporting Hamilton and love interest Suzanne Pleshette are a plethora of familiar faces from sci-fi filmdom: the aforementioned Rennie, Richard Carlson, Earl Holliman, Arthur O'Connell, and others. And supporting them is a dazzling score by Miklos Rozsa, who ignores the expected electronic clichés and delivers a baroque, diabolical main theme that dramatically counterpoints the coldness of super-science and high-technology. Its timeless evil on display here, with Rennie's ruthless futureman every bit as flamboyantly menacing as *Thief of Bagdad*'s wicked sorcerer. Also earning high marks is veteran MGM make-up wizard Bill Tuttle, who blows O'Connell's eyes and tongue out, and subjects Hamilton to extreme temps.

Kafka's 'Metamorphosis' retooled as sci-fi, with political overtones...

DISTRICT 9 2009

⏱112 1.85 🎧

Poster/photos: © 2009 TriStar Pictures

PETER JACKSON
PRESENTS
A FILM BY NEILL BLOMKAMP

NO HUMANS ALLOWED

DISTRICT 9
YOU ARE NOT WELCOME HERE.

IN THEATERS AUGUST 14 District9movie.com

WHO MADE IT:

TriStar Pictures (New Zealand/U.S.). Director: Neill Blomkamp. Producers: Peter Jackson, Bill Block, Ken Kamins, Carolynne Cunningham, Elliot Ferwerda, Paul Hanson. Writers: Neill Blomkamp, Terri Tatchell. Cinematography (color): Trent Opaloch. Music: Clinton Shorter. Starring Sharlto Copley (Wikus Van De Merwe), Jason Cope (Grey Bradman/Christopher Johnson), Nathalie Boltt (Sarah Livingstone), Sylvaine Strike (Dr. Katrina McKenzie), John Sumner (Les Feldman), William Allen Yoing (Dirk Michaels), Jed Brophy (James Hope), Vanessa Haywood (Tania Van De Merwe).

WHAT IT'S ABOUT:

An alien ship appears in the skies of South Africa, and eventually its occupants, insectoid humanoids, come to live in a segregated, ghetto-like community on Earth. An official government re-locator named Wikus Van De Merwe tries to smooth over differences between the defensive aliens and increasingly impatient human population, but finds himself transforming into one of the extraterrestrials after he's accidentally splattered with their rocket fuel. Now torn between two worlds, Wikus must hold onto his humanity and sense of morality as human-alien conflicts escalate.

WHY IT'S IMPORTANT:

District 9 seemed to come out of nowhere in 2009, proudly presented to the world by Peter (*Lord of the Rings*) Jackson. Although variations of Arthur C. Clarke's *Childhood's End* have been appearing on film ever since Kenneth Johnson's *V* in the early '80s (spaceships arrive and hover in our skies just long enough to drive us crazy with wonder and fear), this one is a bit different. Director/co-writer Neill Blomkamp has less familiar conceptual and thematic fish to fry, and he does so with an assurance rarely seen in a first-time feature filmmaker. Although the South Africa locale instantly draws comparisons to apartheid, it's a relatively superficial comparison given the true theme of Blomkamp's story. "Don't give up on me!" implores protagonist Wikus Van De Merwe (played to heartbreaking perfection by Sharito Copley), an official "Prawn" re-locator who is gradually transformed into an alien after he's accidentally splashed by one of their chemicals. Pushed past the point of all desperation, viewed as both traitor and progressive hero by a divided public, Wikus is in truth an inherently decent person and loving husband, thrust into an exotic conflict that forces him into desperate, violent action. His rewarding relationship with one of the aliens is perhaps the most encouraging thing to happen since the uninvited spaceship arrived. Finally a full-fledged Prawn by movie's end, one is left with the impression that Wikus has found an odd kind of contentment in his new biological incarnation. Who knows? Maybe his loving, long-suffering and loyal wife might join him in this alien form. For the record, Best Picture-nominated *District 9* has more than its share of illogic and contrivance. Alien rocket fuel causes one species to transform into another? That's like mutating into a rabbit after getting splattered with some gasoline! And couldn't the aliens have made better use of their international celebrity status? Or hired a helicopter to get them up to the mother ship that much sooner? But relatively superficial flaws aside, the film never loses sight of its human focus. It's ultimately about perseverance in the face of astonishing adversity, the importance of holding onto one's self no matter what happens. *District 9* explores this theme with sensitivity and originality.

Dino-master Lourie's most spectacular and heartfelt saga...

50 ∎∎∎

GORGO 1961

WHO MADE IT:

British Lion-Columbia (U.K.)/Metro-Goldwyn-Mayer (U.S.). Director: Eugene Lourie. Producers: Frank King, Maurice King, Herman King, Wilfred Eades. Writers: John Loring aka Robert L. Richards, Daniel Hyatt aka Daniel James. Cinematography (Technicolor): F.A. aka Freddie Young. Music: Angelo Lavagnino. Starring Bill Travers (Joe Ryan), William Sylvester (Sam Slade), Vincent Winter (Sean), Christopher Rhodes (McCartin), Joseph O'Conor (Prof. Hendricks), Bruce Seton (Prof. Flaherty), Martin Benson (Dorkin), Mick Dillon (Gorgo).

WHAT IT'S ABOUT:

Salvage dealers Joe Ryan and Sam Slade capture a live prehistoric monster off the coast of Ireland and make arrangements to exhibit it in London. Despite warnings from little Sean, a sad-faced boy from the island where the creature was caught, "Gorgo" becomes an internationally-famed attraction at Dorkins' Circus. Before long, however, the beast's enormous, enraged parent rises from the ocean and ultimately attacks London as it searches for its offspring, reducing several famous landmarks to smoking wreckage in the process. Ultimately, mother monster and child are reunited and return to the sea, leaving a burning metropolis and some sadder-but-wiser entrepreneurs behind.

WHY IT'S IMPORTANT:

After giving the world *The Beast from 20,000 Fathoms* and *The Giant Behemoth*, director Eugene Lourie took his little daughter's advice and made a movie where, for once, the titular monster prevails at tale's end. He found exactly the right vehicle in *Gorgo*, where mother love is the motivation for a city-smashing 200-footer from the dawn of time. More mythic and lyrical than Lourie's previous dinosaur films, *Gorgo* also enjoyed the largest budget, which enabled blazing, three-strip Technicolor to be part of the equation. Released through MGM by the King Brothers, who had recently imported the equally colorful *Rodan* with considerable success, this *Godzilla*-like variation would be the *Quo Vadis* of its sub-genre, filled with dazzling, multi-leveled optical effects of every kind. One significant effect *Gorgo* doesn't offer is stop-motion animation, its director opting for the "guy-in-a-suit" approach instead. As is typical of the celebrated filmmaker, Lourie fashions a finely-detailed made-up dinosaur costume, complete with distinctive, wiggling ears. Using thoughtful lighting and artful edits, the illusion of a living animal is achieved.

Bravely eliminating a female from the cast altogether (except, of course, for Big Mama), *Gorgo* weaves a simple tale of semi-scrupulous salvagers hoping to turn their capture of a live prehistoric monster into the greatest money-making stunt of all time. Greed and a lack of respect for nature shatters this Denhamesque goal (not to mention most of London's landmarks) before the recognizable power of maternal love sets things straight. Acting like David Lean's at the helm with a mega-budgeted epic, *Gorgo* pushes its already considerable production values to the max in Act III, literally overwhelming the viewer with astonishing images of mass-destruction. But the poetry and childlike simplicity of the film is never far away. "They're going back now," says ethereal little Sean, Gorgo's omnipresent conscience, of ultimately triumphant mother monster and child. "Back to the Sea."

Enhanced by a sensitive Angelo Lavagnino score and fierce, pulse-pounding editing, *Gorgo* impressed many but didn't spawn a rash of sequels like its Japanese brethren. And perhaps that's just as well. The movie provides a fitting conclusion to Eugene Lourie's agreeable study of reptilian throwbacks in a modern world, turning the familiar formula on its head with spectacular, heartfelt results.

After an erupting volcano tears the ocean apart, a massive prehistoric creature menaces Nara Island. Enterprising adventurers ultimately capture the creature and set course for England. The full-size Gorgo prop was actually transported through London streets in a jaw-dropping sequence. It served to represent both the baby Gorgo and his 200-foot marauding mother.

TOP: London Bridge is falling down as Mama Gorgo does her thing in one of the film's most accomplished fx set-pieces. BELOW: Sam Slade (William Sylvester) and Joe Ryan (Bill Travers) come to grips with their ultra-tragic mistake.

"They're going back now, back to the sea" offers Vincent (Sean) Winter.

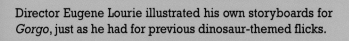

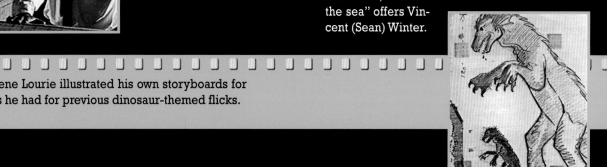

Director Eugene Lourie illustrated his own storyboards for *Gorgo*, just as he had for previous dinosaur-themed flicks.

BIGGER THAN LIFE

Unlike most of his atomic-radiated insect colleagues, *Gorgo* happened to be born impossibly huge, even for a dinosaur. Still, he's nothing more than an agitated pup compared to his city-smashing momma. The movie itself was well publicized and licensed by MGM, providing fans with official tie-ins that included a sexy novelization and a successful series of Charlton comic books that often featured art by *Spider-Man* co-creator Steve Ditko. *Gorgo* was also previewed rather famously in Famous Monsters magazine, enabling most readers to anticipate the arrival of this Godzilla-like superstar at their local movie theater months before the event.

ABOVE: *Them!* female lead Joan Weldon comes face-to-face with a very
big ant, and it's certainly no picnic. As scientist Edmund Gwenn points
out with grandfatherly gloom, beasts may inevitably reign over the Earth
unless we reckless humans a) face up to the nightmare that's been unleashed and b) recognize the inherent danger of atomic testing in general. LEFT: "Get the antennae! He's helpless without them!" Policeman
James Whitmore tries to make his bullets count as our heroes face their

49 THEM! 1954

94 1.37

WHO MADE IT:

Warner Bros. (U.S.). Director: Gordon Douglas. Producer: David Weisbart. Writers: Ted Sherdeman, Russell Hughes, from a story by George Worthing Yates. Cinematography (b/w): Sid Hickox. Music: Bronislau Kaper. Starring James Whitmore (Ben Peterson), James Arness (Robert Graham), Edmund Gwenn (Dr. Medford), Joan Weldon (Dr. 'Pat' Medford), Onslow Stevens (Brig. Gen. Robert O'Brien), Sean McClory (Major Kibbee), Chris Drake (Ed Blackburn), Sandy Descher (The Ellinson Girl), Fess Parker (Alan Crotty), Olin Howlin (Jensen).

WHAT IT'S ABOUT:

Policemen find a little girl wandering alone in the desert, shocked into a numbed and speechless state. Investigating, they discover her shattered house and an equally wrecked local store, along with the body of its slain owner. The FBI is called in when authorities are unable to identify a weird footprint found near these crimes, and it soon becomes apparent that a horde of giant, mutated ants, the product of atomic bomb testing, is responsible. Efforts are made to seal the creatures inside their desert nest, but a fertile, winged Queen Ant manages to escape. Soon ships at sea, unsuspecting pedestrians and even modern cities are threatened by the outsized monsters, who finally settle in the tunneled storm drains of Los Angeles. Soldiers and scientists corner these deadly insects and finally succeed in burning their primary nest, ending this horrific threat to humankind.

WHY IT'S IMPORTANT:

After Warner Bros. made a boxoffice killing with their independent pick-up, *The Beast from 20,000 Fathoms*, the studio immediately began searching for another "sired by radiation" shock-fest to produce. *Them!* enabled them to exploit a horde of giant insects instead of a reborn dinosaur, inventing a whole new sub-genre for the monster-happy '50s.

Taking its cue from *The Thing* and *Day the Earth Stood Still* as much as *Beast*, Gordon Douglas's thriller comes at us in full adult mode, more like a serious murder mystery than a monster-on-the-loose extravaganza. First a cop story (Whitmore), then an FBI procedural (Arness), finally a fully-fledged sci-fi adventure (Gwenn and Weldon), *Them!* is never anything less than a polished studio production, Warner Bros. recognizing the importance of maintaining credibility throughout. And although atomic testing is indeed blamed for the nightmarish threat, this is not an edgy protest film (as is, say, Honda's *Gojira*). Scientist Gwenn's closing speech makes it clear that these unknown dangers are simply an unavoidable byproduct of the nuclear age, problems we simply "must be prepared for." Apparently Earth-threatening mutants represent the inevitable price of human progress, a down side all forward-thinkers are expected to tolerate without thinking twice.

Solid and sturdily-paced, *Them!* manages the unique feat of bringing respectability to a big bug movie, partially because it's inventing the form. Only Jack Arnold's *Tarantula* comes close to challenging it, and Warners' 1957 pseudo-follow-up, *The Black Scorpion*, is ultimately just a pale imitation with some striking effects sequences.

Best scenes: Ed Blackburn's final moments; exploring the catacombs; the ship at sea; sewer patrol; Peterson rescues the kids and gets killed for his trouble; soldiers cut loose with a barrage of firepower.

Reflecting the studio's desire for credibility, writer Ted Sherdeman starts off *Them!* as an enigmatic mystery, with the discovery of a wandering, numbed child (Sandy Descher) triggering a local police investigation (Chris Drake, James Whitmore, LEFT).

Authorities raid a desert nest and ultimately the catacombs of LA's sewers.

James Whitmore's heroic, gruesome death came as something of a surprise to 1954 audiences.

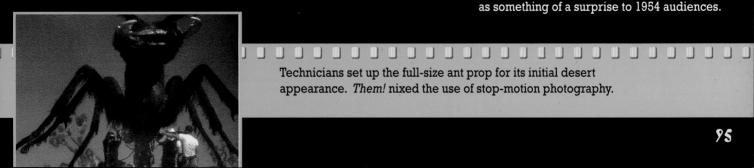

Technicians set up the full-size ant prop for its initial desert appearance. *Them!* nixed the use of stop-motion photography.

95

THE MIGHTIEST MOTION PICTURE OF THEM ALL!

Walt Disney presents

20,000 Leagues UNDER THE Sea

TECHNICOLOR

Starring KIRK DOUGLAS · JAMES MASON
PAUL LUKAS · PETER LORRE

CINEMASCOPE

WHO MADE IT:

Walt Disney Productions, Buena Vista Film Distribution Co. (U.S.). Director: Richard Fleischer. Producer: Walt Disney. Writer: Earl Felton, based on the novel by Jules Verne. Cinematography (Technicolor): Franz Planer. Music: Paul Smith. Starring Kirk Douglas (Ned Land), James Mason (Captain Nemo), Paul Lukas (Prof. Aronnax), Peter Lorre (Conseil), Robert Wilke (Nautilus First Mate), Ted de Corsia (Farragut).

WHAT IT'S ABOUT:

Disappearing ships and reports of a sea monster inspire scientist Prof. Aronnax and his nervous assistant Conseil to investigate. Their search vessel is indeed sunk by the mysterious creature, but they and brash harpooner Ned Land somehow survive. They soon learn that the sea monster they are pursuing is not a living beast at all, but the futuristic submarine Nautilus, captained by renegade genius Nemo. He spares their lives but the three remain captives aboard his well-guarded vessel. With the aid of nuclear energy, Nemo has embarked on a one-man crusade against war ships of every kind, sinking them and their crew without mercy. Although Aronnax comes to understand the tormented genius' motives, Land manages to get word to the authorities, and Nemo is finally cornered on a volcanic island that serves as his base of operations. Rather than have such unlimited power fall into the hands of war-mongering simpletons, the Captain destroys his remarkable discoveries... and himself.

WHY IT'S IMPORTANT:

Although "straight" science fiction concepts were deemed iffy by prestige-conscious Hollywood majors, period pieces based on the works of Wells and Jules Verne were another matter entirely. These projects had the advantage of built-in respectability, as everyone – even studio execs – had brushed against the original classics at one point or another in school. First to receive a lavish movie treatment was this Disney adaptation of *20,000 Leagues Under the Sea*, a major undertaking for the studio, being their first live-action feature of any kind. Disney surprised many by hiring Richard Fleischer, son of former animation rival Dave Fleischer, to helm this all-important project. But the resourceful first-time director came through with flying Technicolors, assembling a star-laden cast – James Mason, Kirk Douglas, Peter Lorre – for a lavish CinemaScope epic that pleased movie critics and made a fortune. Earl Felton's screenplay is filled with colorful set-pieces carefully designed for all members of the viewing audience: a marauding sea monster, in actuality a Victorian super-sub; enraged, attacking cannibals; a giant squid attack; and other widescreen diversions. But Captain Nemo's torment and motivation for his exotic "war against war" is intelligently charted (blame for his wife's murder is placed with "that most hated nation," meaning England), and his ideological duel with Ned Land clarifies how far the Captain has fallen in terms of his own precious humanity. Land may be a self-centered fool, but that doesn't stop him from rescuing Nemo from a grisly death, in spite of the fact that Land and his companions are prisoners aboard the Nautilus. Given *Sea's* plot trajectory, it's inevitable that the Captain will take his atom-age discoveries with him in a massive binge of self-destruction. The world of Queen Victoria is clearly not ready for such unlimited power; tragically, the worlds of 1954 and 2011 really aren't much different.

By not sanitizing Verne's novel and keeping aspects of its political and moral purpose intact, Disney showed Hollywood that its live-action product, while fanciful, should and would have a backbone. In many ways, both *Journey to the Center of the Earth* and *Mysterious Island* are richer, more fully cinematic entertainments. But *20,000 Leagues* was the high-profile groundbreaker, making mainstream movies safe for literature-based science fiction adventures.

Professor Aronnax (Paul Lukas) and loyal assistant Conseil (Peter Lorre) react to a newspaper story about ships being destroyed by a sea monster, in reality Captain Nemo's underwater marvel, the atomic submarine Nautilus.

Nemo (James Mason) is courteous to his unexpected guests (Lukas, Lorre, and trouble-maker Kirk Douglas), but runs his futuristic submarine with an iron fist.

The exciting, nocturnal squid attack was re-filmed after an initial daylight version was deemed too serene.

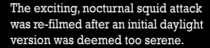

An original production painting depicting the Nautilus and one of its undersea explorers, possibly Captain Nemo.

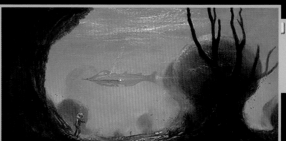

WHO MADE IT:

Amblin Entertainment/Universal Pictures (U.S.). Director: Steven Spielberg. Producers: Kathleen Kennedy, Gerald R. Molen, Lata Ryan, Colin Wilson. Writer: David Koepp, based on the novel by Michael Crichton. Cinematography (Eastmancolor): Dean Cundey. Special Visual Effects: Stan Winston Studio, Phil Tippett Studio, others. Music: John Williams. Starring Sam Neill (Dr. Alan Grant), Laura Dern (Dr. Ellie Sattler), Jeff Goldblum (Dr. Ian Malcolm), Richard Attenborough (John Hammond), Bob Peck (Robert Muldoon), Martin Ferrero (Donald Gennaro), Joseph Mazzello (Tim), Ariana Richards (Lex), Samuel L. Jackson (Ray Arnold), Wayne Knight (Dennis Nedry), B.D. Wong (Henry Wu), Jerry Molen (Gerry Harding).

WHAT IT'S ABOUT:

Living dinosaurs are biologically engineered by millionaire John Hammond, who intends to present them to the world via his new, state-of-the-art tour attraction, Jurassic Park, located on a remote island. Hammond invites noted paleontologists and his own grandkids for a sneak preview, but things go terribly wrong after one of the JP workers attempts to steal ultra-valuable dinosaur embryos. Soon a handful of terrified humans must fight for survival against very real – and very hungry – prehistoric animals, who are no longer confined to their pens.

WHY IT'S IMPORTANT:

At some point, Michael Crichton's ingeniously credible sci-fi premise and the groundbreaking sfx techniques used for Spielberg's movie version seem to have merged: "They've found a way to bring dinosaurs back to life!" the public joyously proclaimed, and stormed theaters across the world to see these fantastic creatures in action. Benefiting from the wonders of computer-generated imagery, the museum-style dinosaurs presented in *Jurassic Park* are indeed the most realistic ever depicted on film, from fluidity of movement to authenticity of design. And Crichton's high concept is so brilliantly simple (dino-blood extracted from insects preserved in prehistoric amber can be used to replicate living dinos) that even now, while acknowledging that this notion is fictional flapdoodle, it still seems strangely credible. As for Spielberg, he rightly reasoned that dinosaurs were "hot" as the century was about to turn, so he connected with the classiest and most timely work of fiction on this subject. It's no secret *Jurassic Park* the novel was cannily conceived for a movie afterlife. Crichton's storyline, like his premise, is easily graspable: Hoping to launch an island theme park featuring live dinosaurs, a handful of characters must fight for survival when technical snafus and human weakness cause things to go terribly wrong. In other words, it's Crichton's own *Westworld* scenario with a prehistoric twist. Hoping to infuse this sci-fi tale with more than just the usual drab scientist heroics, its screenplay gives lead paleontologist Sam Neill a discernable arc: he learns how to think and feel like a parent (i.e., an "adult"), rather than just a grown-up little boy obsessed with dinosaurs, because this crisis situation forces him into the unwanted role of child-protector. The main lesson everyone else learns is even simpler: Don't mess with Mother Nature, or she'll bite you on the ass.

On balance, *Jurassic Park* emerges as an exotic, exciting "under siege" thriller, with landmark special effects its primary asset. And while our hearts may still belong to childhood favorites like *The Beast from 20,000 Fathoms* and *Gorgo*, one cannot dismiss the significance of this smartly-premised, lavishly-produced movie that dared to show us "real" dinosaurs for the very first time.

ABOVE: It all starts with prehistoric amber and a daring experiment. BELOW: Birth of a cloned dinosaur!

ABOVE: Scientists come to the aid of a triceratops with a tummy ache. LEFT: The bellowing Tyrannosaurus rex lets everyone know who's king of Jurassic Park.

LEFT: The colorful Spitter was a semi-fictionalized 'saur. RIGHT: Raptors invade a kitchen, forcing Tim (Joseph Mazzello) to take cover.

Steven Spielberg, seen here chatting with a steg, directed *Jurassic Park* and its equally successful sequel, *Jurassic Park 2: The Lost World*.

Poster/photos © 1966 20th Century Fox

FANTASTIC AND SPECTACULAR VOYAGE...
THROUGH THE HUMAN BODY...INTO THE BRAIN.

STARRING
Stephen Boyd
Raquel Welch
Edmond O'Brien
Arthur Kennedy

fantastic voyage

CinemaScope, Color by DeLuxe 20.

PRODUCED BY SAUL DAVID
DIRECTED BY RICHARD FLEISCHER

WHO MADE IT:

20th Century-Fox (U.S.). Director: Richard Fleischer. Producer: Saul David. Writers: Harry Kleiner, David Duncan, from a story by Jerome Bixby and Otto Klement. Cinematography (Deluxe Color): Ernest Laszlo. Music: Leonard Rosenman. Starring Stephen Boyd (Grant), Raquel Welch (Cora), Edmond O'Brien (General Carter), Donald Pleasence (Dr. Michaels), Arthur O'Connell (Col. Donald Reid), Arthur Kennedy (Dr. Duval), William Redfield (Capt. Bill Owens), Barry Coe (Aide).

WHAT IT'S ABOUT:

A great scientist who knows the secret of maintaining miniaturization for an extended time, is seriously wounded during an assassination attempt. U.S. agent Grant is assigned to be part of a "surgical team" that will be miniaturized and injected into the scientist's bloodstream so that a delicate brain operation can be performed from within. A small nuclear-powered ship named the Proteus propels this select group on a truly fantastic voyage, as scientists monitor their progress from a futuristic laboratory. Although garrulous Dr. Duval is vaguely suspected of being disloyal, it is panicky Dr. Michaels who ultimately proves to be the real traitor, imperiling their all-important mission. Ultimately, Grant and his companions succeed in removing the scientist's life-threatening blood clots. Although the Proteus is destroyed and Michaels becomes engulfed by their patient's "natural defenses," the surviving rescuers manage to escape by swimming to their subject's eye, where they are removed in a teardrop before growing back to normal size.

WHY IT'S IMPORTANT:

Fantastic Voyage is a one-of-a-kind movie experience, the ultimate "high concept" sci-fi premise decades before Hollywood coined the term. A curious, well-received combination of cold war thriller and exotic science lesson, it bridges the mod spy adventures that were defining fantastic cinema mid-decade with a hint of Kubrickian advances that were just around the corner. The first few scenes alone, depicting an assassination attempt, are grown-up, textural and free of background scoring. As a matter of fact, music doesn't enter the picture at all until *Voyage*'s mini-rescuers enter the victim's bloodstream, wisely establishing a tone of no-nonsense believability. Gruff government official Edmond O'Brien even throws his all-important explanatory lines away in a remarkable escalator chat with Boyd, director Fleischer wisely understanding the difference between this kind of science fiction movie and his fanciful period classic, *20,000 Leagues Under the Sea*. Ironically, the more-or-less conventional twists of *Voyage*'s mystery/adventure plot (who among the Proteus crew is a traitor?) come to the rescue whenever scientific jargon gets a little thick. It also has all the benefits of a ticking-clock scenario, smartly employing conceptual aspects ("With time running out, I'd head for the eye!") for a memorable resolution – and a logical icon for the movie's advertising campaign.

More so than the other major studios, 20th Century-Fox understood the enormous boxoffice potential of a carefully-prepared science fiction project (they'd hit the jackpot two years later with *Planet of the Apes*, and a decade after that, with *Star Wars*). *Fantastic Voyage* got there first, though, satisfying audiences with a monster-less sci-fi adventure that dared to stimulate the imagination.

Best scenes: Opening assassination attempt; first entry into the bloodstream; doctors remaining absolutely quiet during Proteus' passage through the ear; "They're tightening!"; O'Connell and the teardrop.

Proteus crew members prepare for their unique, life-saving mission.

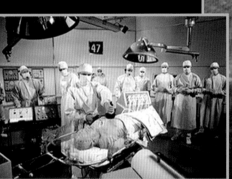

RIGHT: Arthur O'Connell explores an eyeball for signs of the desperate voyagers.

Sparing no expense, 20th Century-Fox created amazing, one-of-a-kind sets for the film.

Fantastic Voyage, along with Fox/Hammer's *One Million Years B.C.*, made statuesque beauty Raquel Welch a household name.

45 STAR TREK II: THE WRATH OF KAHN 1982 -113- 2.20

Poster/photos: © 1982 Paramount Pictures

the end of the universe ... lies the beginning of vengeance.

STAR TREK II
THE WRATH OF KHAN

WHO MADE IT:

Paramount Pictures (U.S.). Director: Nicholas Meyer. Producer: Harve Bennett. Writers: Jack B. Sowards, from a story by Harve Bennett and Jack B. Sowards. Cinematography (color): Gayne Rescher. Music: James Horner. Starring William Shatner (Captain James Kirk), Leonard Nimoy (Mr. Spock), DeForest Kelley (Dr. McCoy), Ricardo Montalban (Khan), Kirstie Alley (Lt. Saavik), James Doohan (Scotty), Walter Koenig (Mr. Chekov), Bibi Besch (Dr. Carol Marcus), Nichelle Nichols (Comdr. Uhura), Merritt Butrick (David Marcus), Paul Winfield (Capt. Terrell).

WHAT IT'S ABOUT:

Although he diverts himself by visiting Starfleet training sessions, retired Admiral James T. Kirk would prefer to be "hopping galaxies" again, as loyal friend Dr. McCoy points out. Kirk gets his chance while on a routine inspection tour of cadets aboard his signature starship, the Enterprise. An old enemy, the genetically-superior Kahn, was marooned by Kirk years earlier, resulting in the death of Kahn's beloved wife. Now he's escaped from exile and passionately seeks vengeance. Part of his  scheme involves the securing of "Genesis," a device which is capable of creating new life on a planetary scale, but could easily be perverted into a super-deadly weapon. In the midst of his tense but reinvigorating battle of wits with Kahn, Kirk is reunited with former wife Carol Marcus, the inventor of Genesis, along with his estranged son. Ultimately, Kahn is thwarted, but the Genesis device is activated, threatening a disabled Enterprise. Only a valiant sacrifice by Mr. Spock enables Kirk and his crew to escape.

WHY IT'S IMPORTANT:

In a deep funk after the creative failure of 1979's *Star Trek: The Motion Picture*, sci-fi fans were endlessly thankful for Nicholas Meyer's spirited reboot, which pushes all the right thematic buttons with an agreeably light touch. Where that first special effects-driven spectacle lost sight of *Trek*'s all-important personal side, this movie embraces it with open arms and a heartfelt hug. True, it's unfortunate that a character as intellectually stimulating as Kahn needed to be reduced to a one-dimensional, vengeance-craving madman. But *Star Trek II* required a strong villain, and a scenario built around Kirk coming to grips with age and death couldn't also accommodate an even-handed portrait of Kahn's remarkable approach to Empire-building. Disheartened viewers needed to be reminded of just how engaging the original *Star Trek* cast was, and still could be, given the proper creative treatment. What emerges from Meyer's wistful blend are some worthwhile observations about friendship and obligation, scene-chewing melodramatics ("Kahn!!!"), an agreeably dialed-down score, and enough spectacular starship duels to keep the special effects junkies happy. Live Long and Prosper, *Star Trek*!

44

ENEMY FROM SPACE 1957

85   1.66

aka Quatermass II

Poster/photos: © 1957 United Artists

WHO MADE IT:

Hammer Films (U.K.)/United Artists (U.S.). Director: Val Guest. Producer: Anthony Hinds, Michael Carreras. Writers: Nigel Kneale, Val Guest, based on the BBC serial by Nigel Kneale. Cinematography (b/w): Gerald Gibbs. Music: James Bernard. Starring Brian Donlevy (Prof. Quatermass), John Longdon (Lomax), Sydney James (Jimmy Hall), Bryan Forbes (Marsh), William Franklyn (Brand), Vera Day (Sheila), Charles Lloyd Pack (Dawson), Tom Chatto (Broadhead), John Van Eyssen (The P.R.O.), Percy Herbert (Gorman), Michael Ripper (Ernie).

WHAT IT'S ABOUT:

Frustrated by efforts to obtain funding for a moon base, Professor Quatermass is stunned to see an identical installation built upon the ruins of a once-thriving community. Related to this weird discovery is a shower of meteorite-like objects containing a deadly contagion that burns and scars. Although this hush-hush secret government project is supposedly engaged in the development of a new food source, Quatermass eventually deduces that it's run by infected, zombie-like victims of the alien contagion. Inside enormous domes are giant alien monsters being fed the ammonia atmosphere of their native world. Only the desperate efforts of Quatermass, Inspector Lomax and a handful of locals thwart this galactic threat, with the orbiting asteroid that sent the meteorites to Earth finally obliterated by a rocket bomb.

WHY IT'S IMPORTANT:

The success of Hammer's *The Creeping Unknown*, based on the popular BBC-TV serial, inspired this no-nonsense follow-up, logically based on the TV sequel to that original serial. Bullish (the word seems designed for him) Dr. Bernard Quatermass is once again at odds with the bureaucratic peabrains in his midst, this time because they fail to see the wisdom of a sophisticated moon base he's proposing. As in *Unknown*, he is teamed with down-to-earth police inspector Lomax (John Longdon, replacing Jack Warner), and the two make for an enjoyable odd couple as their probe of a secret base thickens and the personal danger increases. There are two memorable moments of "high horror": the grotesque appearance of a contaminated victim, blackened head-to-foot; and the sadistic stuffing of a peace-offering civilian ("human pulp") to clog pipes being filled with anti-alien poison by Quatermass. Val Guest's direction is less "on the streets" docu-style for *Enemy from Space*, staying mostly at the project and sometimes covering dramatic moments with indifferent long shots. He revs things up considerably for the spectacular finale, as giant blob creatures emerge from various dome-cocoons and stomp about miniature sets. Making smart use of a real location (the Shell Haven Refinery), *Enemy from Space* is possibly the first sci-fi film to suggest that our democratically-elected governments may not be telling us the truth. Granted, this secret operation is commandeered by alien-infested zombies, not *Seven Days In May*-types, but it's still a federally-funded project, and a chilly, trust-no-one atmosphere prevails. Appropriately enough, if "bullish," anti-establishment Dr. Quatermass can't bring this dark mystery to light, nobody can.

WHO MADE IT:

Paramount Pictures (U.S.). Director: Rudolph Mate. Producer: George Pal. Writer: Sydney Boehm, based on novels by Philip Wylie and Edwin Balmer. Cinematography (Technicolor): W. Howard Greene, John F. Seitz. Music: Leith Stevens. Starring Richard Derr (David Randall), Barbara Rush (Joyce Hendron), Peter Hansen (Dr. Tony Drake), John Hoyt (Sydney Stanton), Larry Keating (Dr. Cole Hendron), Stephen Chase (Dr. George Fyre), Frank Cady (Ferris), Hayden Rorke (Dr. Bronson).

WHAT IT'S ABOUT:

Scientists grimly conclude that Earth's survival is threatened by two planets now rushing into our orbit. The first, named Zyra, will pass over, causing tidal waves and other apocalyptic disasters; the second, Bellus, is expected to collide and completely crush our planet a month later. Although world leaders are skeptical at first, it isn't long before the doomsday crisis becomes obvious, and resourceful Dr. Hendron spearheads the building of a Noah's Ark-like rocketship that can transport a handful of human survivors to Zyra. Financed by a selfish industrialist, the completed craft manages to take off just before Earth is destroyed. After a brief journey, this rocket-ark safely lands on Zyra, which has a breathable atmosphere, and the transplanted Earthlings begin a new life on an alien world they now call home.

WHY IT'S IMPORTANT:

Cecil B. DeMille hoped to make *When Worlds Collide* during Hollywood's golden age as a vehicle for *Lost Horizon* star Ronald Colman; if he had, the picture would have decisively changed the course of science fiction in American cinema. Instead, it was George Pal who seized this Paramount-owned property as the follow-up to his successful *Destination Moon*, with DeMille serving as uncredited advisor. The result is a modest spectacle that divides its Oscar-winning special effects between some carefully-designed "end of the world" images (the flooding of New York City being the most iconic) and "rocket trip to another planet" material, culminating in the '50s' most fanciful depiction of an alien world. Hero Richard Derr, who sort of resembles Danny Kaye, had a limited career in Hollywood (he can be spotted briefly as the doomed starship captain in "The Mutant" episode of *Outer Limits*), but he plays his nice guy leading man part reasonably well. More interesting is a young Barbara Rush, ravishing in Technicolor, who would pop up as Richard Carlson's girlfriend/alien double in *It Came from Outer Space* two years later. Larry Keating, perhaps best known as a fussy husband on TV's *Burns and Allen Show*, is perfectly convincing as the venerable scientist hoping to rescue a disbelieving humanity with his Noah's Ark option. But, in the end, it's John Hoyt's wheelchair-bound, scene-chewing capitalist that registers most strongly, doing a pre-*Strangelove* "I can walk!" gag as his last chance for survival speeds away on a ramp. Clearly, no Republicans are being allowed on the New World. And neither is anyone of color, apparently. Reflecting the "play it safe" attitudes of Pal and Paramount, it's a spaceship of well-fed Caucasian faces that finally makes it to Zyra, its occupants ready to start a whitebread world anew, complete with waggy-tailed puppies and poetic Christian platitudes. A vague mention is made of "other ships" having been launched from Earth just before doomsday, but as far as we movie viewers can tell, this is pretty much it.

Perhaps not as good as it should be, but still respectable and always worth a gander, *When Worlds Collide* obviously can't measure up to 21st Century disaster epics like *The Day After Tomorrow* and *2012*, at least technically. But as a clear-eyed view of unprecedented global destruction and the need to move forward into humanity's final frontier, it neatly captures the "can do" spirit of early '50s America.

Planet Zyra's passing causes fantastic tidal waves on Earth, including the one that engulfs NYC in this breathtaking matte painting. A 20th Century Noak's Ark in rocketship form seems the only possible way to salvage the human race.

ABOVE: The worst fears of Prof. Hendron (Larry Keating) are confirmed. Act I of *When Worlds Collide* concerns the acceptance of Earth's inevitable destruction, not exactly the easiest pill for humanity to swallow.

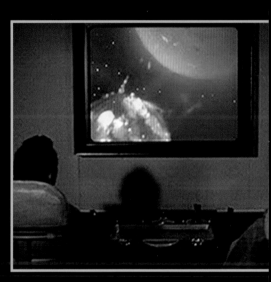

Hendron's spaceship takes off and zooms into space, even as planet Earth meets an apocalyptic end. Ultimately, the escapees land safely on Zyra, a curious planet blessed with *Alice In Wonderland*-style topography and, thankfully, a breathable atmosphere.

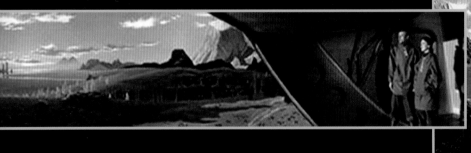

Pal's fx crew prepares the miniature rocketship and ramp for the climactic take-off. *Collide* nabbed an Oscar for its colorful effects.

Poster/photos: © 2005 Paramount Pictures

WHO MADE IT:

Paramount Pictures (U.S.). Director: Steven Spielberg. Producers: Colin Wilson, Kathleen Kennedy, Paula Wagner, Damian Collier. Writers: David Koepp, Josh Friedman, based on the novel by H.G. Wells. Cinematography (color): Janusz Kaminski. Music: John Williams. Starring Tom Cruise (Ray Ferrier), Dakota Fanning (Rachel Ferrier), Miranda Otto (Mary Ann), Justin Chatwin (Robbie), Tim Robbins (Harlan Ogilvy), Rick Gonzalez (Vincent), Lenny Venito (Manny).

WHAT IT'S ABOUT:

Triggered by storms, strange alien craft from beneath the Earth suddenly emerge and wreak havoc. Divorced crane operator Ray Ferrier, a poorly-skilled parent, finds he must protect his two children from the unthinkable as they make their fear-frenzied way from Bayonne, New Jersey to the imagined sanctuary of Boston. During the course of this horrific trek, Ray must contend not only with the dreaded Tripod attacks, but with panic, a rebellious son, and growing madness among the human survivors. In the end, it is Ferrier who first notices that the war machine's protective shields seem to be down, enabling U.S. military forces to vanquish a Tripod. With no resistance to Earthly bacteria, the invaders soon perish.

WHY IT'S IMPORTANT:

Like most kids who grew up watching sci-fi thrillers of the '50s, Steven Spielberg was fascinated by the horrific possibilities of a devastating, full-scale outer space invasion. For his new version of H.G. Wells' alien attack classic, the celebrated director felt obliged to honor three significant creative ingredients – the original Victorian-era novel, Orson Welles' infamous radio broadcast, and George Pal's beloved 1953 movie version – while fashioning a gritty, modern take that would resonate with 21st Century audiences. Several fairly dramatic changes were required. Updating the story to current day New Jersey (where Wells' broadcast set the action) enabled Spielberg to directly tap into the fresh, relatable emotions of his post 9/11 audience. Even more surprising was the decision to turn these ruthless space invaders into generic aliens rather than Martians, a name synonymous with extraterrestrials in the '50s, but dated and perhaps goofy-sounding today, given what science has learned about the red planet in the last fifty years. Spielberg and ILM conjure fashionable, bio-sleek Tripod war machines that honk ominously as they power-up, while at the same time suggesting Wah Chang's spectacular 1953 "manta ray" design and the distinctive, suction-cupped talon of Charlie Gemora's Martian. Deliberately resisting the "postcard" approach of *Independence Day*, *War of the Worlds* avoids showing the destruction of iconic landmarks, presenting its "money shot" moments selectively and infrequently. For the true power of this thriller is its caught-on-the-fly reality, nicely combined with the Hollywood star presence of Tom Cruise. Handsome but weather-beaten, he's ideally suited to his role of deadbeat dad who discovers his better lights as a parent and human being during the course of this harrowing ordeal. We taste the unique terror of alien-inflicted doomsday every step of the way, from the astonishing first attack (Spielberg reminds us why he's Spielberg with partial coverage of this assault through a fallen camcorder), to that incredible "train in flames" roaring past numbed and horrified spectators. The director is also careful balancing Cruise's action-star heroics with a reasonable measure of guy-next-door believability. Equally impressive, daughter Dakota Fanning is at the heart of several well-crafted set-pieces, most memorably her horrific discovery of a dead body in the stream... which is promptly followed by countless floating bodies. Dark and properly disturbing, *War of the Worlds* ultimately has more in common with the solemn *Schindler's List* than *Close Encounters*, or even *Jaws*. In spite of his showman's instincts, Spielberg correctly recognizes that the worldwide slaughter and subjugation of humanity is no picnic, but rather a harsh poetic tragedy unlike anything our species has ever experienced.

TOM CRUISE

WAR OF THE WORLDS

THEY'RE ALREADY HERE

SUMMER

LEFT: the devastating First Attack, in New Jersey. ABOVE: Ray (Tom Cruise) and daughter Rachel (Dakota Fanning) watch in numbed horror as a burning train flashes by.

Three scared survivors try to elude an alien spy device.

Spielberg's warship design pays homage to George Pal's 1953 classic. As in Wells' novel, the Earth itself is gradually transformed into a toxic, alien landscape.

As in all versions of this story, the invading aliens are defeated by Earthly bacteria.

Director Steven Spielberg discusses a tense scene with stars Tom Cruise and Dakota Fanning.

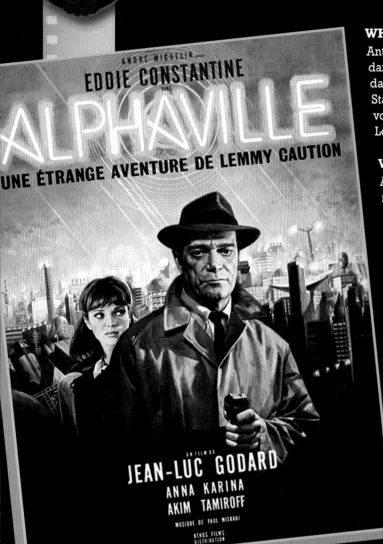

WHO MADE IT:

Anthos Films/Chaumiane/Filmstudio (France). Director: Jean-Luc Godard. Producer: Andre Michelin (uncredited). Writer: Jean-Luc Godard. Cinematography (b/w): Raoul Coutard. Music: Paul Misraki. Starring Eddie Constantine (Lemmy Caution), Anna Karina (Natacha von Braun), Akim Tamiroff (Henri Dickson), Howard Vernon (Prof. Leonard Nosferatu aka von Braun – uncredited).

WHAT IT'S ABOUT:

A hard-boiled American detective named Lemmy Caution arrives in Alphaville, a futuristic city on another planet that is governed by a master computer and it's evil creator/programmer, a scientist named Vonbraun. Artists, musicians and other creative forces are banned from the world, eliminating poetry and personal expression...even love. It is through a relationship with Vonbraun's lovely daughter, Natasha, that the dark heart of Alphaville is finally vanquished. The master computer is thwarted, eliminating the threat Dr. Vonbraun posed to other planets and free civilizations.

WHY IT'S IMPORTANT:

Jean-Luc Godard's *Alphaville* is commonly referred to as "the science fiction movie without special effects." Critic Andrew Sarris is correct when he asserts that Godard couldn't afford them, and wouldn't want them if he could. Instead of planning and building elaborate spaceship shots, why not use the reflections of overhead highway lamps on a car windshield, speeding by at a rapid clip, to suggest interstellar flight? This kind of "light speed" is far more poetic and, of course, way less expensive. To understand what this movie is doing one must re-live the significance of French New Wave cinema in the late '50s and early '60s, a movement Godard was at the heart of. Today, the easy sense of documentary-style reality captured in these films is still quite liberating, especially given what commercial cinema has become in the 21st Century.

Lead Eddie Constantine's character of Lemmy Caution is a comic strip-like recreation of Sam Spade and Mike Hammer, his face, fedora and up-collared trenchcoat suggesting both spy and shamus. He's a tough guy, all right, nasty to strangers and sometimes sadistic to those he kills, and the film actually slips into an unexpected bloodbath three quarters of the way through. Yet Caution is gentle, even poetic with "Princess" Vonbraun (Anna Karina), explaining to this relative innocent (all of *Alphaville*'s citizens serve a central computer) that sex is empty without love behind it – quite a statement from a macho secret agent with a license to slaughter. Although freeing Alphaville's population from this machine's dark clutches is Caution's primary goal, the movie takes in a lot more, including references to everything from French movie critics to at least one specific cinematic setup that's a homage to Orson Welles (with Welles favorite Akim Tarmiroff in the shot to certify the connection).

Driving about industrial Paris streets in his Ford Galaxy as the futuristic retro main theme blasts continually, second-rate movie dick Lemmy Caution is a fine symbol of director Godard's admirable need to irk his viewing audience with the unexpected. And that is pretty much what the French New Wave was all about to begin with.

40

ON THE BEACH 1959

134 1.66

WHO MADE IT:

United Artists (U.S.). Director/Producer: Stanley Kramer. Writer: John Paxton, based on the novel by Nevil Shute. Cinematography (b/w): Giuseppe Rotunno. Music: Ernest Gold. Starring Gregory Peck (Cmdr. Dwight Towers), Ava Gardner (Moira Davidson), Fred Astaire (Julian Osborne), Anthony Perkins (Lt. Peter Holmes), Donna Anderson (Mary Holmes), John Tate (Adm. Bridie), Harp McGuire (Lt. Sunderstrom), Lola Brooks (Lt. Hosgood, Bridie's secretary), Guy Doleman (Lt. Cmdr. Farrel).

WHAT IT'S ABOUT:

A nuclear war spreads deadly radioactive particles across the world, extinguishing life in all but a few locations, such as Australia. Commander Dwight Towers arrives with his American submarine crew and befriends many of the locals, who, like all survivors, are living on borrowed time. Hoping to find a place on Earth where life can be sustained, Towers takes his sub to an empty San Francisco and other remote locations, investigating mysterious Morse code signals that wind up being bogus. Unable to accept the death of his wife and children, Dwight has a difficult time dealing with the passionate needs of beautiful, drunkard Moira, who doesn't want to die without love. As doomsday approaches, those remaining must poison their loved ones and take their own lives. And Towers, granting the wishes of his crew, sets a submarine course for home as heartsick Moiria looks on. Soon, not a soul is living on the radiated planet.

WHY IT'S IMPORTANT:

The *Inconvenient Truth* of its day, *On the Beach* mixes social diatribes with Hollywood star power, and for the most part, this odd combination works: the warning of nuclear folly comes through loud and clear, and audiences are equally interested in the steamy Gregory Peck-Ava Gardner romance (will they have sex before the world ends?).

A narrative like this was practically made for "message" producer Stanley Kramer, enabling him to preach and soul-search without restraint, although he backs away from holding America directly responsible for doomsday. He also has the opportunity to experiment with some arresting new filmmaking techniques. The empty street visuals speak for themselves, eerie, haunting snapshots of a once-living society. Still, Kramer took some heat for not showing bodies ("...armageddon's too neat and clean..."). Given the darkly romantic tone of *On the Beach* and the delicate balance its director was striving to maintain, this appears to have been the correct creative choice.

Australia's own "Waltzing Matilda" warbles throughout the movie in one form or another, frequently associated with life in general, and passionate love-making. Its final rendering, a ghostly echo in permanently empty Melbourne, is joltingly interrupted by Ernest Gold's commanding final notes, tinged with his fallout motif, that sledge-hammer the inevitable on-screen message: There Is Still Time, Brother! Heavy-handed or not, Stanley Kramer's most crucial message movie still resonates.

39 THE CREEPING UNKNOWN 1956 ⟨78⟩ 1.66 ◖

aka The Quatermass Experiment

WHO MADE IT:

Hammer Films/Exclusive Films (U.K.)/United Artists (U.S.). Director: Val Guest. Producer: Anthony Hinds. Writers: Richard H. Landau & Val Guest, based on the BBC TV play by Nigel Kneale. Cinematography (b/w): Walter Harvey. Music: James Bernard. Starring Brian Donlevy (Prof. Quatermass), Jack Warner (Lomax), Richard Wordsworth (Victor Carroon), Margia Dean (Mrs. Judith Carroon), Thora Hird (Rosemary Rigly), David King-Wood (Briscoe), Jane Asher (Little Girl).

WHAT IT'S ABOUT:

Only one of three astronauts survives the crash-landing of a returning spaceship; he's rescued and scrutinized scientifically. Through an investigation led by Prof. Bernard Quatermass, authorities soon discover that an alien force invaded the ship, overwhelmed all aboard and turned two of the men to jelly. Both astronauts now live on within mute, stricken Carroon, a human carrier for this weird and sentient extraterrestrial disease. After wife Judith hires a private detective to spirit her husband away from Quatermass, Carroon kills the man and escapes, threatening all of London as he gradually takes on the form of a crablike alien entity.

WHY IT'S IMPORTANT:

Writer Nigel Kneale introduced a new type of science fiction story to British audiences with his BBC TV serial *The Quatermass Experiment*. It was very much like a police procedural, but with scientists rather than cops asking most of the questions. When it came time for this property to be adapted into a feature movie, Val Guest took charge as director, using Kneale's original story and ideas but hiring a different scripter to adapt them. The result is an early sci-fi noir, shot in a raw, documentary-style mostly at night, with bleak British sidestreets, hospitals and zoos becoming pivotal locations. Also key is Westminster Abbey, where the tale's titular astronaut-turned-tentacled monstrosity meets an electrifying end. Guest carefully builds to this climax with a methodical investigation (scientists *and* policemen) that also focuses on the victim before he has completely "gone over"; actor Richard Wordsworth is perfection as back-from-the-brink Victor Carroon, his mute performance conjuring memories of Karloff from the first *Frankenstein* (he sits solemnly in his chair in exactly the same manner, and even has a encounter with an unsuspecting little girl while on the run). It was standard practice during this period for low-budget British movies to cast fading U.S. stars to help sell their product in American markets. Brian Donlevy certainly fits the bill; but to many, the gruff, gangster-like politician of Preston Sturges's *The Great McGinty* seems woefully miscast as an ingenious British astro-physicist. Then director Guest really pulls a fast one, a creative move that infuriated Kneale: he turns the admirable Prof. Quatermass into a driven perfectionist, completely devoid of charm, tact and sentiment. It was quite daring to have a hero with the aura and flavor of a villain. But Donlevy's "bullish" Q ultimately becomes an unexpected plus, and many current viewers prefer this petulant, crabby old buzzard to more typical casting choices for this usually ultra-civilized part (such as Andre Morell or Andrew Keir).

With a bizarre monster (courtesy of Les Bowie) that looks like a snail on steroids, *The Creeping Unknown* introduces fans to a specific sub-genre that we'd re-visit in later films (*X the Unknown* among them, and even Italy got into the act with 1960's *Caltiki the Immortal Monster*). It's all about pitch-black night photography, nervous grunts with regional accents, breath vapor, and dingy working class locations that conceal nameless horrors.

Authorities rescue sole survivor Carroon (Richard Wordsworth, RIGHT, under the lamp) from his crash-landed spaceship. Driven Prof. Quatermass (RIGHT, Brian Donlevy) is in charge.

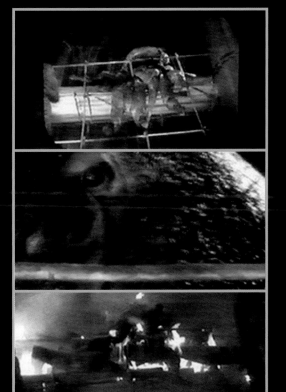

LEFT: Carroon's final metamorphosis and electrocution at Westminster Abbey. Standout scene: the shadowy horror lurches through a local zoo in the dead of night, witnessed only by terrified caged animals. RIGHT: Richard Wordsworth as cactus-fisted Carroon.

Terrified TV producers at Westminster Abbey wind up with more of a show than they bargained for as *Unknown* swells to its climax.

Director Val Guest (left) and actor Brian Donlevy made two *Quatermass* movies together, both based on Nigel Kneale's teleplays.

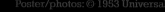

WHO MADE IT:

Universal-International (U.S.). Director: Jack Arnold. Producer: William Alland. Writer: Harry Essex, based on a screen treatment by Ray Bradbury. Cinematography (b/w 3D): Music: Irving Gertz, Herman Stein, Henry Mancini (all uncredited). Starring Richard Carlson (John Putnam), Barbara Rush (Helen Fields), Charles Drake (Sheriff Matt Warren), Joe Sawyer (Frank Daylon), Russell Johnson (George), Kathleen Hughes (June).

WHAT IT'S ABOUT:

Astronomer John Putnam and schoolteacher girlfriend Ellen Fields witness the crash-landing of what they believe to be a meteor. But after investigating the resulting crater, Putnam is astounded to see a circular spaceship rammed into the mountainside. An ensuing landslide covers all evidence; much to his annoyance, the astronomer is disbelieved by Arizona locals. But soon mysterious events convince gruff Sheriff Matt Warren that Putnam may be on to something. It turns out that the space visitors are ambassadors from another galaxy on an important mission to another world; they crashed on Earth by mistake and are desperately trying to repair their craft and leave. Shape-shifters by nature, they take on human form to move about freely and gather needed equipment. Although a last-minute posse threatens to undo these efforts, Putnam keeps the angry mob at bay, allowing the extraterrestrials to escape in their now-functioning spaceship.

WHY IT'S IMPORTANT:

Director Jack Arnold's sci-fi debut, *It Came from Outer Space* was Universal's first "serious" science fiction movie (the *Flash Gordon* serials and *The Invisible Ray* were more fantasy than sci-fi). With the '50s underway and futuristic subjects in vogue, it was inevitable that Big U would throw its considerable resources into a project of this nature, even marrying it to 3D for additional thrills. And who should pen this tale of tomorrow? Who better than author Ray Bradbury, since, then as now, his name is synonymous with science fiction. Working with Bradbury's lengthy treatment, screenwriter Harry Essex fashioned a tidy melodrama, intelligently presenting its "visitors from outer space" as frustrated intergalactic ambassadors delayed on their mission (presumably of peace) because of an error that "dragged" them to Earth. Conveniently shape-shifters by nature, they disguise themselves as humans to move about freely and steal materials needed to repair their disabled spaceship. And while talking in a monotone is the order of the day for these aliens, each manages to display some individual character traits. The one impersonating Barbara Rush's character, for example, happens to be a trigger-happy bitch. A word about star Richard Carlson. Like Bradbury, this handsome, intelligent-looking actor came to represent sci-fi, at least in early '50s cinema. Here, in one of his seminal performances, he's the Bradburian ideal fleshed-out: a courageous young scientist bucking the system and fighting prejudice in the midst of a potentially deadly alien encounter.

According to producer William Alland, *It Came from Outer Space* was originally filmed without a single clear shot of the titular monster. A suggestion of some unearthly presence would be required (those circular POV shots, or some wispy angel hair), but nothing specific. When a cut of the movie in this form was screened for Universal execs, they insisted a tangible 3D "monster" be added, so the makeup/fx department was called into play and some new scenes were shot.

A fine combination of suspense, chills and sense of wonder, *It Came from Outer Space* makes especially splendid use of 3D, particularly in the evocative desert scenes. Best moment: Joe Sawyer's telephone lineman soliloquy, straight out of Bradbury's treatment.

ABOVE: Astronomer John Putnam (Richard Carlson) and love interest Helen Fields (Barbara Rush) are wishing upon a star when a real one hurtles across the night sky. RIGHT: Putnam (actually a stick figure) stands before the globe-like spaceship now rammed into a shaky mountainside. No one in town believes his story… at first.

Shape-shifting aliens kidnap local humans and assume their form, much to the consternation of Putnam and an increasing irritable Sheriff Warren (Charles Drake), the astronomer's foil and semi-romantic rival.

Some of the stranded visitors have short tempers, especially the one impersonating Ellen Fields.

LEFT: The Xenomorph model. RIGHT: Director Jack Arnold (center) and cast members chat with producer William Alland (seated).

113

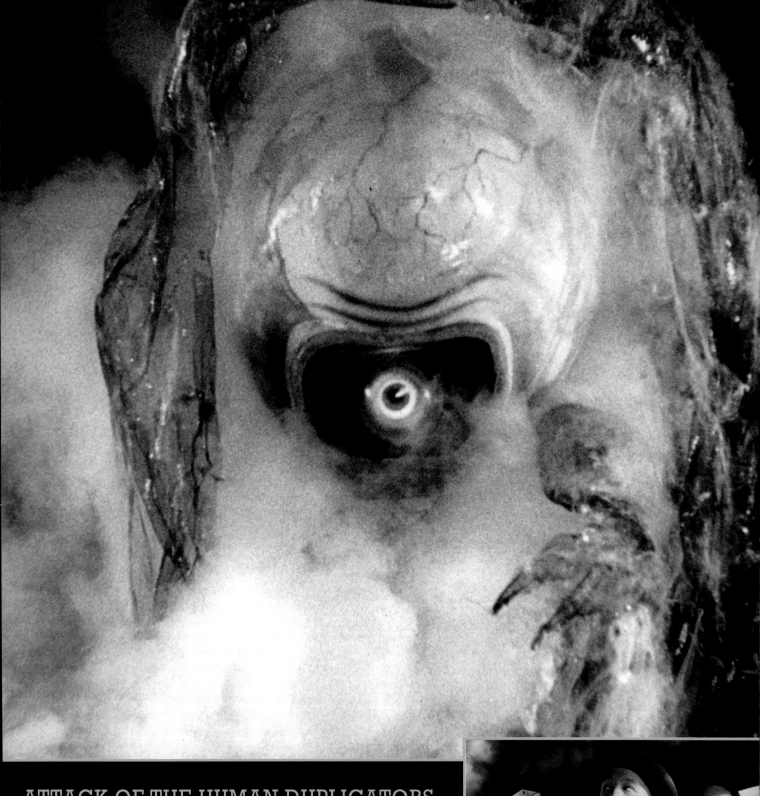

ATTACK OF THE HUMAN DUPLICATORS

ABOVE: The glowering Xenomorphs of *It Came from Outer Space* capture and copy unsuspecting humans (RIGHT), much to the horror of telephone linemen Frank (Joe Sawyer) and George (Russell Johnson).   OPPOSITE PAGE: An especially sinister alien replicates Frank. *Outer Space* author Ray Bradbury employed alien shape-shifters in many of his stories, most notably *The Martian Chronicles*. Other significant '50s sci-fi films that showcase the concept include *Invaders from Mars*, *Invasion of the Body Snatchers*, and *I Married a Monster from Outer Space*.

WHO MADE IT:

Columbia Pictures (U.S.). Director: Steven Spielberg. Producers: Michael Phillips, Julia Phillips, Clark Paylow. Writer: Steven Spielberg. Cinematography (color): Vilmos Zsigmond. Music: John Williams. Special Photographic Effects Supervisor: Douglas Trumbull. Alien design: Carlo Rambaldi. Starring Richard Dreyfuss (Roy Neary), Francois Truffaut (Claude Lacombe), Teri Garr (Ronnie Neary), Melinda Dillon (Jillian Guiler), Bob Balaban (David Laughlin), Roberts Blossom (farmer), Cary Guffey (Barry Guiler).

WHAT IT'S ABOUT:

A rash of UFO sightings affects civilians and government professionals alike. Telephone lineman Roy Neary's life changes dramatically; he becomes obsessed with an image he's compelled to pursue, much to the consternation of his wife and family. Another eyewitness, Jillian, is visited by the extraterrestrials, and her little boy Barry is abducted. Soon Neary and Jillian are off to Wyoming, driven by their compulsion, where they are intercepted by officials preparing for a major event: the landing of an alien craft, based on information and coordinates provided by the space beings. Roy and Jillian witness this monumental close encounter between scientifically-prepared humans and entities from outer space, who astonish all with their amazing spaceships. Ultimately, little Barry and other abductees from times past are returned. A surprised Neary is chosen to accompany the aliens back to their planet, and the giant ship lifts off for the return voyage.

WHY IT'S IMPORTANT:

Like Spielberg's seminal thriller *Jaws*, *Close Encounters* is neatly divided into two story sections: the first half covers average American Roy Neary's obsessive journey after witnessing a UFO display, the second half is an almost documentary-like representation of what an actual government-arranged first encounter might play like. Both parts of the film are handled with passion and the kind of exciting, colorful cinematic syntax viewers came to expect from SS during this period. Oscar-winning Richard Dreyfuss is an excellent choice for Neary, his schmuck-next-door quality exactly right as he and other bewildered civilians follow their abstract obsession simply because they must. Yet, as much as their compulsive journey interests Spielberg, it's the event itself that probably inspired him to make *CE3K*. Calling upon all the newfangled special effects technologies and related expertise available, he fashions a captivating first contact display that dwarfs anything previously attempted. There is no major distrust of government here, as would become standard for *The X-Files* and almost everything along these lines that followed. We're actually grateful that the U.S. is so scientifically prepared, so the full impact of this historic meeting can be absorbed and processed for maximum benefit. Doug Trumbull's astonishing fx produce buzzing, ethereal spacecraft, along with the ultimate "mother ship," a glorious upside-down chandelier that can't help but steal this extraterrestrial light show. Delivering his second knockout sci-fi score of 1977, John Williams provides a five-note motif that enables scientists to establish contact with the aliens, which, by a bizarre coincidence, duplicates the same five notes used by Peter Graves to contact ETs in 1952's cold war polemic, *Red Planet Mars*. Getting the childlike space beings to look convincing proved to be an issue, so Spielberg conceals most of them in evocative silhouettes, his trademark back lighting making that task relatively easy. More emotional and visual than intellectual, *Close Encounters of the Third Kind* is nevertheless a sci-fi masterpiece, introducing modern viewers to the pure bliss of following one's instinctive passions, come what may. At this juncture of his career, and life, Mr. Spielberg was the ideal filmmaker to escort us down this reinvigorating path.

ABOVE, LEFT: Jillian Guiler (Melinda Dillon) and her son Barry (Cary Guffey) have to dodge a speeding UFO on the roadway. ABOVE, RIGHT: Roy Neary (Richard Dreyfuss) begins sculpting the image of the Devil's Tower mountain in Wyoming, which is somehow implanted into his psyche. FAR RIGHT: Barry faces his cosmic abductors.

The climax of *Close Encounters of the Third Kind* is the arrival of an immense "mothership," a city of light co-conceived by director Spielberg that dwarfed anything previously seen on the sci-fi screen. The Oscar-nominated effects were created by Doug Trumbull.

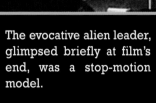

The evocative alien leader, glimpsed briefly at film's end, was a stop-motion model.

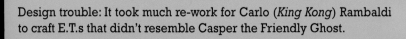

Design trouble: It took much re-work for Carlo (*King Kong*) Rambaldi to craft E.T.s that didn't resemble Casper the Friendly Ghost.

117

Poster/photos: © 1972 Universal Studios

WINNER 1972 CANNES FILM FESTIVAL JURY PRIZE AWARD
Only American Film to be so Honored

SLAUGHTERHOUSE-FIVE

Billy
Pilgrim
lives
from time
to time
to time...

A GEORGE ROY HILL · PAUL MONASH PRODUCTION

SLAUGHTERHOUSE-FIVE

"One of the most daring, original, and totally fascinating pictures ever made."
Rex Reed,
N.Y. Daily News

MICHAEL SACKS · RON LEIBMAN · VALERIE PERRINE
Based on the novel by KURT VONNEGUT, Jr. · Screenplay by Stephen Geller · Directed by George Roy Hill · Produced by Paul Monash
Music by Glenn Gould · A Universal Picture · TECHNICOLOR

R

WHO MADE IT:

Universal Pictures (U.S.). Director: George Roy Hill. Producers: Paul Monash, Jennings Lang. Writer: Stephen Geller, based on a novel by Kurt Vonnegut Jr. Cinematography (Technicolor): Miroslav Ondricek. Music: Glenn Gould. Starring Michael Sacks (Billy Pilgrim), Ron Liebman (Paul Lazzaro), Eugene Roche (Edgar Derby), Sharon Gans (Valencia Merble Pilgrim), Valerie Perrine (Montana Wildhack), Holly Near (Barbara Pilgrim), Perry King (Robert Pilgrim).

WHAT IT'S ABOUT:

Emotionally scarred by his World War II experiences, a gentle, decent man named Billy Pilgrim has apparently become "unstuck in time," jumping from one period of his curious life to another. And these unexpected interludes aren't necessarily confined to the Earthly realm. On the wedding day of his daughter, for example, Billy is kidnapped by inquisitive aliens and comfortably maintained in a space zoo with a comely companion of his choice. He explains his bizarre life's experience to interested listeners everywhere, but no one is entirely sure if Pilgrim is mad or merely recounting true, often outrageous and in many cases traumatic events.

WHY IT'S IMPORTANT:

Novels have no problem jumping around from one period of time to another, but movies are generally a more linear, grounded experience, making an adaptation of Kurt Vonnegut Jr.'s celebrated story *Slaughterhouse-Five* a tad problematic. Gentle lead character Billy Pilgrim (Michael Sacks in an difficult performance) has become "unstuck in time," which means viewers follow him from the desolation of World War II all the way to an intergalactic zoo on distant world Tralfamadore, where he enjoys senior life and even parenthood with the vivacious centerfold model (Valerie Perrine) of his choice. Pilgrim even comes to know exactly how he is going to die, assassinated by an obsessed, psychotic idiot (Ron Liebman) he crossed paths with during the war. As with the accidental loss of Billy's wife in a traffic accident on her way to the hospital, death is presented as a random, often darkly humorous event.

Ultimately, it's the heart-wrenching recreation of 1945's fire-bombing of Dresden that becomes this movie's most memorable sequence and emotional powderkeg. Director George Roy Hill carefully sets things up with fanciful views of picturesque, fairy tale-like exteriors, soon to be blasted into smoking ash and rubble. For the most part, Hill allows this controversial event to be judged objectively (though veteran character actor John Dehner has a funny bit as an egotistical historian who recently completed a book on the subject, but has no interest in talking to an actual survivor).

Aimed at the art house crowd, *Slaughterhouse Five* opened to excellent reviews and mediocre box office, becoming something of a cult item on cable and video over the years. Arguably the most offbeat and original time-travel story ever conceived, it renders the experience both personal and existential, providing a very different, very welcome new slant on a familiar sci-fi premise.

Ken Russell's outré vision of obsession, truth-seeking and primal screams...

35 ALTERED STATES 1981

Poster/photos: © 1981 Warner Bros.

In the basement of a university medical school Dr. Jessup floats naked in total darkness. The most terrifying experiment in the history of science is out of control.

ALTERED STATES

'ALTERED STATES' WILLIAM HURT BLAIR BROWN BOB BALABAN CHARLES HAID
DANIEL MELNICK · JOHN CORIGLIANO · SIDNEY AARON · PADDY CHAYEFSKY
HOWARD GOTTFRIED · KEN RUSSELL [X]

WHO MADE IT:

Warner Bros. (U.S.). Director: Ken Russell. Producers: Daniel Melnick, Stuart Baird, Howard Gottfried. Writer: Sidney Aaron, based on the novel by Paddy Chayefsky. Cinematography (Technicolor): Jordan Cronenweth. Music: John Corigliano. Starring William Hurt (Eddie Jessup), Blair Brown (Emily Jessup), Bob Balaban (Arthur Rosenberg), Charles Haid (Mason Parrish), Miguel Godreau (Primal Man), Peter Brandon (Hobart), Drew Barrymore (Margaret Jessup), Charles White-Eagle (The Brujo).

WHAT IT'S ABOUT:

Conducting experiments in an isolation chamber, driven, unorthodox young scientist Eddie Jessup makes use of hallucinogens, specifically untested ones used in mystical Mexican rituals. Before long, Dr. Jessup pushes himself to an unbelievable extreme, briefly regressing into a prehistoric man. Although his wife Emily becomes greatly concerned, Jessup keeps pushing himself further, seeking answers to eternal conundrums while abandoning his family in the process. Finally, only Eddie's love for Emily, grounded in reality, is able to bring him back from the cosmic brink.

WHY IT'S IMPORTANT:

At a time when most big studio fantasy films were aggressively comic book-like (Lucas' *Star Wars* and *Raiders*, the Salkinds' *Superman* series), *Altered States* dared to be grown-up, far out and dark, as befits a Ken Russell experience. Also befitting the colorful filmmaker is an opportunity for wildly extravagant visual set-pieces, conveniently plot-motivated in that *States* concerns itself with a brash young scientist who takes mind-screwing trips on a regular basis. Sure, this movie's decidedly adult; but that doesn't mean that a prehistoric ape-man and a bunch of misshapen monsters can't figure into the narrative. And they're not even a part of the wacked-out hallucinatory sequences, which offer their own over-the-top pleasures. At the heart of this modern-day Faust scenario is Dr. Jekyll – sorry, Dr. Jessup (William Hurt) a charming young genius obsessed with a driving passion to find "God" within himself. He's perfectly suited to another advanced specimen, Emily (Blair Brown), and the movie significantly charts their relationship from first meeting through marriage, break-up, and final metaphysical denouement. These two practically eat up Paddy Chayefsky's sidewinding scientific patter, and listening to them spar with advanced theorems instead of traditional domestic issues is one of the film's pleasures. Both well-cast performers are ably supported by Bob Balaban and Charles Haid as worried colleagues. The centerpiece of *States* and the thing that apparently drove writer Chayefsky up the wall (and possibly swinging from the ceiling) is the devolution of Jessup into a prehistoric man-ape, beautifully enacted by Miquel Godreau. His appearance is brief but powerful enough to dominate the film, racing into oncoming cars like a crazed animal and making a bloody killing at the zoo.

Finally, after the full catalogue of special effects has been exploited (with state-of-the-art depictions of Jessup's twisted, inhuman incarnations), it's his love for Emily that provides our tortured explorer with the answer he's been seeking. There's no higher state to "transcend to" when the only significant thing in the universe is something already achieved, the tangible love he and his wife have for each other. True, this is the old "there's no place like home" theme made shiny with a PhD and some *Outer Limits*esque poetry, but it happens to be exactly what this odd little story has been about all along. Here's to love, Dr. Jessup: the ultimate trip.

34 ALIENS 1986

 137 1.85

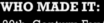

Poster/photos: © 1986 20th Century Fox

WHO MADE IT:

20th Century-Fox/Brandywine Productions (U.S.). Director: James Cameron. Producer: Gale Anne Hurd, Walter Hill, David Giler, Gordon Carroll. Writer: James Cameron, from a story by Cameron, Giler and Hill. Cinematography (Eastmancolor): Adrian Biddle. Music: James Horner. Alien Effects Creator: Stan Winston. Starring Sigourney Weaver (Ellen Ripley), Michael Biehn (Cpl. Dwayne Hicks), Lance Henriksen (Bishop), Paul Reiser (Carter Burke), Bill Paxton (Pvt. Hudson), Carrie Henn ('Newt'), William Hope (Lt. Gorman), Jenette Goldstein (Pvt. Vasquez).

WHAT IT'S ABOUT:

After years of deep-space hibernation, warrant officer Ellen Ripley is picked up in a shuttle ejected from the mining craft Nostromo. Questioned, she warns superiors about a deadly, elemental alien life form that slaughtered her crewmates, but she is widely disbelieved. Not long after, Ripley is asked for assistance when contact is lost with colonies believed to be in the Alien danger zone. To cure herself of incessant nightmares, Ripley returns to the stricken planet with eager marines and becomes a second mother to stranded little Newt, a girl who lost her parents to the marauding monsters. Ripley must contend not only with Alien enemies, including a monstrous, multi-armed Queen, but a treacherous Company man and a synthetic human with uncertain motives.

WHY IT'S IMPORTANT:

The unexpected success of *The Terminator* got James Cameron *Aliens*, and it's a fit so perfect even Ridley Scott purists can't really argue the point. Although Scott's cinematic vision is more self-consciously artful, Cameron is no slouch in the poetry department himself, giving the film a languid texture and pace that had Fox execs somewhat concerned initially (even cut down dramatically for theatrical release, it's nearly an hour before the first genuine monster attack occurs). Cameron provides his trademark obsession with macho military action, transforming Scott's elegant Old Dark Spaceship into an opportunity for muscular marines (male and female) to strut their stuff, with plenty of "lock and load"-style dialogue to please the *Rambo* audience and six year-old boys. Fortunately, Ellen Ripley is the soul of this sequel story, a rational, deep-feeling civilian with enough personal moxie to mix it up with the machos. Sigourney Weaver was a nobody when she made *Alien*; in *Aliens*, she's a confident A-list actress confirming her position as the cinema's foremost female action star. Equally adept at other roles, Weaver continues to have a special fondness for this career-launching character; she played the part in four movies before Fox decided to mix *Aliens* and *Predators* ("An absolutely terrible idea," opined Sigourney). Cameron effortlessly fleshes out the character by giving her a stranded little girl to protect (upgraded from Jones the Cat) and a synthetic human she comes to respect (Lance Henriksen), conquering her understandable prejudices in the process.

Smartly realizing that even a horde of Aliens may not be enough to thoroughly satisfy a thrill-craving audience, Cameron has Stan Winston create the mother of all space monsters, keeping this amazing-looking "Queen" off-camera until the final stages of the drama. Indeed, a character as novel and strong as Ripley requires an adversary of astonishing power, and the female angle allows for an interesting textural analogy: both "women" are risking life and limb to protect their endangered children.

Exciting, smart and with a solid emotional core, *Aliens* solidified Sigourney Weaver's reputation as a mainstream star and elevated James Cameron to the head of the sci-fi movie-making class. It plays to this day as a thrilling rollercoaster ride in the best sense of the term.

ABOVE: Nostromo's shuttle is discovered by Company men. RIGHT: Ellen Ripley (Sigourney Weaver) leads a platoon of buff Marines on a mission that will wipe out most of them.

Aliens slaughter Lt. Gorman's best military operatives, but Vasquez (Jenette Goldstein) "stays frosty" till the bitter end. BELOW: Bishop (Lance Henriksen) ripped in half by the vicious Queen.

Ripley to Queen: "Stay away from her you bitch!"

Makeup genius Stan Winston inspects what may be his greatest full-size creation, the horrific Queen from *Aliens*.

WHO MADE IT:

National Pictures/20th Century-Fox (U.S.). Director: William Cameron Menzies. Producer: Edward L. Alperson. Writers: Richard Blake, from a story by John Tucker Battle. Cinematography (Supercinecolor): John F. Seitz. Music: Raoul Kraushaar and (uncredited) Mort Glickman. Starring Helena Carter (Dr. Pat Blake), Arthur Franz (Dr. Kelston), Jimmy Hunt (David MacLean), Leif Erickson (George MacLean), Hillary Brooke (Mrs. Mary MacLean), Morris Ankrum (Col. Fielding), Max Wagner (Sgt. Rinaldi), Milburn Stone (Capt. Roth), Bill Phipps (Sgt. Baker), Janine Perreau (Kathy Wilson), Luce Potter (Martian intelligence – uncredited).

WHAT IT'S ABOUT:

A little boy named David MacLean witnesses the landing of a flying saucer in the sand pit just beyond his home. His father heads over to investigate, but returns the next day a changed, unfeeling man, the opposite of his true nature. Desperate, David begins noticing more "transformed" people and is disbelieved by most of his elders. Fortunately, Dr. Pat Blake and local astronomer Dr. Kelston are finally convinced, and the armed forces are called in. Apparently these aliens come from a dying world and are using their advanced technology to transform Earthlings into sabotaging spies, all part of their master invasion plan. Ultimately, both David and Pat are swallowed up by opening sand holes and taken to the impassive Martian leader, who orders Blake brainwashed. At the same time U.S. soldiers manage to penetrate the enemy's underground tunnels and plant explosives on their spaceship. Everyone runs from the blast area, even as young David tosses and turns in his sleep... the entire experience is revealed as a dream.

WHY IT'S IMPORTANT:

If Siegel's *Body Snatchers* is the ultimate personal invasion movie for adults, then *Invaders from Mars* should claim a parallel prize for eight year-old viewers. Two generations grew up haunted by the nightmarish sounds and sights of William Cameron Menzies' sci-fi pulpfest, most notably those funky "sand holes" swallowing up unsuspecting victims to the tune of a weird wailing ("That sound!"). Menzies seems to be replicating dream-state throughout the entire movie; sets are designed for their stark, unreal quality (the police station), and even the leisurely revolving of an observatory telescope takes on a curious reverie. As many reviewers have pointed out, the broken fence "that once extended across the sand pit" is ripe with unconscious symbolism.

Clearly, I'm not the first to classify Menzies as an artistic genius. His remarkable production design for *Gone With the Wind* and *Things to Come* puts him in a class by himself. As for his Martians, the bug-eyed, velour-suited slaves who trundle through underground tunnels are reasonably scary, but Menzies saves his greatest conceptual ideas for their leader, an impassive, tentacled brain-being who controls his mutant soldiers from within a transparent globe. Little Jimmy Hunt pounding his fists on this bubble as the evil Martian Intelligence glowers at him is one of the movie's highlights. Also worth mentioning is Kraushaar/Glickman's evocative and wildly energetic music score, which is heard almost non-stop (the alien "wail" associated with the ground opening up is an unforgettable aural creation).

In the early '80s, a tongue-in-cheek remake of *Invaders from Mars* was produced, complete with Stan Winston-designed aliens. Lacking even the stylish pleasures of *Strange Invaders*, this retro redo pales in comparison with Menzies' celebrated original.

Little David MacLean (Jimmy Hunt) witnesses the nocturnal landing of a spaceship. Soon, the sand pit area behind his house becomes a focal point in this battle against alien invasion. INSERT, RIGHT: A frantic Sgt. Rinaldi (Max Wagner) is pulled under by "swallowing" sand.

LEFT: Director Menzies keeps the colorful interior of his Martian flying saucer under wraps until Act III, as military forces finally penetrate the stronghold. BOTTOM: Dr. Blake (Helena Carter) is captured by mute mutants and prepared for crystal mind control.

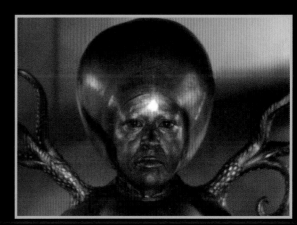

The impassive Martian Intelligence (Luce Potter) earns the fury of young David McLean.

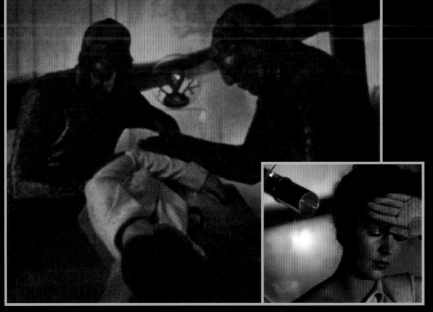

The British release of *Mars* ends differently: no "dream" twist, just Drs. Blake and Kelston saying good-night to tuckered-out alien fighter David.

32 DESTINATION MOON 1950

91 1.37

TWO YEARS IN THE MAKING!

DESTINATION MOON
COLOR BY TECHNICOLOR

Produced by GEORGE PAL · Directed by IRVING PICHEL
Screenplay by RIP VAN RONKEL, ROBERT HEINLEIN and JAMES O'HANLON

WHO MADE IT:

Eagle Lion (U.S.). Director: Irving Pichel. Producer: George Pal. Writers: James O'Hanlon, Rip Van Ronkel, Robert A. Heinlein, based on the novel "Rocketship Galileo" by Heinlein. Cinematography (Technicolor): Lionel Lindon. Music: Leith Stevens. Starring John Archer (Jim Barnes), Warner Anderson (Dr. Charles Cargraves), Tom Powers (General Thayer), Dick Wesson (Joe Sweeney), Erin O'Brien-Moore (Emily Cargraves), Grace Stafford (Woody Woodpecker's Voice).

WHAT IT'S ABOUT:

Committed to the idea of a lunar landing, General Thayer enlists the aid of American production man Jim Barnes to raise funds for the building of a rocketship. Red tape and political heat nearly scuttle their voyage, but the constructed ship manages to blast off, carrying a four-man crew: Barnes, Thayer, scientist Charles Cargraves, and Brooklyn-based civilian Joe Sweeny, a last-minute addition. In space, the voyagers deal with weightlessness and some anxious moments outside the ship, but finally set down on the lunar surface without incident. It's a spectacular moment for the human race as a flag of peace is planted by Cargraves. But the accidental loss of rocket fuel threatens to cut short their historic visit, and for a while it seems as if someone is going to be left behind. Stripping the ship down to its essentials, they avoid the problem, and all expedition members return home safely.

WHY IT'S IMPORTANT:

After years of producing short-subject *Puppetoons* for Paramount, George Pal decided to take on space travel for his first feature-length movie, tapping into the public's post-war fascination with all things futuristic. At some point, Pal nixed the idea of outright fantasy and took a calculated risk with a pseudo-documentary, based very much on scientific fact, about a privately-financed expedition to the moon undertaken by three civilians. Ironically, the film was adapted from a far more fanciful novel by Robert Heinlein, with the rocketship crew discovering more than unexpected cracks on the lunar surface (would you believe Nazi refugees planning a takeover of Earth?).

Still, Pal and director-actor Irving Pichel, familiar to horror movie fans as Zander from *Dracula's Daughter* (1936), manage to keep *Destination Moon* interesting even without the pulpy pleasures of bug-eyed monsters and other B-movie distractions. Recognizing the pitfalls of a technology-themed storyline, Pal insisted on an earthy, fish-out-of-water crew member audiences could identify with. The result is comedian Dick Wesson as Joe Sweeney, the kid from Brooklyn, a last minute addition to Warner Anderson's space flight when one of the scientists falls ill. This wound up being a brand new cliché for sci-fi movies, along with meteorite showers and the suspenseful gambit of insufficient rocket fuel for a return ship.

Eschewing romance and excessive melodrama, *Destination Moon* offers a succinct, satisfying three act structure: Act I is concerned with preparing for the trip, Act II is the space voyage itself, Act III involves lunar exploration and figuring out how to get home. It's that simple. Shot in glorious Technicolor (check out those day-glow space suits) and filled with rational-sounding technical jargon, *Destination Moon* makes the most of its limited goals, and goes a long way in establishing credibility for its newly-minted movie genre.

Tidbit: Leith Stevens composed the grandiose, "can do" background music for *Destination Moon*, the first of three scores for producer George Pal (*When Worlds Collide* and *The War of the Worlds* followed).

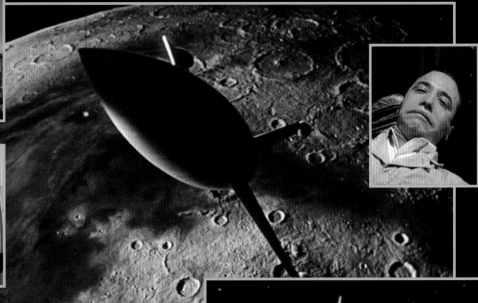

Producer George Pal was determined to imbue his space film with down-to-earth credibility, from practical considerations like funding (Woody Woodpecker recruited as a salesman, ABOVE INSERT), to the imagined gravitational pressures associated with take-off (that's Dick Wesson with the grimace, INSERT RIGHT).

ABOVE: Renowned celestial painter Chesley Bonestell prepared this magnificent rendering of the moon's surface. RIGHT: The astronauts set up a telescope. To create the illusion of size on a small set, resourceful designers added perspective-cheating cracks to the lunar crust.

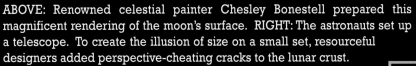

RIGHT (A): Prepping a space walk. RIGHT (B): Author Robert A. Heinlein and wife visit the *Destination Moon* set.

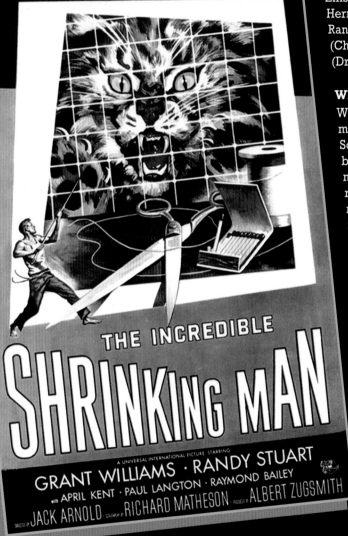

A FASCINATING ADVENTURE INTO THE UNKNOWN!

THE INCREDIBLE SHRINKING MAN

A UNIVERSAL INTERNATIONAL PICTURE STARRING
GRANT WILLIAMS · RANDY STUART
with APRIL KENT · PAUL LANGTON · RAYMOND BAILEY
JACK ARNOLD · RICHARD MATHESON · ALBERT ZUGSMITH

WHO MADE IT:

Universal-International (U.S.). Director: Jack Arnold. Producer: Albert Zugsmith. Writer: Richard Matheson, based on his novel "The Shrinking Man"; Richard Alan Simmons (uncredited). Cinematography (b/w): Ellis W. Carter. Music: Earl E. Lawrence, Irving Gertz, Hans J. Salter, Herman Stein (all uncredited). Starring Grant Williams (Scott Carey), Randy Stuart (Louise Carey), April Kent (Clarice), Paul Langton (Charlie Carey), Raymond Bailey (Dr. Thomas Silver), William Schallert (Dr. Bramson), Billy Curtis (Midget).

WHAT IT'S ABOUT:

While on vacation, Robert Scott Carey is engulfed in a strange sea mist that covers his body with shimmering particles. Not long after, Scott discovers that his clothes don't fit properly, and soon it becomes apparent that, astonishingly enough, he is shrinking a little more each day. Scientists deduce that the mist was some kind of radioactive cloud and search frantically for a cure. Although they manage to stop the process for a brief time, the contamination reasserts itself, and soon Carey is living in a dollhouse. After an attack from an ordinary housecat, the Shrinking Man is plunged into his own basement, and grieving wife Louise gives him up for dead. But Carey somehow endures, calling upon his intelligence and ingenuity to survive. The challenges of procuring food (cheese stolen from a mouse-rap), not drowning in a flood (the water heater explodes) and avoiding death in the jaws of a local black widow spider become his primary concerns. In the end, still shrinking at an alarming rate, triumphant Carey finds acceptance as a legitimate force of nature with every right to exist.

WHY IT'S IMPORTANT:

Jack Arnold's best science fiction film for Universal, *The Incredible Shrinking Man* is a relatively ambitious adaptation of Richard Matheson's novel, with Matheson himself co-scripting. Its melancholy trumpet theme and the silhouette-graphic of a man getting smaller in the opening titles indicate that we're already on a somewhat higher level of sophistication than, say, *Creature from the Black Lagoon*. Indeed, *Shrinking* owes something to *The Man in the Gray Flannel Suit* and other '50s social dramas dealing with the "diminished" post-war American male. The metaphor may be buried, as it should be, but it's still a part of Jack Arnold's thesis, subtly elevating the overall experience. Matheson's novel is told in flashbacks, with miniaturized Scott Carey, preparing for his fateful battle with the spider, recalling "how it all began." The author hoped to approach his screen adaptation in much the same manner, but Universal balked, feeling *Shrinking Man*'s exotic premise required a grounded, linear plot progression. In any case, the scenario is pretty much divided between the discovery/unsuccessful treatment of Carey's unprecedented condition, and the little guy's mythic battle for survival in his peril-laden "basement universe." Bland and uninteresting Grant Williams is a fine choice for Matheson's bland and uninteresting protagonist. But as the cliché goes, special optical effects are the real stars of this film. Universal's fx veterans provide a number of memorable set-pieces, from radioactive ocean mist to the housecat attack (down, Rhubarb!) and the final, carefully-choreographed climax. The ambiguous ending of *Shrinking Man* also enhances Matheson's material, with the religious themes better earned than similar talking points in George Pal films. "To God, there is no zero" is simply another way of saying that every living entity matters, that it's special and worthwhile. Amen to that. Jack Arnold's sometimes awkward, mostly impressive "social" sci-fi masterpiece captures this forward-thinking psychology with commendable style and vigor. It doesn't matter that the Shrinking Man isn't "rescued" in the conventional sense or restored to "normalcy" in the final reel; he inevitably rescues himself with a uniquely personal form of self-acceptance. End of sermon.

ABOVE: Scott Carey (Grant Williams) stares at an oncoming radioactive cloud, the enigmatic source of his "shrinking problem." BELOW: Carey defends himself against family pet Butch, a housecat-turned-predatory monster. Butch was played by famous movie feline Rhubarb (aka "Orangy"), who also popped up as Neutron in Universal's *This Island Earth.*

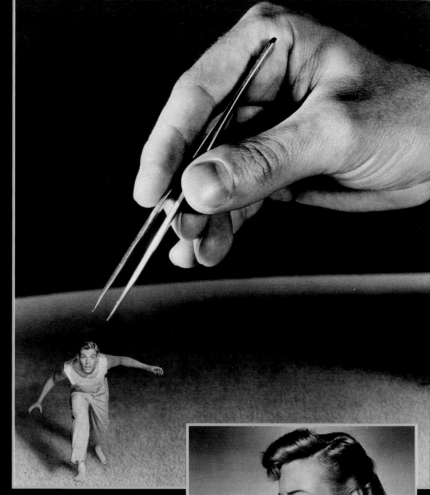

RIGHT: Carey's disintegrating marriage to Louise (Randy Stuart) parallels his fantastic physical diminishment.

Searching for food (some mousetrap cheese will do) and battling local predators (like an especially aggressive spider) keeps Scott busy during his basement odyssey.

LEFT: Director Arnold, star Williams, and the "piece of cake" prop. RIGHT: Jose Ferrer (far right) visits the *Shrinking Man* set.

127

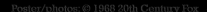
Poster/photos: © 1968 20th Century Fox

WHO MADE IT:

20th Century-Fox/APJAC Productions (U.S.). Director: Franklin J. Schaffner. Producers: Mort Abrahams, Arthur P. Jacobs. Writers: Michael Wilson, Rod Serling, based on the novel by Pierre Boulle. Cinematography (DeLuxe Color): Leon Shamroy. Music: Jerry Goldsmith. Special Make-Up: John Chambers. Starring Charlton Heston (Col. George Taylor), Roddy McDowall (Cornelius), Kim Hunter (Dr. Zira), Maurice Evans (Dr. Zaius), James Whitmore (Assembly President), James Daly (Dr. Honorious), Linda Harrison (Nova).

WHAT IT'S ABOUT:

Astronaut George Taylor and his mini-crew crash land on a barren planet where apes have evolved into the dominant species, and humans are hunted like animals. His companions killed or butchered, Taylor fights for his life against formidable Dr. Zauis, an orangutan who knows a great deal about his planet's checkered past. Befriended by progressive chimpanzees Zira and Cornelius, the stranded, abused astronaut escapes and finally learns the terrible truth while staring up at half-buried remains of the Statue of Liberty: he's been on Earth all along, but an Earth of the distant future that was all-but destroyed by atomic war.

WHY IT'S IMPORTANT:

The mid-1960s were the "cold years" for science fiction movie fans. The Verne-Wells classical approach had run its course after a solid decade (beginning with Disney's *20,000 Leagues Under the Sea* in '54), and only a handful of futuristic movies were being produced, possibly because major studios were still concerned about the stigma of B-cheesiness wafting about them. One stalwart film company that always seemed willing to take a chance on the downtrodden genre was 20th Century Fox. They had just rolled the dice and came up smiling with *Fantastic Voyage*, a high-profile, critically-acclaimed Oscar winner that made a fortune. *Planet of the Apes*, developed by artists with substantial pedigrees, would be Fox's next mega-project along these lines.

Although the plot resembles some *Twilight Zone* storylines (guess that's why you hire Rod Serling as screenwriter), the presence of mega-star Charlton Heston and *Apes'* overall muscular, widescreen, outdoor flavors lend it an impressive movie identity of its own, and almost immediately. The odd notes of Jerry Goldsmith's theme, matched with floating starbursts, signal a very different kind of experience ahead. There is a most welcome gritty reality to all of those early scenes dealing with survival and preliminary exploration, culminating in *Apes'* finest set-piece, the hunt. And even if Taylor's cynicism is a tad ham-fisted, the sight of Charlton Heston laughing derisively at the planting of an American flag says very clearly that this is a late '60s movie, reflecting the frustration and anxiety of that volatile period. And then there are the Apes. The closest things we fans had to science fiction "monsters" in 1968, they are imaginative, persuasive simian-human hybrids, conceived and developed by makeup impresario John Chambers, who would earn an Oscar for his work. It's perhaps a bizarre twist of fate that another group of intelligent apes would be fascinating sci-fi movie audiences the very same year (in Kubrick's *2001*). But Zira, Cornelius, and wily Dr. Zaius became instant superstars of the genre regardless, turning up in less-satisfying sequels and other spinoffs for the next decade or so.

Although Tim Burton made a game (some say lame) attempt to re-invent the franchise in *2001*, 1968's *Planet of the Apes* remains the one to beat, a winning combination of fantasy, action-adventure and surprisingly bitter social commentary.

Col. George Taylor (Charlton Heston) is a cynical sono-fabitch who re-discovers his faith in humanity…

…only to have it dashed to Hell again. ABOVE: Taylor tries to let the arguing Apes know he's not just another dumb human.

Taylor makes a few loyal friends among the simians. RIGHT: Nova (Linda Harrison) joins her new suitor at the end of a leash.

ABOVE: Captured! BELOW: Taylor holds Dr. Zaius (Maurice Evans) prisoner. BELOW, RIGHT: Zira (Kim Hunter) kisses her human friend in spite of the fact that he's "so damned ugly." BELOW, FAR RIGHT: "You blew it up!"

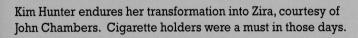
Kim Hunter endures her transformation into Zira, courtesy of John Chambers. Cigarette holders were a must in those days.

129

FUTURE SHOCK

There were five *Planet of the Apes* movies produced by 20th Century Fox in the late '60s and early-to-mid '70s, followed by both a live-action network TV series and an animated incarnation. Critics and audiences seem to delight in these colorful but cynical sci-fi adventures, which forecast the bleakest of all possible futures for humanity. Tim Burton took a crack at the franchise in 2001 with his much-despised "re-imagining" (a term now replaced by "re-boot" in Hollywood parlance). The original '68 *Apes*, a showcase for brawny Charlton Heston and the Fox make-up department, still towers over all. BELOW: Maurice Evans as Dr. Zaius drives home a point before the imposing statue of the simian Lawgiver. OPPOSITE PAGE: Kim Hunter gave her chimpanzee doctor character Zira a distinctive and irresistible personality; equally fine was Roddy McDowall (not pictured) playing her inquisitive scientist husband Cornelius. Fox's resident make-up genius John Chambers won an Oscar for his unforgettable and iconic creature designs, which evolved basic chimpanzees, orangutans and gorillas into sentient, quasi-human individuals.

WHO MADE IT:

Universal Pictures (U.S.). Director/Producer: Robert Wise. Writer: Nelson Gidding, based on a novel by Michael Crichton. Cinematography (Technicolor): Richard H. Kline. Music: Gil Melle. Starring Arthur Hill (Dr. Jeremy Stone), David Wayne (Dr. Charles Dutton), James Olson (Dr. Mark Hall), Kate Reid (Dr. Ruth Leavitt), Paula Kelly (Karen Anson), George Mitchell (Jackson), Ramon Bieri (Major Manchek), Peter Hobbs (General Sparks).

WHAT IT'S ABOUT:

Scoop VII, a U.S. Army satellite, crashes to Earth in New Mexico, leaving countless dead bodies in its wake. It appears something retrieved from outer space has contaminated the local population, and only an old man and an infant survive this tragedy. An elite scientific team headed by no-nonsense Dr. Jeremy Stone examines what is ultimately dubbed "the Andromeda strain" in Stone's massive, state-of-the-art bio-investigating facility, Wildfire. It's ultimately a race against time to solve Andromeda's mystery and stop this vile contagion from spreading and threatening our planet.

WHY IT'S IMPORTANT:

Although director Robert Wise is praised for his genre versatility, he has made a few high-profile science fiction movies, ranging from classic (*The Day the Earth Stood Still*), to inadequate (*Star Trek: the Motion Picture*). Somewhere in between is this ambitious adaptation of Michael Crichton's best seller, *The Andromeda Strain*. Shot only a few years after Kubrick's *2001* and boasting color-coordinated high-tech sets, *Strain* actually belongs to the sub-genre of biological infestation thrillers (you can count on the hero wearing a bulky protection suit at some point, complete with hood). Still, the focus and ambience is strictly sci-fi, as the "nemesis" is a microscopic alien life form with the capacity to infect our entire species instantaneously (shades of Carpenter's *The Thing*, which clearly owes something to Crichton's concept).

One of *Andromeda Strain*'s most obvious assets are reliable cast members who seem thoroughly at home in their highly-professional roles. Arthur Hill is progressive authority personified as the unflappable driving force behind Wildfire, an ultra-sophisticated underground facility in Nevada designed to handle scientific emergencies such as the one depicted in this scenario. It's actually newcomer to the team James Olson who provides some inevitable conflict, as he's saddled with the unenviable task of being the only member who can prevent Wildfire from atomically self-destructing if the contaminating virus under investigation should break loose. Olson's desperate efforts to stop this pre-arranged nuclear detonation provide the breathless climax, a conceptual 'ticking clock' cannily revisited by Ridley Scott in his equally tense conclusion to *Alien*. Other members of Arthur Hill's grim-faced scientific team have their moments as well, in particular David Wayne as a casual believer in extraterrestrial life ("Sounds a little far-fetched," complains Olsen), and stocky Kate Reid as an argumentative, no-nonsense physicist burdened by epilepsy.

In some ways more of a science class engaged in a technical challenge than a movie driven by characters with relatable problems, *The Andromeda Strain* is certainly not for the casual, half-thinking viewer. But fans of both "outbreak" thrillers and smartly speculative science fiction stories should find satisfaction in this consistently intriguing, well-polished ride.

WHO MADE IT:

J. Arthur Rank Organization (U.K.)/Universal Pictures (U.S.). Director: Alexander Mackendrick. Producers: Michael Balcon, Sidney Cole. Writers: Roger MacDougall, John Dighton, Alexander Mackendrick, from a play by Roger MacDougall. Cinematography (b/w): Douglas Slocombe. Music: Benjamin Frankel. Starring Alec Guinness (Sidney Stratton), Joan Greenwood (Daphne Birnley), Cecil Parker (Alan Birnley), Michael Gough (Michael Corland), Ernest Thesiger (Sir John Kierlaw), Duncan Lamont (Harry).

WHAT IT'S ABOUT:

Pathologically dedicated scientist Sidney Stratton invents a fabric that is both indestructible and stain-proof, alarming various aspects of his community. Enterprising businessmen want to buy Stratton's formula to

suppress it (the garment industry will be destroyed if clothes never need to be replaced), and local workers are terrified that his discovery will end their production jobs. Ultimately, it's Sidney that everyone turns their anger toward, finally cornering the white-suited (and luminous) scientist in an alley. It is then and there that his formula proves unstable – amusing the crowd, but depressing the visionary inventor.

WHY IT'S IMPORTANT:

Sometimes mistaken for "yet another" Alec Guinness comedy from this period, *The Man in the White Suit* is without question a science fiction movie – it plays fast-and-loose with a real scientific principle, spins an enjoyable yarn, and winds up saying something significant about the human condition. In some circles, an sf story or movie that doesn't accomplish all of the above is a failed example of the form, no matter how many colorful spaceships or aliens are hurled at the audience. *Man* requires none of this pulp iconography to dramatize its potent story points, although Guinness' glowing white suit has the whiff of sci-fi gimmickry about it, even while it neatly dovetails with the thematically accurate "knight in shining armor" motif. Guinness plays Sidney Stratton, a pure, incorruptible breed of visionary scientist that might be described as progress personified. Granted, this is another thinly-veiled Christ analogy, but smartly incorporated into a sharp social satire that smoothly balances absurd-seeming fantasy with an even-handed condemnation of all political sides. Stratton's miracles are feared; he becomes the despised "Enemy of the People," turns into an object of ridicule when his fantastic suit decomposes, and finally exits the film triumphantly, a figure of eccentric, unstoppable dignity. In constant motion, great-as-always Guinness gets fabulous support from a wonderful, instantly recognizable group of character actors (that's *Bride of Frankenstein*'s Dr. Pretorious himself, Ernest Thesiger, as the venal and diseased representative of old-school capitalism), and not one, but two loyal lovers (Joan Greenwood being his true sweetheart).

As both social commentary and sci-fi fable, *The Man in the White Suit* continues to wear well, earning new admirers with each passing decade.

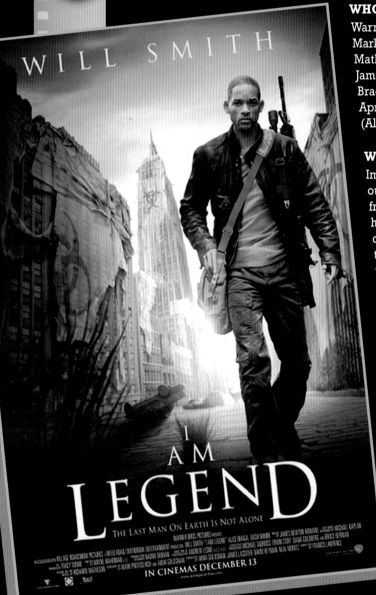

WHO MADE IT:
Warner Bros. (U.S.). Director: Francis Lawrence. Producers: Writers: Mark Protosevich and Akiva Goldsman, based on the novel by Richard Matheson. Cinematography (Technicolor): Andrew Lesnie. Music: James Newton Howard. Starring Will Smith (Robert Neville), Alice Braga (Anna), Charlie Tahan (Ethan), Salli Richardson (Zoe Neville), April Grace (TV Personality), Dash Mihok (Alpha Male), Joanna Numata (Alpha Female), Emma Thompson (Dr. Alice Krippin) - uncredited.

WHAT IT'S ABOUT:
Immune to an incredible, man-made virus that has apparently wiped out most of the human race, scientist Robert Neville searches frantically for a cure in the eerily empty streets of New York City. He has only a loyal pet dog and memories of his loving family for comfort. Meanwhile, lurking in the shadows are mutant victims of this plague, known as The Infected, who watch Neville's every move, waiting for him to make a fatal mistake. Using his own immune blood, Neville tries desperately to reverse the effects of the virus and save what's left of his species. But The Infected are not so easily vanquished, and the creatures manage to corner Neville in his own lab. Nothing less than the future of life on Earth hangs in the balance as these two opposing races confront one another...

WHY IT'S IMPORTANT:
They say third time's the charm. After two interesting but imperfect attempts to film Richard Matheson's seminal novel of a contaminated future, superstar Will Smith, himself no stranger to sci-fi properties, took on the juicy role of Neville, the last man on Earth... who is not alone.

Matheson's original conceit was right out of the old pulps. Our infected planet becomes a world of blood-sucking vampires, with all the reliable clichés of this classic horror sub-genre (repelled by garlic, can't stand mirrors, etc.) lovingly addressed with a sly spin. Morose but committed Neville literally drives wooden stakes through these corrupted hearts in the best Carl Kolchak tradition. This traditional angle was maintained in the first movie based on *I Am Legend*, Italy's scarifying *The Last Man on Earth*, starring Vincent Price. Vampires became blanched and preachy mutations (possibly influenced by *Beneath the Planet of the Apes'* telepaths) with eerie white pupils in 1972's *Omega Man*, with a more heavily-armed Neville, played by still-buff Charlton Heston, patrolling empty LA streets in search of his wretched enemies. By the time Smith got around to the character, a lot had happened, both in the world and in the movies. AIDS brought a greater awareness of the widespread dangers of disease, especially the ones we never see coming. Although Neville (Morgan in the Price version) was originally Caucasian, we're at a point in our culture where no one blinks at the choice of a black actor taking on such a role (as long as it works; Smith bombed famously as gun-totin' secret agent James T. West a few years earlier). Finally, the era of CG effects has fully bloomed, for better or worse. In the case of *Legend*'s nocturnal wretches, many film buffs deemed it "worse," as there was no real justification for animated monsters in this scenario. Then again, modern filmmakers have problems with slow-moving shamblers, even in zombie movies proper. Frankly, I have less of a problem with the special effects method than with the ultimate dramatic use of these characters. If *I Am Legend* has any real flaw, it's an awkward, makeshift ending necessitated by unresolved plot issues relating to Matheson's original theme: Neville may be "legend" because of his Christlike attempt to save humanity (a cure for the disease), but he's infamous to the world's "new" population, a heinous mass murderer who captures and conducts foul experiments on innocent mutants. A different ending that tried to address this dichotomy was actually filmed, but it proved emotionally unsatisfying and was scrapped.

Neville (Will Smith) inherits a world that can still be saved... if it wants to be. BELOW: Man's best friend is his pet German Shepherd. Sleep tight, guys.

The Brooklyn Bridge doesn't fare well in this adaptation of Matheson's novel. Other doomsday survivor thrillers include Arch Obler's *Five*, MGM's *The World, the Flesh and the Devil*, and a couple of Roger Corman quickies.

"Normal" Robert Neville confronts monstrous Infected leader Alpha Male (Dash Mihok), understandably distressed after Neville experimented on his girlfriend.

More end-of-the-world wreckage, nicely crafted.

Will Smith is at his intense best in the "escape from New York" sequence, the most ambitious scene in the film.

WHO MADE IT:

Paramount Pictures (U.S.). Director: Byron Haskin. Producer: George Pal. Writer: Barre Lyndon, based on the novel by H.G. Wells. Cinematography (Technicolor): George Barnes. Music: Leith Stevens. Starring Gene Barry (Dr. Clayton Forrester), Ann Robinson (Sylvia Van Buren), Les Treymane (General Mann), Robert Cornthwaite (Dr. Pryor), Sandro Giglio (Dr. Bilderbeck), Lewis Martin (Pastor Dr. Matthews Collins), Bill Phipps (Wash Perry), Vernon Rich (Col. Heffner), Jack Kruschen (Salvatore), Cedric Hardwicke (Narrator).

WHAT IT'S ABOUT:

A mysterious meteor-like object streaks across the heavens and crash-lands in California. Investigating scientist Dr. Clayton Forrester suspects that there's more to this curious event than meets the eye, and he's right: the object is actually a Martian cylinder containing deadly war machines that blast unsuspecting humans to ashes. The U.S. military is called in, but these monster saucers are simply too powerful; they protect themselves from retaliation with an "electronic umbrella." Soon the entire world is under siege, and even thermonuclear weapons have no effect on the awesome invaders. A chance encounter with an actual Martian in a crushed farmhouse enables Forrester and Sylvia Van Buren to escape with a sample of alien blood. Although the scientists attempt to regroup and fight the Martians with a biological approach, they are thwarted as the world's social order begins to crumble. Ultimately, the ruthless aliens are stopped cold and humanity is saved by the "littlest things" residing on our planet – invisible germs that indigenous Earth species have no problem with.

WHY IT'S IMPORTANT:

It's interesting to consider the various movie incarnations of this story that almost happened. Like *When Worlds Collide*, *War of the Worlds* was once a property Cecil B. DeMille had been toying with. When Orson Welles first came to Hollywood in 1939, RKO practically begged him to do a film adaptation so they could capitalize on his infamous radio hoax (Lord, what a picture that would have made; but we did get *Citizen Kane* as compensation). Finally, it took the 1950s and George Pal to realize this seminal tale of planetary invasion and the undefeatable power of nature's infrastructure, not to mention the soothing balm of religious faith.

Challenge Number One: updating Wells' Victorian-era classic. Pal had his screenwriters throw out the book's dated characters and replace them with more logical substitutes, most notably Gene Barry as a handsome young scientist. This enables the savvy protagonist to track events and even impact on them with fresh insights and discoveries. The standout sequence in the farmhouse gives director Byron Haskin a chance to scare audiences with ominous shadows and clutching talons, but also provides Barry with a sample of Martian blood, allowing a key plot point to be established a couple of scenes later (the invaders are biologically vulnerable). And giving love interest Ann Robinson a priestly uncle to be martyred sets the semi-appropriate religious motif in motion.

Technically, this is as good as it gets in the 1950s. The manta ray-like war machines and the barely-glimpsed Martian make a lasting impression, the later a truly bizarre take on H.G. Wells' squid-like entities, designed and inhabited by Paramount's resident creature creator Charles Gemora. And while those cables holding up the machines are painfully visible, viewers tend to cut pre-digital fx a good deal of slack, especially when the craftsmanship and design are as brilliant as this.

ABOVE: the Martian landscape. RIGHT: a cylinder lands, bringing death and disintegration with it.

ABOVE: Hero Clayton Forrester (Gene Barry) and local Sheriff Bodony (Walter Sande) witness Martian ruthlessness first hand. RIGHT: The sleek alien warships protect themselves with transparent, electrically-generated shields ("Guns... tanks... bombs... They're like toys against them!" proclaims a frustrated General Mann).

The Martians are thwarted by bacteria harmless to humans.

Sylvia Van Buren (Ann Robinson) has a memorable farmhouse encounter with an inquisitive alien.

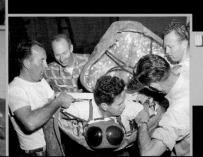

The ultra-weird Martian was designed and inhabited by Charles Gemora, Paramount's resident makeup master.

FEAR OF A RED PLANET

With inspiration and uncredited involvement from Cecil B. DeMille, producer George Pal launched his Technicolor adaptation of H.G. Wells' *The War of the Worlds* in 1953. Left: Charlie Gemora as an inquisitive Martian, exploring an abandoned farmhouse in one of the film's most frightening sequences . Above: The wired war machine miniatures are set up by technicians on a Paramount soundstage. Right: Dr. Clayton Forrester (Gene Barry) and Sylvia van Buren (Ann Robinson) are rightfully terrified by hostile aliens in their midst. Paramount revisited this classic property twice, once in the '80s with a TV series that served as a direct sequel to Pal's film (Robinson even appeared in an episode), and later in the 21st century with Spielberg's compelling remake.

WHO MADE IT:

TriStar Pictures/Carolco Pictures (U.S.). Director: James Cameron. Producers: Gale Anne Hurd, Mario Kassar, James Cameron. Writers: James Cameron, William Wisher. Cinematography (color): Adam Greenberg. Music: Brad Fiedel. Special Makeup Producer: Stan Winston. Starring Arnold Schwarzenegger (The Terminator), Linda Hamilton (Sarah Connor), Edward Furlong (John Connor), Robert Patrick (T-1000), Earl Boen (Dr. Silberman), Joe Morton (Miles Dyson), S. Epatha Merkerson (Dyson), Jenette Goldstein (Janelle Voight).

WHAT IT'S ABOUT:

Young John Connor, son of Sarah Connor and future soldier Kyle Reese, is targeted for termination by Cyberdyne, a super-advanced robot society that rules the world of tomorrow and fights human resisters with android assassins. Two Terminators are sent through time with John as their objective: one is identical to the robot that menaced Sara and killed Reese, but it functions as an ally; the other is an advanced, liquid-metal changing T-1000, programmed to destroy young John. On the run, the Connors and their Terminator bodyguard endure astonishing assaults, before both battle-scarred robots fight an awesome battle to the death in a refinery. John Connor survives, and humanity has a future.

WHY IT'S IMPORTANT:

The original *Terminator* was a low-budget movie that built its reputation mainly on video. Not so the inevitable sequel: between 1984 and 1990, body-builder Arnold Schwarzenegger had become a major Hollywood superstar, having made a splash in *Raw Deal*, *Predator*, and *Commando* – all as a result of his *Terminator* success and a newly-minted tough guy persona, complete with quotable one-liners. Director James Cameron had also graduated to the big leagues, earning critical raves and boffo boxoffice for his action-oriented sequel to Ridley Scott's *Alien*. Now, with total confidence, both filmmaker and star embarked on the most expensive movie ever produced, and Hollywood's bean counters held their breath.

Like *Titanic* and ultimately *Avatar*, *Terminator 2: Judgment Day* achieved tremendous commercial success, justifying the enormous sums invested in it. Moreover, it accomplished the neat trick of being a sequel to a relative cheapie without a noticeable difference in style or flavor. Like the 1984 film, *Judgment Day* deftly combines action, sci-fi concepts, pathos and darkly evocative, doomsday poetry. Schwarzenegger is a protecting android this time around, with villainous duties falling to a new adversary, a highly-advanced liquid-metal Terminator (Robert Patrick) like nothing we'd seen on movie screens before... except, of course, for Cameron's own *Abyss*, which had introduced the computer-generated liquid effects honed to perfection here. The character of Sara Connor (Linda Hamilton), a soft and relatively demure girl-next-store in the first movie, has become a buffed and borderline psychotic "soldier" prepping for the inevitable nightmare of Judgment Day. She and her rebellious teenage son John (Edmund Furlong), the offspring of now-dead Kyle Reese and the eventual protector of future humankind, bond with their hulking bodyguard, forming the ultimate functional/dysfunctional family unit. As expected in a James Cameron film, the action set-pieces are superb, even the ones without obvious special effects: a thrilling motorcycle and diesel truck chase come to mind.

For the record, this property inspired two more theatrical movies (including an ambitious misfire boasting the stars of *The Dark Knight* and *Avatar*), neither helmed by Cameron, and a short-lived television series, *The Sarah Connor Chronicles*. With the arrival of Michael Bay's brain-dead *Transformers* flicks, the distinctions between dark poetry enlivened by action in robot-themed scenarios and rapid-paced action for its own sake have been forever blurred.

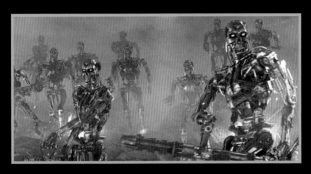

LEFT: A full-scale war sequence boasting metallic skeletal warriors starts the film off on an exhilarating high-note. BELOW: The most disturbing sequence in *T2* (other than, perhaps, the child's playground in flames under the opening credits), is Sarah's horrific nightmare of Judgment Day, where she (Linda Hamilton) is blasted into radioactive dust. RIGHT: Cool publicity portrait of Mr. Terminator himself (Arnold Schwarzenegger).

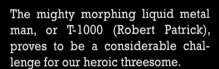

The mighty morphing liquid metal man, or T-1000 (Robert Patrick), proves to be a considerable challenge for our heroic threesome.

Inspecting the damage: Schwarzengger's robot character is put through quite a beating, requiring some Stan Winston makeup wizardry.

BE AFRAID.
BE VERY AFRAID.

WHO MADE IT:

20th Century-Fox/Brooksfilm (U.S.). Director: David Cronenberg. Producers: Stuart Cornfeld, Marc Boyman, Kip Ohman. Writers: Charles Edward Pogue, David Lynch, based on a short story by George Langelaan. Cinematography (color): Mark Irwin. Music: Howard Shore. Creature Effects: Chris Walas. Starring Jeff Goldblum (Seth Brundle), Geena Davis (Veronica Quaife), John Getz (Stathis Borans), Joy Boushel (Tawny), David Cronenberg (Gynecologist).

WHAT IT'S ABOUT:

Seth Brundle is an introverted genius on the cutting edge of teleportation, an amazing process that will "change the world as we know it." Veronica Quaife, an attractive reporter for a science magazine, becomes his personal documentarian, covering various experiments and some grotesque failures. Drunk and disappointed with himself personally, Seth enters the telepod and successfully transports himself, unaware of a fly inside the pod that winds up bonding with him on a molecular level. At first, Brundle is a new man, strong, confident and sexually insatiable. But before long he degenerates, the "fly" side of his chemistry gradually becoming dominant. Brundle ultimately becomes an insect-like monstrosity, merging with his own telepod as it explodes, before he's mercifully shot to death by an aghast Veronica.

WHY IT'S IMPORTANT:

David Cronenberg has always been fascinated by strange contortions of the human body. Fox's remake of *The Fly* enabled him to explore this premise with state-of-the-art makeup effects and an excellent, well-cast A-list actor, quite an effective combination. Produced by Brooksfilm, this modern fable of hope and tragedy is every bit as good as Kurt Neumann's 1958 original, decidedly better in certain ways. It pushes the envelope of both gore and pathos with a plot that ingeniously re-thinks the nature of the protagonist's metamorphosis, allowing for a fuller exploration of both his personality and the weird process of ongoing change that he's unleashed within himself. The 1958 movie was a romantic husband-and-wife affair, closer in many ways to *Altered States*. In contrast, new Fly Dr. Brundle is presented as the quintessential nerd, lovable but sheltered and inexperienced with the opposite sex. For his female companion, the script provides a beautiful but somewhat self-loathing journalist clawing her way to the top, and seizing upon Brundle's ground-breaking experiments as the possible key to her success. The nerd becomes a self-confident macho man after his first teleportation, reveling in primal pleasures long denied him. But when the Fly portion of his chemical makeup begins to assert itself, his inevitable degeneration cannot help but be heartfelt and tragic ("I was an insect who dreamed he was a man, and now the dream is over."). Well, not quite. Chris Walas' appropriately grotesque makeup designs dominate the second half of the drama. Instead of simply "swapped body parts" as in the original movie (and George Langelaan's short story), Cronenberg and company opt for the deterioration approach – a kind of sad analogy to AIDS, with the victim checking his worsening physical condition daily – before Brundle's persona is completely submerged. This final design (or I should say next-to-final design) bravely abandons humanity altogether, with Brundlefly now a full-fledged, multi-appendaged monstrosity. He changes one final time before his beloved summons the courage to shoot him to pieces, and that's when he literally bonds with his exploded teleportation pod, producing a partially metallic mutilation of his Fly physiognomy. The symbolism here is complete... Dr. Brundle and his work are literally one and the same, and he dies as he had lived. An engrossing film with memorable performances, *The Fly* is also enhanced by Howard Shore's lush score, which replaces the heavily romantic motif of the 1958 version with an equally compelling, more exploratory theme that captures the melancholy of Brundle's beautiful dream gone awry.

ABOVE: Modern Einstein Seth Brundle (Jeff Goldblum) "doesn't get out much," observes comely new documentarian Veronica (Geena Davis). BELOW: Brundle, made sexier and stronger by his impromptu teleportation, soon begins to degenerate. BELOW, LEFT A: Veronica's monstrous nightmare.

ABOVE: Brundlfly spews corrosive, mutilating saliva on "rival" Stathis Borans (John Getz). BELOW RIGHT: There is no separating Seth Brundle from his work, literally: the final metal-monster metamorphosis.

Director John Carpenter clowns with Chris Walas' full-size Fly prop. Walas would go on to direct this movie's well-cast, but less successful sequel.

23 ETERNAL SUNSHINE OF THE SPOTLESS MIND 2004 (108) 1.85

Jim CARREY Kate WINSLET Kirsten DUNST Mark RUFFALO Elijah WOOD Tom WILKINSON

LACUNA

I'M FINE WITHOUT YOU.

a revolutionary process

Eternal Sunshine of the spotless mind

This Spring, Clear Your Mind

WHO MADE IT:

Focus Features (U.S.). Director: Michel Gondry. Producers: Anthony Bregman, Steve Golin, David Bushell, Charlie Kaufman, Glenn Williamson. Writers: Charlie Kaufman, from a story by Kaufman, Michel Gondry and Pierre Bismuth. Cinematography (color): Ellen Kuras. Music: Joe Brion. Starring Jim Carrey (Joel Barish), Kate Winslet (Clementine Kruczynski), Gerry Robert Byrne (Train Conductor), Elijah Wood (Patrick), Thomas Jay Ryan (Frank), Mark Ruffalo (Stan), Jane Sdams (Carrie), David Cross (Rob), Kirsten Dunst (Mary), Tom Wilkinson (Dr. Howard Mierzwiak).

WHAT IT'S ABOUT:

Joel Barish is a quiet, decent guy who is horrified to discover that his ex-girlfriend, free-spirited Clementine, has undergone an experimental procedure that erases him from her memory. Deeply hurt, he decides to do the same thing. But before long, both former lovers begin to realize that the wonderful memories they share are simply too precious to loose. As hired erasure experts redouble their efforts, Joel and Clem resort to desperate, bizarre ways to counteract this morally-questionable process that now threatens to split them up forever.

WHY IT'S IMPORTANT:

Be forewarned: this offbeat confection from decidedly offbeat writer/director Charlie Kaufman requires lots of patience and a willingness to disconnect emotionally from any given scene at a moment's notice. This is the deliberate result of a realitybending premise that plunges its viewers through the same, perplexing and challenging situations as its protagonists are forced to endure. It's a risky approach that pays off big-time with audiences that are capable of comprehending these bewildering shifts; those who can't (or won't) will probably turnthe movie off half-way through so their headache can subside.

At the heart of this bizarre relationship drama is the dream-wish of every broken-hearted lover: to remove the profound emotional disturbance of an affair turned sour. "I wish I never met you" is given a simple yet ingenious sci-fi treatment with the implementation a wonky electronic process that can selectively erase human memories. Although this kind of twisty tampering is bound to result in some unexpected consequences, *Sunshine* stays focused on the obsessive, literally mind-blowing need to hold onto love no matter what, obviously reflected in our lead couple (Jim Carey and Kate Winslet), but also with at least two parallel relationships that Kaufman and his writers cannily set up.

Carry is quite excellent as *Sunshine*'s nice-guy protagonist Joel Barish, using but not abusing his comedic skills when called upon to portray Joel as a child, or indulge in some other far-fetched memory requirement. Winslet's Clementine ranges from shallow irritant to someone even the casual viewer can't help falling in love with, just as Joel does. A standout scene has Joel and Clem enduring each other's "honest" evaluation of one another after the break-up, which was recorded on tape to initiate the memory erasing procedure. It's one of the most heartbreaking little scenes ever created for movies, the emotional apex of a very often confusing, but generally inspired sci-fi parable.

22 VOYAGE TO THE END OF THE UNIVERSE 1964 (81) 2.35

aka Ikarie-XB1

WHO MADE IT:

Filmove Studio Barrandov (Czech Republic)/American International Pictures (U.S.). Director: Jindrich Polak. Writers: Pavel Juracek, Jindrich Polak. Cinematography (b/w): Jan Kalis, Sasa Rasilov. Music: Zdenek Liska. Starring Zdenek Stepanek (Captain Vladimir Abajev), Frantisek Smolik (Anthony Hopkins), Dana Medrika (Nina Kirova), Irena Kacirkova (Brigitta), Radovan Lukavsky (Commander MacDonald), Otto Lackovic (Michal the Coordinator).

WHAT IT'S ABOUT:

A sophisticated city-in-space known as Ikarie-XB1 leaves recognizable planetary systems and zooms into deep space, beginning a long, sometimes tedious voyage to a distant world. Along the way, brave crewmembers live their lives as normally as possible, with human fears, jealousies and other emotions presenting personal challenges. At one point, a derelict spaceship from the 20th Century is discovered, and a pair of investigating Ikarians lose their

lives. Members are also threatened by a strange sleeping sickness and a sabotaging crew member on the brink of madness. Ultimately, even as new life asserts itself aboard ship, the star voyagers reach their long-sought destination... a planet very much like the Earth.

WHY IT'S IMPORTANT:

Space flight in science fiction films generally results in a planetary landing, with most of the story centering around events on that world. This Russian-made epic is one of the few films to make the journey itself the story, involving us in the lives of a small community of hardy interstellar voyagers. In many ways, the quietly ground-breaking *Universe* is a precursor to Kubrick's *2001*, with melancholy astronauts (in this case, futuristic cosmonauts) watching old movies or chatting with loved ones via telescreens, thinking about the cherished world they're leaving behind, and wondering about what profound mysteries may lie ahead. Although the ensemble is convincing and several characters resonate (even the dorky robot with his monotonic "An-tony!" is memorable), it's space cruiser Ikarie that is the true star of this movie, a zooming galactic township on an all-important, predetermined mission. Given the (for the most part) single location of the film, Ikarie's interior sets are vast and meticulously designed, with cameras gliding in and around them for maximum effect. In what is perhaps *Voyage*'s finest sequence, the travelers encounter a derelict spaceship from the 20th Century, with eerily preserved crewmembers still playing cards or indulging in recreational activities when doom obviously engulfed them. Intended as a contrast to the more civilized, forward-thinking denizens of Ikarie, these glimpses of the past serve as a dark reminder of mankind's volatile heritage.

The U.S. release of *Voyage to the End of the Universe* was slightly re-edited to accommodate a "twist" ending: the planet our voyagers ultimately reach is Earth, as they are (are you ready?) extraterrestrials. Fortunately, the film's inherent power and novelty shine through, adding up to a *Voyage* that all science fiction film historians should take with great pleasure.

aka The Forbin Project

THIS IS THE DAWNING OF THE AGE OF COLOSSUS

(where peace is compulsory...freedom is forbidden... and Man's greatest invention could be Man's greatest mistake)

"THE FORBIN PROJECT"

Co-starring
ERIC BRAEDEN · SUSAN CLARK · GORDON PINSENT
Screenplay by JAMES BRIDGES · Based on the Novel 'Colossus' by D.F. JONES
Directed by JOSEPH SARGENT · Produced by STANLEY CHASE
A UNIVERSAL PICTURE · TECHNICOLOR® · PANAVISION®

WHO MADE IT:

Universal Pictures (U.S.). Director: Joseph Sargent. Producer: Stanley Chase. Writer: James Bridges, based on the novel "Colossus" by D.F. Jones. Cinematography (Technicolor): Gene Polito. Music: Michel Colombier. Starring Eric Braeden (Dr. Charles Forbin), Susan Clark (Dr. Cleo Markham), Gordon Pinsent (The President), William Schallert (CIA Director Grauber), Leonid Rostoff (Russian Chairman), Georg Stanford Brown (Dr. John F. Fisher), Martin E. Brooks (Dr. Johnson), Marion Ross (Angela Fields), William Sage (Dr. Blake).

WHAT IT'S ABOUT:

In an historic moment, the armed defenses of the U.S. are turned over to a super-computer called Colossus. Dr. Charles Forbin, inventor of this remarkable machine, is meeting with the American President when Colossus reveals "there is another system," meaning another super-computer, Guardian, just recently activated by the Soviet Union. Both computers wish to share information, which greatly concerns the rival world powers. When this exchange is denied, Colossus launches a missile attack, as does Guardian; it is clear that these imperious machines now control human destiny, for better or worse. Forbin is permitted to remain alive in order to interact effectively with his ruthless creation. Colossus also allows him a lover – colleague Dr. Cleo Markham, who is actually working secretly with the scientist in a daring scheme to end computer control. But Colossus sees through the plan and thwarts it, spilling more blood. Forbin begins to realize that his logical, unemotional approach to life is at least partially responsible for the technological nightmare he's unleashed. But Colossus promises a brave new world, one that, he projects, the good doctor himself will someday come to appreciate.

WHY IT'S IMPORTANT:

This modest masterpiece began life as a TV movie, but was elevated to theatrical status when Universal realized they had something better than usual on their hands. *The Forbin Project* as it was originally called was shot in Technicolor and full Panavision; the intellectual importance of its theme and the lack of conventional action convinced the studio to market it as a "prestige item" (this was one year after Kubrick's *2001*, the hardest act for any sci-fi film to follow). Unfortunately, this well-reviewed, John Frankenheimer-esque, futuristic message film wound up bombing at the boxoffice, forcing Universal to re-title and re-release the picture a year later. Selling headaches aside, what Sargent and company provide is a taut and compelling Cold War nail-biter, a sci-fi suspense thriller with genuine smarts, loosely inspired by *Frankenstein* (Forbin himself brings up the analogy), but in truth a study of suppressed emotion and, ultimately, an unwitting loss of humanity. Robotlike yet sympathetic and appealing, Eric Braeden is an excellent choice as star-crossed Dr. Charles Forbin, who remakes the world via his computer doppelganger, and lives to regret it. One must congratulate the screenwriters for including a bedroom scene that a) advances the plot, b) ties into *Forbin*'s semi-buried repression theme, and c) keeps less sophisticated viewers interested.

Except for a few necessary global stops (generally accomplished with stock footage), most of the film takes place in a central laboratory, complete with war room-level technology. Its downbeat resolution is not only in keeping with the bleak tenor of the times, but it actually ups the thematic ante, pushing already difficult questions to the next moral/ethical level: Will Dr. Forbin come to respect, even love, his renegade brainchild for "saving" mankind by eliminating the "illusion" of freedom? Yep, it's that's kind of sci-fi movie. No bloodthirsty monsters, no fist fights, just a few necessary gunshots fired in an unglamorous context. Thank you, Joseph Sargent, for a thought-provoking example of politically astute science fiction.

ABOVE: This spectacular matte painting opens the movie impressively. *Forbin* began life as a made-for-TV movie; director Joe Sargent would helm *Tribes* and *The Glass House* a few years later. BELOW: Susan Clark radiates intelligence and fresh-scrubbed beauty as Dr. Cleo Markham. The same year she'd appear opposite Burt Reynolds in Universal's semi sci-fi adventure, *Skullduggery*.

Dr. Charles Forbin and the Kennedyesque President (Gordon Pinset) monitor super-computer Colossus' latest strategic moves.

Joseph Sargent also directed *Nightmares* (1982), a theatrical feature made up of unaired episodes of Universal TV's short-lived *Darkroom* anthology.

WHO MADE IT:

Paramount Pictures/Spyglass Entertainment/Bad Robot (U.S.). Director: J.J. Abrams. Producers: J.J. Abrams, Alex Kurtzman, Damon Lindelof, Bryan Burk, Jeffrey Chernov. Writers: Robert Orci & Alex Kurtzman, based on the television series created by Gene Roddenberry. Cinematography (color): Dan Mindel. Music: Michael Giacchino. Starring Chris Pine (James T. Kirk), Zachary Quinto (Spock), Leonard Nimoy (Spock Prime), Eric Bana (Nero), Bruce Greenwood (Christopher Pike), Karl Urban (Dr. McCoy), Zoe Saldana (Nyota Uhura), Simon Pegg (Montgomery 'Scotty' Scott), John Cho (Hikaru Sulu), Anton Yelchin (Pabel Chekov), Ben Cross (Sarek), Winona Ryder (Amanda).

WHAT IT'S ABOUT:

James Kirk is born on the very day his father George dies on a starship under attack by a mysterious alien vessel. Twenty years later, Kirk has grown into a rebellious youth, but he's persuaded by mentor Captain Christopher Pike to pursue a career in Starfleet and live up to his enormous potential. This puts him on a collision course with a no-nonsense instructor, Lt. Spock, and the brash cadet continues to get himself into jams, big and small. A sudden emergency on Vulcan brings Kirk, his grousing friend Leonard McCoy, and several other promising young Fleeters to the newly-commissioned USS Enterprise, and eventually a confrontation with the alien vessel that destroyed George Kirk's ship twenty years before. Two different realities emerge as the Enterprise crew embarks on a desperate mission to save not only Vulcan, but imperiled planet Earth.

WHY IT'S IMPORTANT:

At a time when most sci-fi films and TV series were still "shockers" (with *Outer Limits* topping the list), Gene Roddenberry's *Star Trek* humanized the genre for a mass audience, making pop cultural history in the process. The daunting task of re-creating Captain James T. Kirk, along with Spock and the other iconic Trek heroes, fell to enterprising producer J.J. Abrams in 2009, who seemed strangely calm about the whole thing. Thankfully, this ease permeates his movie, an excellent, character-driven space adventure that captures the heart and soul of *Star Trek* proper with no apology. Ground zero for any remake, of course, is the robust character of Kirk. This film's writers fully understand their central subject; in young, ruddy-faced Chris Pine, Abrams finds his man: physically brash, intellectually smooth, impulsive and determined, but always charmingly self-effacing... Jim Kirk IS humanity, and he knows it. So does everyone in his orbit, including the new Mr. Spock (Zachary Quinto), who serves as principal rival (among other things, they both have the hots for sultry Lt. Uhura). It's a perfectly logical device to maintain tension and conflict throughout the story, while allowing these individuals to gradually appreciate each other's inherent qualities. Hitting exactly the right note, *Star Trek*'s colorful villain (Eric Bana) has a tragic motivation for his current atrocities, but this isn't allowed to interrupt the jaunty flow of life-threatening challenges that characterize Abrams' approach. Exceptionally clever sci-fi concepts are deftly called upon to balance two parallel worlds, one belonging to the Nimoy version of Spock, the other to Quinto's. Through the ingenious use of imaginative fiction, Abrams and company are able to have their classic *Trek* cake and eat it too, not only enabling both mythologies to co-exist, but actually enhancing each by proxy. In addition to getting the "hard stuff" right (writing and casting), *Star Trek* is the first film in the series to offer truly cinematic, breathtaking action-adventure set pieces on the level of a George Lucas fantasy. That three-man dive is breathtaking, and planet Vulcan bites the dust with heart-stopping believability. Although it's not about the special effects, and never was, *Star Trek* in its latest incarnation doesn't retreat from stylish visual exercises. All things considered, modern audiences have been given a splendid new crew of ingratiating explorers to take us where no viewer has gone before... and with all the right creative trimmings.

ABOVE: Young Jim Kirk (Chris Pine) stares up at the Enterprise-in-progress, a magnificent shot showcased in the trailer. RIGHT: Kirk's totally at home in the Captain's chair, while best friend Dr. McCoy (Karl Urban) is lost in troubling thought.

LEFT: Captain Christopher Pike (Bruce Greenwood) is a character re-imagined from the 1966 *Star Trek* TV series (Jeffrey Hunter played him originally) BELOW: Young Spock (Jacob Kogan) is plagued by Vulcan bullies.

BELOW: Villainous Nero, played by Eric Bana. Unlike the original timeline, where Kirk and his famous friends meet during the course of their careers, this re-conception unites them for Enterprise's very first voyage.

The two Spocks (Zachary Quinto, above, strangling Kirk) and Leonard Nimoy ("Live Long and Prosper").

On set, J.J. Abrams discusses the departure scene with his *Star Trek* cast. Abrams' take on the classic sci-fi property pleased audiences and critics alike.

149

THE OPTIMISM FACTOR

Every incarnation of *Star Trek* adheres to creator Gene Roddenberry's original vision of a hopeful, enlightened future for mankind. ABOVE: The perceptive 2009 movie "reboot" by J.J. Abrams was no exception. Pictured are the new Mr. Spock (Zachary Quinto) and Captain Kirk (Chris Pine), along with an ultra-streamlined starship Enterprise. INSERT: "With this, he could have explored life on the other planets": *The Day the Earth Stood Still*'s Klaatu (Michael Rennie) offers an extraordinary gift for the U.S. President… OPPOSITE PAGE: …but it's shot to pieces by a fidgety soldier upon the alien's arrival. Just as well, perhaps; such privileged knowledge of the cosmos might've upset the delicate balance of power during this crucial period of Earth's history.

WHO MADE IT:

20th Century-Fox (U.S.). Director: Robert Wise. Producer: Julian Blaustein. Writer: Edmund H. North, based on the story "Farewell to the Master" by Harry Bates. Cinematography (b/w): Leo Tover. Music: Bernard Herrmann. Starring Michael Rennie (Klaatu), Patricia Neal (Helen Benson), Hugh Marlowe (Tom Stevens), Sam Jaffe (Professor Jacob Barnhardt), Billy Gray (Bobby Benson), Frances Bavier (Mrs. Barley), Lock Martin (Gort).

WHAT IT'S ABOUT:

An alien ambassador named Klaatu lands his flying saucer in Washington D.C. and is promptly shot by a trigger-happy soldier. Recovering, Klaatu requests a meeting with all of Earth's leaders to discuss a most urgent problem, but is refused. Attempting to understand human behavior, he escapes government captivity and spends some quality time incognito with ordinary folk, including widow Helen Benson and her inquisitive son Bobby. Meanwhile, Klaatu and sympathetic scientific genius Prof. Barnhardt ponder how to get a distracted world's attention, and the alien decides to stop all electricity on Earth for an hour. It's little Bobby who ultimately discovers the true identity of "Major Carpenter," and Helen's suitor Tom Stevens who informs the authorities, hoping to be rewarded as a hero. Helen is soon pressed into service by an injured and dying Klaatu; she gives ultra-destructive robot Gort an imperative message, and the android, pre-programmed to destroy Earth, retrieves his companion's now-dead body instead. Using advanced technology, Klaatu is restored to life long enough to deliver his long-awaited warning: extend human violence into outer space, and the Earth will be obliterated. After biding Helen farewell, he and Gort take off in their spacecraft, leaving that all-important decision to us.

WHY IT'S IMPORTANT:

Perhaps more so than any movie in this book, *The Day the Earth Stood Still* is adored by fans of the sci-fi genre. Something about distinguished alien Klaatu's style and demeanor seems to push geekboy buttons, making him the role model for smart kids in the '50s (Mr. Spock would carry on the tradition a decade later). The idea of wedding futuristic sci-fi visuals and concepts with a sober warning about the very real dangers of nuclear testing seemed to justify the offbeat project to Fox's front office, although you'd never know it from the lurid ad campaign they dreamed up. True, Gort shoots death beams and vaporizes his share of soldiers and tanks. But the movie at its core is an intellectual polemic that uses a variation of Hollywood's fugitive formula to maintain suspense. There are two highly significant set-pieces: the title-inspired event, and Klaatu's final, clarifying speech to Earth's gathered leaders. Many critics have perhaps correctly concluded that the alien's suggested "police state" remedy for mankind's ills is fascistic, or at the very least reckless (see *Colossus: The Forbin Project*). This curious paradox is even more pronounced in the original story, where Gort's (or Gnut's) dominance over Klaatu has more bite; "He is the Master," the alien diplomat explains, turning to his implacable robot superior. And those in the galaxy who obey him are apparently the noble slaves of a peaceful and well-ordered cosmos. Klaatu claims we have a choice, but do we really?

Day is blessed with letter-perfect "new face" Michael Rennie as Klaatu (Spencer Tracy and Claude Rains were considered), and Patricia Neal's Helen Benson is one of the very few realistically portrayed female leads in 1950s sci-fi movies. Sam (*Lost Horizon*) Jaffe as the Einstein figure Barnhardt adds another element of class to Julian Blaustein's already impressive production. Oh, and yes, Bernard Herrmann's therimen-driven music score is a groundbreaking masterpiece.

ABOVE: The landed saucer in Washington D.C. – a flawless fx composite. LEFT: Klaatu is wounded by a fidgety soldier. Gort dramatically appears, reducing tanks and guns to molten pools.

LEFT: Judas figure Stevens (Hugh Marlowe), Helen (Patricia Neal), Prof. Barnhardt (Sam Jaffe, ABOVE). RIGHT: arranging for the global power blackout.

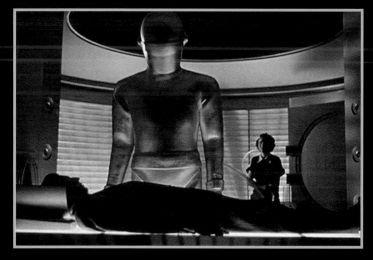

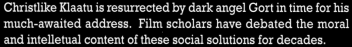

Christlike Klaatu is resurrected by dark angel Gort in time for his much-awaited address. Film scholars have debated the moral and intelletual content of these social solutions for decades.

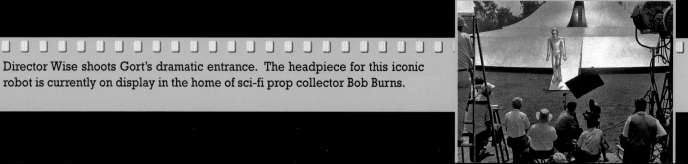

Director Wise shoots Gort's dramatic entrance. The headpiece for this iconic robot is currently on display in the home of sci-fi prop collector Bob Burns.

Poster/photos: © 1982 Universal Studios

The ultimate in alien terror.

THE THING

WHO MADE IT:

Universal Pictures (U.S.). Director: John Carpenter. Producers: Lawrence Turman, David Foster, Wilbur Stark, Larry Franco, Stuart Cohen. Writer: Bill Lancaster, based on "Who Goes There?" by John W. Campbell Jr. Cinematography (Technicolor): Dean Cundey. Music: Ennio Morricone. Special Makeup Effects Designer: Rob Bottin. Starring Kurt Russell (R.J. MacReady), Wilford Brimley (Dr. Blair), T.K. Carter (Nauls), David Clennon (Palmer), Keith David (Childs), Richard Dysart (Dr. Cooper), Charles Hallahan (Vance Norris), Peter Maloney (Bennings), Richard Masur (Clark), Donald Moffat (Garry), Joel Polis (Fuchs).

WHAT IT'S ABOUT:

In the Antarctic, members of an American scientific expedition are suddenly under siege by an apparent madman pursuing and shooting a running dog, before the pursuer himself is killed. Investigating a nearby Norwegian base, helicopter pilot MacReady and other team members discover that everyone there is dead; they also learn that these men had stumbled upon a crashed UFO, and the frozen corpse of a weirdly twisted creature that was recovered is now brought back to the American base. During the night, it becomes grotesquely clear than a malevolent alien life-form is imitating organisms on Earth, and soon our entire world will be infected. Trying to determine who is human and who is enemy in order to survive this horrific ordeal, MacReady and the others, armed with flamethrowers and TNT, become increasingly hostile and paranoid. In the end, only two team members are left. But are they both real, or is one an extraterrestrial imitation?

WHY IT'S IMPORTANT:

After reinvigorating the horror genre with *Halloween* (1977), John Carpenter was determined to re-imagine one of his favorite sci-fi films, *The Thing*, this time basing its scenario more directly on the original source material, a tense little story called "Who Goes There?" Fortunately, the recent success of Ridley Scott's *Alien* set the boxoffice stage for yet another bloody sci-fi chiller in a remote location, again with a bunch of cynical, self-interested malcontents trying to hold on as their numbers start to dwindle. At the time of release, most critics and fans were convinced that Carpenter lost his head (so to speak) over Rob Bottin's aggressively outlandish physical effects, which clearly dominate the film. Comparisons with the truly groundbreaking *Alien*, let alone Hawks' cherished original, were generally unfavorable. But as so often happens over the years, the qualities of Carpenter's film began to override a hasty, thoughtless dismissal. It's actually one of his best-directed films; comfortable as he was with the talented nymphs of *Halloween*, Mr. C's equally at ease with the grizzled macho men and sweaty slackers of this harrowing spook show. Moreover, physical (on set) special effects such as the kind Bottin provides are now viewed with something of a golden glow by movie buffs, who often roll their eyes at the "artificiality" of CGI in the same breath. The idea of an alien imitating other life forms has always been potent in fiction, allowing a mystery element to enhance an already exciting battle for survival. In one of the film's finest set-pieces, *Thing*'s alien is grotesquely revealed as he sits tied to a chair alongside equally restrained humans in what begins as a scientific test to unmask the invader. With a bunch of believable actors shouting like stuck pigs as Bottin's wildest effects explode around them, it's an incredible, exhilarating scene that never fails to amaze.

Combining elements of *Body Snatchers* and *Alien*, this juicy approach to alien invasion/human duplication seems to have hit an elemental nerve. Whether Carpenter's unique creative magic can be replicated in a newly-planned follow-up remains to be seen, however.

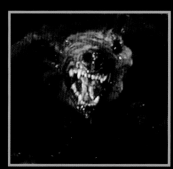

ABOVE: The alien saucer, resplendent with oscillating lights, spins to Earth in an earlier age. RIGHT: Helicopter pilot MacReady (Kurt Russell) makes a gruesome discovery in the alien-assaulted Norwegian base. BELOW: the UFO (matte painting by Albert Whitlock). BELOW RIGHT: More deadly duplications, and a fiery counterattack.

BELOW: the contaminated dog... or rather, the alien-duplicated dog. Replication and contamination go hand-in-hand in Bill Lancaster's bizarre, chilling screenplay.

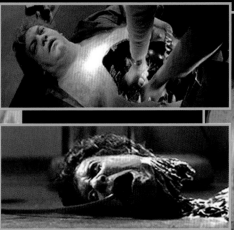

Some critics felt that director Carpenter got carried away with Rob Bottin's far-out horrors; today, these ambitious scenes are celebrated. LEFT: Bottin's infamous "spider-head" in all its grotesque glory.

RIGHT: Team members are tied together during a test to reveal who's human and who isn't, resulting in a geyser-like alien explosion that the others literally can't escape from.

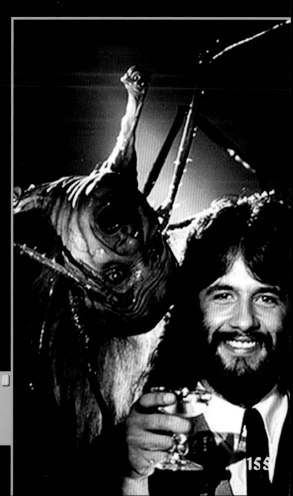

Special effects guru Rob Bottin, and friend. Acclaimed Bottin had recently provided the impressive werewolf fx for Joe Dante's *The Howling*.

155

WHO MADE IT:

Embassy International Pictures (U.K.)/Universal Pictures (U.S.). Director: Terry Gilliam. Producers: Arnon Milchan, Patrick Cassavetti. Writers: Terry Gilliam & Tom Stoppard, Charles McKeown. Cinematography (Technicolor): Roger Pratt. Music: Michael Kamen. Starring Jonathan Pryce (Sam Lowry), Robert De Niro (Archibald 'Harry' Tuttle), Katherine Helmond (Mrs. Ida Lowry), Ian Holm (Mr. M. Kurtzmann), Bob Hoskins (Spoor), Michael Palin (Jack Lint), Peter Vaughan (Mr. Helpmann), Ian Richardson (Mr. Warrenn), Kim Griest (Jill).

WHAT IT'S ABOUT:

Overwhelmed by a ruthless future society that is bureaucratic to the point of absurdity, harried technocrat Sam Lowry looks into the

killing of a wrongly-pegged terrorist, opening up a can of societal worms in the process. As Sam's problems escalate, he plunges into a relationship with the girl of his literal dreams, and soon finds himself branded a traitor himself. Pursued by nameless authorities, he is finally apprehended and is about to be subjected to a grueling interrogation, when Sam finds a simple, irreversible way of thwarting their venal goals.

WHY IT'S IMPORTANT:

Director Terry Gilliam had already proven himself a master of visual fantasy before embarking on *Brazil*, an expensive, studio-financed sci-fi movie that horrified execs, who came very close to "reshaping" it for audience accessibility. Fortunately, an emergency screening earned Gilliam's offbeat comedy-drama a flurry of awards and Oscar nominations, convincing Universal to release it just as presented to them. Prompted by the filmmaker's own rebellious nature, *Brazil* deals with a futuristic society ("...somewhere in the 20th Century...") that is Orwellian by way of overwhelming bureaucracy, apathy and ultra-indulgence – in other words, a parody of capitalism gone amok, where the privileged class lives a pampered good life even as terrorist bombs explode all around them. Caught in the middle of this societal muddle is nice-guy technocrat Sam Lowry (Jonathan Pryce), who escapes from the horror of day-to-day life through imaginative dreams, where he finds himself battling the system (a monstrous Samurai warrior) and rescuing a lady fair... who happens to have a real-life equivalent. Sam's efforts to assist this rebellious heartthrob lead to his own persecution, until, finally, only one form of escape is left to him. Over-the-top and certainly not for all tastes, *Brazil*, like *Dr. Strangelove*, uses pitch-black humor to make its devastating points about human stupidity and perfidy,

abandoning hope and ultimately embracing whatever personal catharsis hapless humans can find for themselves, whether it's sleep, death, or the questionable bliss of insanity. It is a significant visionary work by one of the most gifted filmmakers who ever stared through a camera lens.

16 GATTACA 1997

106 2.35

Poster/photos: © 1997 Columbia Pictures

WHO MADE IT:

Columbia Pictures (U.S.). Director/Writer: Andrew Niccol. Producers: Danny DeVito, Michael Shamberg, Stacey Sher. Cinematography (color): Slawomir Idziak. Music: Michael Nyman. Starring Ethan Hawke (Vincent Freeman), Uma Thurman (Irene Cassini), Gore Vidal (Director Josef), Xander Berkeley (Dr. Lamar), Jayne Brook (Marie Freeman), Maya Rudolph (Delivery Nurse), Elizabeth Dennehy (Preschool Teacher), Blair Underwood (Geneticist), Jude Law (Jerome Morrow), Alan Arkin (Det. Hugo).

WHAT IT'S ABOUT:

In the near future, genetically-imperfect Vincent Freeman, driven to explore outer space but denied this opportunity because of "biological deficiencies," assumes the identity of "perfect" Jerome Morrow. Using his surrogate's fluids, Vincent is able to escape detection at aerospace company Gattaca and ultimately finds himself scheduled for an actual space mission. But the unexpected murder of his program director spurs a police investigation, resulting in Freeman being suspected of the crime and imperiling his great dream of seeing the stars.

WHY IT'S IMPORTANT:

A welcome relief from action-adventure sci-fi movies, Andrew Niccol's *Gattaca* looks at tomorrow's bleak world with a hopeful eye. Playing God with advanced genetics is a new and potentially traumatic moral test for the human race. Not surprisingly, those born 'traditionally' are saddled with a profound disadvantage in this ultra- competitive society's eyes and instantly become second-class citizens, a new minority made up of all races. In ways good and bad, Niccol's well-ordered but borderline soulless futureworld is a clear extrapolation of our current unhappy social condition, where overpopulation, unavoidable self-awareness and a primal fear of survival have taken the smiles off human faces. Perhaps this is why Hawke's character Vincent Freeman (we'll forgive the emblematic name) is so refreshing. Motivated by twin compulsions of escape and discovery, he plunges into the riskiest of con jobs while navigating his way through perilous moral waters. The inclusion of a random murder into this scenario provides plenty of suspense for our hero, and, briefly, threatens to turn this smartly-conceived drama into something less fine. But Niccol knows what he's doing as a storyteller, and never loses sight of the specific story he is telling.

Hawke is exactly right as Freeman, intensely driven but never personally compromised by a grand dream to visit the stars and fulfill his potential. He receives first-rate support from wheelchair-bound Jude Law as designated surrogate Jerome and Loren Dean as Vincent's genetically-perfect brother, Anton. Also adding class to this cast are veteran performers Alan Arkin as a smart cop and Gore Vidal playing the Gattaca project director. Xander Berkeley also has a nice turn as a by-the-numbers doctor who discovers his latent humanity at a crucial moment.

Whatever else may be wrong with Niccol's class-driven future, it's gratifying to see those rockets zooming into the heavens almost nonstop. We simply have to escape planet Earth if our species is to survive, morally-intact or not. *Gattaca*'s writer/director is very aware of this imperative, deftly incorporating it into a rewarding and insightful scenario that acknowledges the worst in humanity, while celebrating the very best.

Poster/photos: © 1980 Lucasfilm & 20th Century Fox

THE STAR WARS SAGA CONTINUES

WHO MADE IT:

Lucasfilm/20th Century-Fox (U.S.). Director: Irvin Kershner. Producers: Gary Kurtz, George Lucas. Writers: Lawrence Kasdan, Leigh Brackett, from a story by George Lucas. Cinematography (color): Peter Suschitzky. Music: John Williams. Special Visual Effects: ILM. Starring Mark Hamill (Luke Skywalker), Harrison Ford (Han Solo), Carrie Fisher (Princess Leia Organa), Billy Dee Williams (Lando Calrissian), Alec Guinness (Ben 'Obi-wan' Kenobi), Anthony Daniels (C-3PO), David Prowse (Darth Vader), James Earl Jones (Voice of Darth Vader), Frank Oz (Voice of Yoda), Peter Mayhew (Chewbacca), Jeremy Bulloch (Boba Fett).

WHAT IT'S ABOUT:

From their secret base on Ice planet Hoth, the heroic Rebel Alliance continues in its struggle against Imperial aggression. But Darth Vader discovers their location, and soon Luke Skywalker is battling massive walking tanks while Han Solo is whisking Princess Leia away on the Millennium Falcon. As Solo and his team elude Imperial capture, Skywalker travels to swamp world Dagobah, where he is trained as a Jedi by wizened master Yoda. Soon he must interrupt these Force lessons to rescue his imperiled friends, who are finally nabbed by Vader in Bespin's Cloud City. Luke can't prevent Han from being encased in carbonite, but he does confront Vader for a monumental showdown... and learns the shocking truth about his father's fate.

WHY IT'S IMPORTANT:

With the seemingly insurmountable task of following and somehow topping *Star Wars*, *The Empire Strikes Back* manages to do just that for a good many viewers, adding some meat to the bones of George Lucas' charming characters and upping the fx ante. Additionally, Irvin Kershner's more casual style of direction allows his actors to ad lib – we'd never have "I love you!"/"I know" without this looser approach. Still, *The Empire Strikes Back* is still very much George Lucas' baby. Not content with turning apple-pie hero Luke Skywalker into the son of Satan, he wins over fawning audiences with a brand new character just as wonderful as anything conceived for the original: Jedi master Yoda, Frank Oz's personality-plus puppet and arguably the heart of the entire *Star Wars* saga. But before we venture to bog-planet Dagobah for our first encounter with this wise and wizened gnome, we are treated to an unforgettable attack of metal behemoths (AT-ATs), followed by an equally spectacular galactic chase through a field of asteroids. No-nonsense Princess Leia and rogue-turned-reluctant-hero Han Solo continue their Saturday morning cartoon romance, this time complicated by Han's semi-trustworthy pal, Lando Calrissian. The movie ends on a cliffhanger, annoying some critics initially, but ultimately proving to be just another aspect of an unusual plot structure that sends main characters in different directions for necessary developmental reasons, then reunites them (with one significant exception) for the finale. Nothing could have prepared audiences for Darth's dark revelation, of course, transforming this *Wizard of Oz*-like scenario into a pop tragedy – it's as if Dorothy had discovered that the Wicked Witch was her real mother. Yikes!

Although alive with imagination and thrilling action sequences, *Empire* nevertheless begins a trend that ultimately transformed Lucas' establishment-challenging '70s-style of cinema, still on display in *Star Wars*, into a more commercial, almost Cecil B. DeMille approach to blockbuster movie production. Later entries in the *SW* series would be even slicker and less surprising cinematically. But no one can ignore the hugely entertaining qualities of this wonderful, carefully-developed follow-up, for many fans the most satisfying two hours in that fanciful galaxy so far, far away...

ABOVE: Han (Harrison Ford), Luke (Mark Hamill) and a "tauntaun." RIGHT: Imperial Walkers on the march!

Luke is trained by Yoda on Dagobah, even as the Falcon dodges Imperial gunfire before entering an asteroid field.

RIGHT: Han Solo's fate. BELOW: Luke versus the Dark Lord.

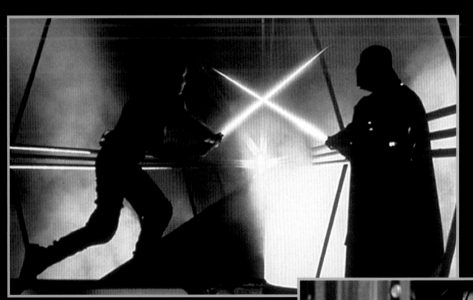

LEFT: Phil Tippett's stop-motion Walker models.
RIGHT: Director Irvin Kershner instructs Vader (David Prowse).

159

WHO MADE IT:

London Film Productions (U.K.)/United Artists (U.S.). Director: William Cameron Menzies. Producer: Alexander Korda. Writer: H.G. Wells, based on his novel "The Shape of Things to Come." Cinematography (b/w): Georges Perinal. Music: Arthur Bliss. Starring Raymond Massey (John Cabal/Oswald Cabal), Edward Chapman (Pippa Passworthy/Raymond Passworthy), Ralph Richardson (The Boss), Margueretta Scott (Roxana/Rowena), Cedric Hardwicke (Theotocopulos), Maurice Braddel (Harding), Sophie Stewart (Mrs. Cabal), Ann Todd (Mary Gordon).

WHAT IT'S ABOUT:

In 1940, a devastating aerial attack leaves cheerful Everytown in ruins, sparking a world war that goes on for decades. Drawn into the conflict is Oswald Cabal, a man of peace horrified by mankind's stupidity and seemingly endless need for self-destruction. As the years roll by, an epidemic called the Wandering Sickness wipes out a good deal of Earth's population. Slowly human society reasserts itself, and Cabal, now part of an advanced scientific union, patrols the world to root out primitive brigades and would-be despots, such as Everytown's ruthless Boss. Using the gas of peace, these feudal communities are quieted, and ultimately welcomed into Cabal's grand new order. A spectacular metropolis is created from the ruins of Everytown, and peace and plenty are provided for its citizens. Still, artists and dissatisfied civilians protest ongoing advancement, and threaten Oswald Cabal's latest symbol of insatiable human progress, the Space Gun.

WHY IT'S IMPORTANT:

Things to Come, a work of fiction inspired by H.G. Wells' speculative book, is a super-production from legendary British magnate Alexander Korda that rivals anything Hollywood was offering during this period. It boasts not only the directorial/design expertise of celebrated craftsman William Cameron Menzies, but also the services of Mr. Wells himself as screenwriter. The resulting epic is more than a little preachy (big surprise, given Wells' emphatic views), with many of its social "solutions" appearing questionable or naïve by current standards. But it dazzled 1936 audiences with the most spectacular and imaginative vision of the future ever presented on film, with the notable exception of Fritz Lang's *Metropolis*. Not only is Korda's City of Tomorrow an iconic masterpiece, but even the film's workaday fashions are striking, John Cabal's bubble-domed flying suit suggesting a touch of Buck Rogers. The film uses the destruction and re-creation of Everytown (a thinly veiled London) to chart mankind's progress over the course of many decades. A powerful civilian aerial attack dominates Act II, and an agonizing return to the Middle Ages, complete with signature plague (the Wandering Sickness), eventually gives way to Cabal's world-changing scientific revolution. Viewers are treated to a succession of jaw-dropping visuals, from futuristic tanks rolling across farmlands to the shattered, bombed out remains of what was once a great city.

Playing two generations of Cabals, star Raymond Massey embodies this forceful personality, creating a distinguished symbol of progressive humanity forever at war with the forces of militarism and "senseless competition." Dueling with a tribal Boss is child's play, but taking on conservative artisan Theotocopulos (Cedric Hardwicke) in a utopian, antiseptically perfect society is another matter entirely. It's here where humanity's perplexing illogic is spelled out: the irate civilian resents "living in the same world" with scientific dreamers who imperil emotional security with constant change; Oswald Cabal, on the other hand, considers advancement the only possible course for humanity ("All the universe, or nothingness. Which shall it be?"). H.G. Wells has clearly decided for himself, and, despite some severe last-minute edits, *Things to Come* represents his agreeably opulent term paper on the subject.

The film's real star is Everytown, sent to a premature grave, then reborn as a heavenly super-city by John Cabal (Raymond Massey), who helped to overthrow petty tyrants before the Age of Science took hold.

Although considered a classic today, *Things* was a boxoffice and critical disappointment back in '36.

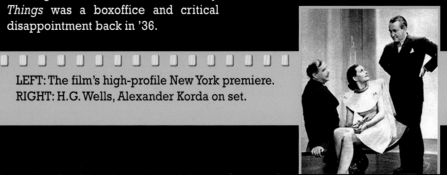

LEFT: The film's high-profile New York premiere.
RIGHT: H.G. Wells, Alexander Korda on set.

Being the adventures of a young man whose principal interests are rape, ultra-violence and Beethoven.

STANLEY KUBRICK'S CLOCKWORK ORANGE

R RESTRICTED

A Stanley Kubrick Production "A CLOCKWORK ORANGE" Starring Malcolm McDowell • Patrick Magee • Adrienne Corri and Miriam Karlin • Screenplay by Stanley Kubrick • Based on the novel by Anthony Burgess • Produced and Directed by Stanley Kubrick • Executive Producers Max L. Raab and S. Litvinoff • From Warner Bros. A Kinney Company

Exciting original soundtrack available on Warner Bros. Records

WHO MADE IT:

Warner Bros. (U.K./U.S.). Director: Stanley Kubrick. Producers: Stanley Kubrick, Si Litvinoff, Max L. Raab. Writer: Stanley Kubrick, from the novel by Anthony Burgess. Cinematography (Warnercolor): John Alcott. Music: Wendy Carlos, Erika Eigen. Starring Malcolm McDowell (Alex), Patrick Magee (Mr. Alexander), Michael Bates (Chief Guard), Warren Clarke (Dim), John Clive (Actor), Adrienne Corri (Mrs. Alexander), Carl Duering (Dr. Brodsky), Paul Farrell (Tramp).

WHAT IT'S ABOUT:

In an England of the not-so-distant future, violence is omnipresent. Young Alex and his gang of misfits wreak havoc on local citizens until he's apprehended and ultimately subjected to an experimental mind-control program.

Conditioned to become sick whenever he sees or experiences violence of any kind, Alex is returned to the mean streets he once terrorized. Bewildered, he accidentally finds his way to a former victim, who plans an especially cruel revenge, all the while planning to exploit the shaken young man politically. It's tainted faction against tainted faction with an alternately tortured and pampered Alex caught in the middle.

WHY IT'S IMPORTANT:

Movie buffs weren't sure what to make of Stanley Kubrick's decision to follow his culture-changing *2001* with yet another science fiction film. But *A Clockwork Orange* is so different, so thoroughly original and unforgettable in its own delirious way, that it plays now as an absolutely perfect follow-up project. Bloodletting and ultra-violence had engulfed American cinema in the late '60s with groundbreaking films from Arthur Penn, Sam Peckinpah and others obviating the very concept of Hollywood censorship. Kubrick always recognized the visceral and thematic potential of unrestrained sadism on film, finding in Anthony Burgess' futuristic novel an ideal property to explore the subject with enough intellectual weight and social commentary to justify flamboyantly-staged rape, murder, and bloody attack interludes.

Young cane-brandishing Alex (Malcolm McDowall) is an amoral murdering monster, but he's also a lovable innocent, victimized by a tainted society even as he victimizes others. "Man is an ignoble savage," Kubrick was fond of saying while promoting the film. As with Ibsen's *Enemy of the People*, there's enough hypocrisy, corruption and primal blame to go around in *A Clockwork Orange*. Right, Left and Center all play their part in the nonstop horror show known as the Human Condition, and all are on display warts and all for equally-guilty viewing audiences to mock. It's Kubrick's darkly joyous tone that gives a damning diatribe like *Orange* its originality, employing a storytelling style almost preternaturally in sync with its subject matter. Made long before Kubrick's directorial flourishes became heavy-handed and intrusive, *A Clockwork Orange* thrives on every majestic slow motion set-up, every austere silhouette, every broadly drawn caricature that indicts humanity at large. In short, we simply have to laugh uproariously at what we see in the mirror or we'll start crying instead, and probably never stop.

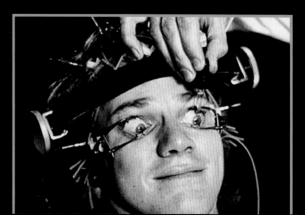

12 INVASION OF THE BODY SNATCHERS 1956

WHO MADE IT:

Allied Artists (U.S.). Director: Don Siegel. Producer: Walter Wanger. Writer: Daniel Mainwaring, based on the Collier's magazine serial "The Body Snatchers" by Jack Finney. Cinematography (b/w): Ellsworth Fredericks. Music: Carmen Dragon. Starring Kevin McCarthy (Dr. Miles J. Bennell), Dana Wynter (Becky Driscoll), Larry Gates (Dr. Dan Kaufman), King Donovan (Jack Belicec), Carolyn Jones (Theodora Belicec), Jean Wiles (Nurse Sally Withers), Virginia Christine (Wilma Lentz), Dabbs Greer (Mac Lomax).

WHAT IT'S ABOUT:

Shaken Dr. Miles Bennell relates a terrifying tale to doctors and authorities: After returning home to Santa Mira from a medical convention, Bennell discovers that many of his patients are experiencing a peculiar emotional estrangement from loved ones... they claim family members have become "strangers." When this happens to his girlfriend Becky, Miles begins to suspect that something unprecedented and diabolical is menacing Santa Mira. In truth, malignant extraterrestrial seed pods have taken root in a famer's field  and are now being distributed across the country. These parasites imitate human bodies perfectly while the hosts are sleeping, but the new entities they produce are devoid of emotion. Striving to hold on to their humanity, the doctor and his beloved become desperate, fleeing fugitives. It isn't long before a weakened Becky finally succumbs to sleep and loses her soul, tragically turning against Miles. Horrified, Bennell manages to escape Santa Mira, shouting for help like a madman while warning about the threat to our species.

WHY IT'S IMPORTANT:

The idea of trusted loved ones becoming unfeeling strangers, and ultimately mortal enemies, taps into our primal insecurities in a way that outsized monsters and marauding alien armies simply can't match. With all due respect to the stylistic pleasures of Menzies' *Invaders from Mars* (1953), it's Don Siegel who shook up viewers on a decidedly adult level with *Invasion of the Body Snatchers*, exploring the always-potent dehumanization theme with a ferocity seldom seen in 1950s sci-fi movies.

Serious actors with major studio credits, leads Kevin McCarthy and Dana Wynter elevate the experience instantly. Their characters' history of failed relationships dovetails nicely with the "cure" for emotional instability provided by the pods ("You've been in love before... It didn't last. It never does..."). McCarthy is particularly memorable as a smoothly rational doctor turned raving fugitive by tale's end, his triangular face and bulging eyes registering every moment of disbelieving, off-the-scale horror.

Since its primary goal is noir-like realism, *Body Snatchers* offers little in the way of traditional sci-fi special effects. This said, the handful of foamy, pod-to-human transformations that are depicted are pretty convincing for their day. McCarthy plunging a pitchfork into his "own" body is an especially sick touch.

Sometimes viewed as a metaphor for the Communist threat, *Invasion of the Body Snatchers* is ultimately about something far more universal: the fear of losing our individual souls, of "evolving past" the basic human capacity for love.

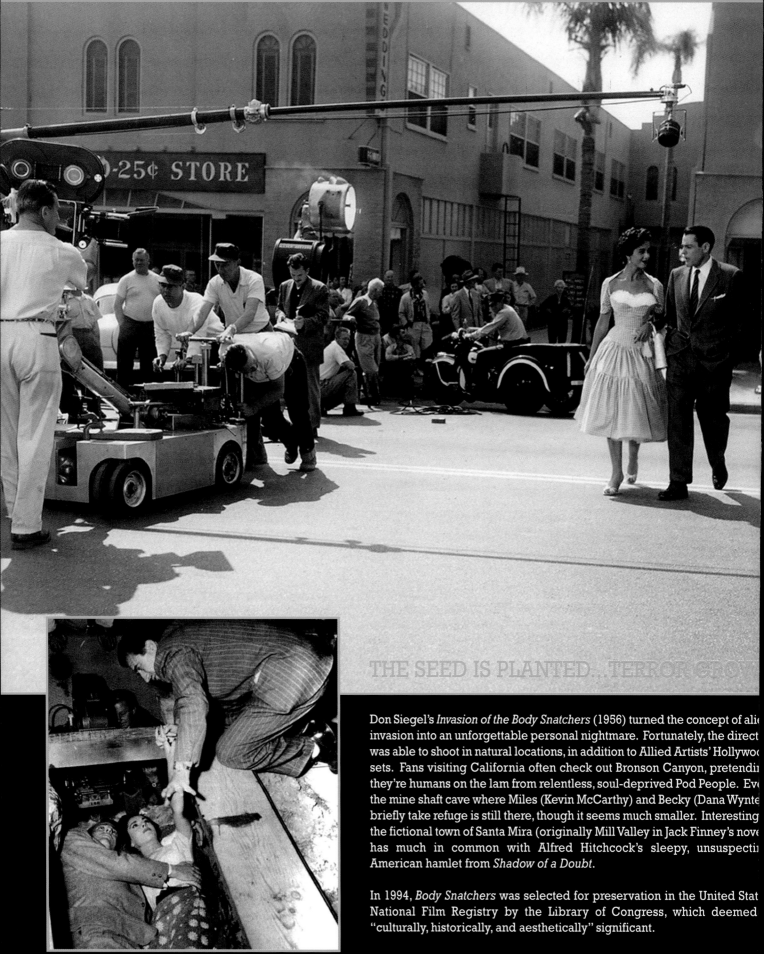

Don Siegel's *Invasion of the Body Snatchers* (1956) turned the concept of ali
invasion into an unforgettable personal nightmare. Fortunately, the direct
was able to shoot in natural locations, in addition to Allied Artists' Hollywo
sets. Fans visiting California often check out Bronson Canyon, pretendin
they're humans on the lam from relentless, soul-deprived Pod People. Eve
the mine shaft cave where Miles (Kevin McCarthy) and Becky (Dana Wynte
briefly take refuge is still there, though it seems much smaller. Interesting
the fictional town of Santa Mira (originally Mill Valley in Jack Finney's nove
has much in common with Alfred Hitchcock's sleepy, unsuspectir
American hamlet from *Shadow of a Doubt*.

In 1994, *Body Snatchers* was selected for preservation in the United Stat
National Film Registry by the Library of Congress, which deemed
"culturally, historically, and aesthetically" significant.

Evolution of an icon: H.R. Giger based the unique, dinosaurian head design for Ridley Scott's Alien on a pre-existing conceptualization. This popular screen creature appeared in six theatrical movies since 1979, with a proposed Scott-helmed prequel due in 2012.

ALIEN 1979

117   2.20

ALIEN

In space no one can hear you scream.

TWENTIETH CENTURY FOX PRESENTS
A L I E N
TOM SKERRITT SIGOURNEY WEAVER VERONICA CARTWRIGHT HARRY DEAN STANTON
JOHN HURT IAN HOLM and YAPHET KOTTO as Parker
EXECUTIVE PRODUCER RONALD SHUSETT SCREENPLAY BY DAN O'BANNON PRODUCED BY GORDON CARROLL, DAVID GILER AND WALTER HILL DIRECTED BY RIDLEY SCOTT
STORY BY DAN O'BANNON & RONALD SHUSETT MUSIC JERRY GOLDSMITH PANAVISION® EASTMAN KODAK COLOR®
PRINTS BY DELUXE® 70MM DOLBY STEREO® IN SELECTED THEATRES MOTION PICTURE SOUNDTRACK AVAILABLE ON 20TH CENTURY-FOX RECORDS & TAPES

WHO MADE IT:

20th Century-Fox (U.S.). Director: Ridley Scott. Producers: Walter Hill, David Giler, Gordon Carroll, Ivor Powell, Ronald Shusett. Writer: Dan O'Bannon, based on a story by O'Bannon and Ronald Shusett. Cinematography (color): Derek Vanlint. Music: Jerry Goldsmith. Concept Artist: Jean 'Moebius' Giraud. Starring Tom Skerritt (Dallas), Sigourney Weaver (Ripley), Veronica Cartwright (Lambert), Harry Dean Stanton (Brett), John Hurt (Kane), Ian Holm (Ash), Yaphet Kotto (Parker), Bolaji Badejo (Alien), Helen Horton (Voice of Mother).

WHAT IT'S ABOUT:

Investigating a distress signal from a remote planetoid, Captain Dallas and his crew of engineers and scientists aboard the Nostromo discover and investigate a derelict alien spaceship. Inside the cavernous craft, a strange life-form attaches itself to one of the crewmembers, Kane. Dallas and his team blast off, but soon the ingested life-form erupts through Kane's stomach and escapes into the bowels of the Nostromo. One-by-one crewmembers are slaughtered by this elusive, acid-blooded alien, who soon evolves into a grotesque humanoid monster. In the end, only warrant officer Ellen Ripley is left to thwart her vicious pursuer. She blows up Nostromo, escapes in a shuttle and fights a final battle for survival with the stowed-away creature.

WHY IT'S IMPORTANT:

The phenomenal success of both *Star Wars* and *Close Encounters* in 1977 opened the floodgates for expensively-mounted, widescreen sci-fi extravaganzas. With "Flash Gordon" and "UFO" subject matter colorfully re-visited, 20th Century-Fox decided to give the long-discarded '50s style "monster" thriller an upgrade, green-lighting a project that had been sitting around the studio for quite some time. What began as a murky B-project from filmmaker Dan (*Dark Star*) O'Bannon became something very different in the hands of stylish auteur Ridley Scott, late of *The Duelists*. Working with extraordinary production/makeup design provided by Jean 'Moebius' Giraud and H.R. Giger, *Alien* is unquestionably the most artistic "space monster on the loose" movie ever conceived. Scott cleverly hides his titular beastie within menacing, often strobing shadows for most of the film's running time, taking a stylistic cue from Howard Hawks' *The Thing*, an obvious thematic inspiration.

Action is set in three pivotal locations: the bizarre hell-like planet Captain Dallas and his crew are diverted to; a derelict alien spaceship discovered there; and Dallas' mining ship Nostromo, a cavernous "old dark house" in space, with enough inviting nooks and crannies for a size-changing monster to conceal himself in. O'Bannon based his plot very directly on a '50s mini-gem called *It! The Terror from Beyond Space*; but Scott and producer Walter Hill bring freshness to these far-out proceedings at every turn. Hard to believe now, but it was a surprise for audiences back in '79 to see a deglamorized female like Ellen Ripley outlast her more macho male crew members and take out this salivating super-beast with ingenuity, raw courage, and just a little bit of luck.

Not surprisingly, *Alien* spawned several sequels, the best being James Cameron's military-themed *Aliens* seven years later. Eventually this franchise crossed bloody paths with another extraterrestrial movie series from the same studio, *Predator*... fun as pulpy entertainment perhaps, but a long way from Scott's original, creatively breathtaking journey into galactic darkness.

Ripley (Sigourney Weaver) monitors her crewmates' entry into an alien spaceship.

The Space Jockey amazes scientist Kane (John Hurt); the Face Hugger attacks him.

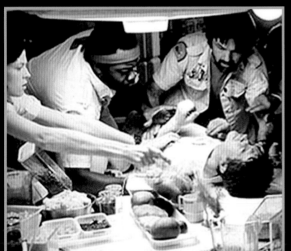

The Alien emerges from Kane, grows into a murderous monster, and is finally slain by Ripley.

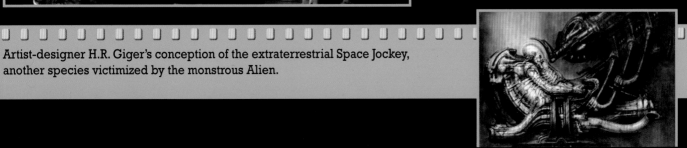

Artist-designer H.R. Giger's conception of the extraterrestrial Space Jockey, another species victimized by the monstrous Alien.

Poster/photos © 1984 Orion Pictures

WHO MADE IT:

Orion Pictures/Hemdale Film (U.S.) Director: James Cameron. Producer: Gale Anne Hurd. Writers: James Cameron & Gale Anne Hurd, William Wisher, inspired by two episodes of TV's *The Outer Limits* by Harlan Ellison. Cinematography (color): Adam Greenberg. Music: Brad Fiedel. Starring Arnold Schwarzenegger (The Terminator), Michael Biehn (Kyle Reese), Linda Hamilton (Sarah Connor), Paul Winfield (Lt. Ed Traxler), Lance Henriksen (Detective Vukovich), Bess Motta (Ginger Ventura), Dick Miller (Pawnshop Owner), Bill Paxton (Punk

WHAT IT'S ABOUT:

Two beings arrive in present day from a war-torn future: one is a hulking android, programmed to kill a specific person; the other is a soldier sent to protect that same person. Sarah Connor is destined to become the mother of a man who will lead a revolution against the sophisticated machines that take over Earth in years hence. At first unsure of who is friend and who is enemy, the terrified young woman ultimately bonds with futuristic bodyguard Reese. Together they narrowly escape the Terminator's murderous grasp, avoiding one deadly attack after another. Reese is killed before this chase is ended, but Sarah, summoning strengths she never suspected she had, manages to destroy her relentless assassin at the last moment.

WHY IT'S IMPORTANT:

In the late '70s and early '80s, George Lucas and Steven Spielberg practically owned sci-fi/fantasy, dazzling movie audiences with a succession of feel-good "event" flicks almost always accompanied by lush, reassuring John Williams scores. Determined to sidestep this Disneyesque reinvention of his favorite movie genre, director James Cameron employed a far more sophisticated, *Outer Limits*-like approach, bringing terror back into play along with adult romance and intellectual notions mostly missing from '80s movie rollercoasters. The result is a film that, in many ways, has outlasted the trumped-up "happy" tone of its more high-profile, bigger-budgeted rivals.

Among other things, *The Terminator* revived the sagging film career of body builder Arnold Schwarzenegger, who had fully embarrassed himself as John Milius' *Conan the Barbarian* two years earlier. A limited actor to say the least, Schwarzenegger is a surprising revelation as the hulking, emotionless man-machine, delivering quotable sound bites like "I'll be back" in his patented, half-accented monotone. Throughout the film he's ably supported by long-suffering Michael Biehn as a bodyguard soldier from tomorrow, and pre-buffed Linda Hamilton as a terrified young woman who becomes humanity's single-handed protector at tale's end.

Although Cameron is rightly credited with bringing gritty reality to fast-paced action sequences, he's just as effective with the film's evocative, haunting moments. Robot killers blasting away are fine, but it's a single shot of a tubeless TV set with a candle inside, being "watched" by numbed survivors in a ruined future, that remains with viewers seeking a little more depth. There is a dark poetry to the end of the world, and Cameron clearly understands this. Indeed, all the flashbacks to tomorrow's battleground are disturbing and rich with high-tech nightmare imagery, all the more impressive given the movie's relatively low budget.

The Terminator (Arnold Schwarzenegger) arrives in modern-day LA in search of Sarah Connor (Linda Hamilton). Like Fox's *Alien* franchise, *Terminator* eventually devolved into a filmed comic book series.

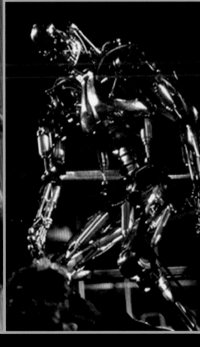

ABOVE: "I'll be back." This robot assassin means business, sending Kyle Reese (Michael Biehn) and Sarah into desperate flight. The Terminator's metal skeleton (achieved by both stop-motion and full-size Stan Winston armatures) proved to be a most welcome third act surprise.

Director James (*Avatar*) Cameron directs wife-to-be Linda Hamilton in an intense scene. They'd reunite seven years later for *Terminator 2: Judgment Day*.

9 THE THING FROM ANOTHER WORLD 1951 ⬤87 ▮1.37▮ ◖

aka The Thing

Poster/photos: © 1951 RKO Radio Pictures. Renewed by Warner Bros.

NATURAL OR SUPERNATURAL ?

THE THING

from another world !

HOWARD HAWKS' *Astounding* **MOVIE**

WHO MADE IT:

RKO Radio Pictures (U.S.). Directors: Christian Nyby, Howard Hawks - uncredited. Producer: Howard Hawks. Writers: Charles Lederer, Howard Hawks and Ben Hecht – uncredited, based on the story "Who Goes There?" by John W. Campbell Jr. Cinematography (b/w): Russell Harlan. Music: Dimitri Tiompkin. Starring Margaret Sheridan (Nikki Nicholson), Kenneth Tobey (Captain Patrick Hendry), Robert Cornthwaite (Dr. Carrington), Douglas Spencer (Ned 'Scotty' Scott), James R. Young (Lt. Eddie Dykes), Dewey Martin (Crew Chief Bob), Robert Nichols (Lt. Ken 'Mac' MacPherson), William Self (Barnes), Eduard Franz (Dr. Stern), James Arness (The Thing).

WHAT IT'S ABOUT:

Captain Hendry and his team are summoned to a military base in the Arctic, where scientists have been tracking the arrival of what can only be described as a flying saucer. After accidentally destroying the ice-covered spacecraft during a retrieval operation, soldiers manage to secure its frozen, still-alive alien occupant. As Hendry and leading scientist Dr. Carrington debate their next move, the alien thaws out, kills several guard dogs and races into the stormy night. Soon everyone at the base is imperiled by the agenda-driven invader, a kind of humanoid vegetable, who slaughters some of the scientists and uses their blood to breed a whole new alien army. Fighting not only for their lives but for the safety of Earth, Hendry and his companions find themselves boxed in by their ruthless enemy, but finally turn the tables and reduce The Thing to smoldering matter with an electrical arc.

WHY IT'S IMPORTANT:

The Thing from Another World represents Howard Hawks' amicably conservative, pro-military approach to dealing with alien encounters. This is no intellectual discourse on mankind's role in the universe, but a crisply-written combat movie, pitting soldiers and civilians against an enemy so one-dimensionally evil he might as well be Satan. Or Hitler. In addition to a tense battle for survival in the claustrophobic confines of a remote Arctic base, the vanguard of a full-scale space invasion needs to be thwarted, with low-key Captain Hendry (Kenneth Tobey) and his intrepid team cast in the unlikely role of Earth's saviors. And although Hawks and director-of-record Christian Nyby attempt some fairness in the depiction of scientists, it's pretty clear where their gung-ho sympathies lie. Standing in for a Russian bad guy is shifty-eyed Dr. Carrington (Robert Cornthwaite), scientific group leader, not exactly in cahoots with the fearsome intruder (like Ash from *Alien*), but a wrong-headed enabler nonetheless.

Craggy-faced, unpretentious Kenneth Tobey is an excellent choice for Captain Hendry, a cautious man-of-action trying to keep an open mind in an increasingly volatile situation. His playful love scenes with earthy-sexy romantic lead Nikki (top-billed Margaret Sheridan) are charming and witty, reminding viewers that this is, after all, a Howard Hawks film, complete with sexual tension, wry homilies and overlapping dialogue. In the title role, pre-Marshal Dillon James Arness is given a vaguely Frankensteinian look by RKO's makeup artist Lee Greenway. He's wisely kept off-camera for most of the movie, which is partially the reason why his actual appearances are so striking (another reason is that these set-ups are especially well-planned and executed, such as Arness' startled, then furious appearance behind a suddenly opened door).

Reflecting World War II movie camaraderie, the heroes of *The Thing* grow closer and more resourceful as their powerful enemy closes in. Quite the opposite happens in John Carpenter's 1984 remake, where the true monster is distrust, fueled by palpable paranoia among the principals. Flip sides of the same suspenseful coin, both sci-fi thrillers are now regarded as classics.

ABOVE: Hendry (Kenneth Tobey) and Dr. Carrington (Robert Cornthwaite) supervise the inspection and inadvertent destruction of a frozen flying saucer. BELOW: The captured alien (James Arness) thaws out, posing a threat to everyone at an isolated military base. Its sudden appearance in the greenhouse doorway provides an odd, off-center thrill for viewers.

Dr. Carrington's colleagues have differing views on his plans to grow new "Things" in the name of scientific research. That's Paul Frees on the right.

"Keep Watching the Skies!" became the perfect catchphrase for this Cold War classic.

The Thing is decidedly pro-military, with recklessly progressive scientist Carrington faring poorly. In real life, Captain Hendry's destructive actions would probably be criticized the world over.

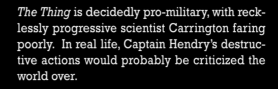

The Thing himself, towering James Arness, takes part in some initial smoke and costume tests.

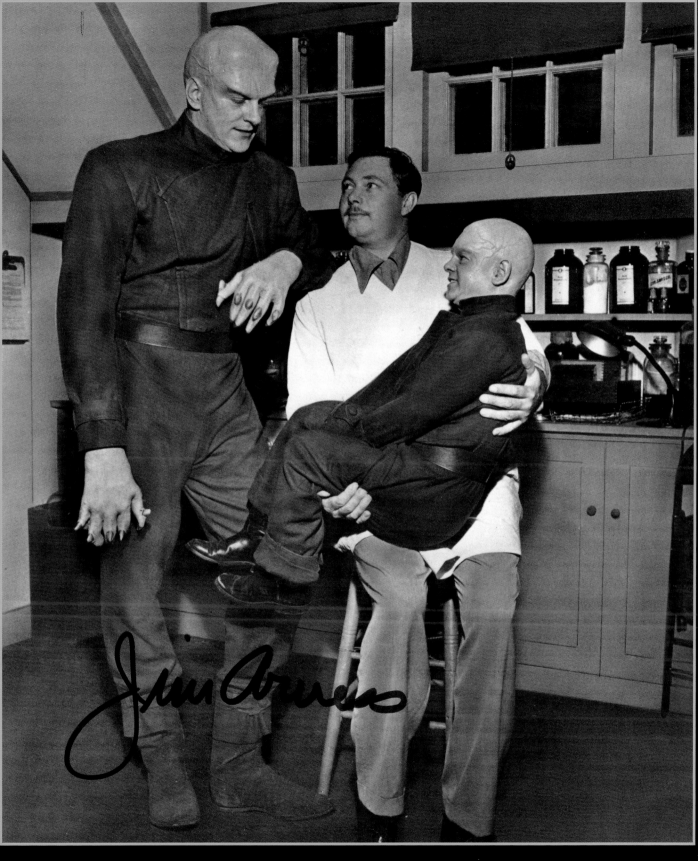

CULTIVATING AN INTELLECTUAL CARROT

One "Thing" or another was required to bring Howard Hawks' blood-lusting (and veggie-based) extraterrestrial to cinematic life. The full-size invader was portrayed by towering, pre-*Gunsmoke* James Arness, while his "mini-me" double, glimpsed briefly in the disintegration sequence (OPPOSITE PAGE, inset), was none other than *The Wizard of Oz*'s Billy Curtis. Startling head/hands make-up prosthetics by Lee Greenway.

8 METROPOLIS 1927

155 1.33 ♂

Poster/photos: © 1927 UFA

WHO MADE IT:

Universum Film aka UFA (Germany)/Paramount Pictures (U.S.). Director: Fritz Lang. Producer: Erich Pommer. Writer: Thea von Harbou, based on her novel. Cinematography (b/w with tinted sequences): Karl Freund, Gunther Rittau, Walter Ruttmann. Special Effects: Ernst Kunstmann; Konstantin Irmen-Tschet and Erich Kettelhut (uncredited). Starring Alfred Abel (Joh Fredersen), Gustav Frohlich (Freder), Rudolf Klein-Rogge (C.A. Rotwang), Fritz Rasp (The Thin Man), Theodor Loos (Josaphat), Erwin Biswanger (11811 – Georgy), Brigitte Helm (Maria).

WHAT IT'S ABOUT:

The futuristic city of Metropolis is ruled with an iron fist by businessman Joh Fredersen, who has little sympathy for the multitudes of tortured workers who keep it running from massive, highly-dangerous stations underground. Horrified by these conditions, Joh's idealistic son, Freder, falls in love with peace-loving spiritual leader of the downtrodden, Maria. But Joh has other plans for this woman: through his corrupt scientist contact Rotwang, Maria's appearance is transferred to a robot, intended to discredit the original and leave her followers demoralized. Instead, the witchlike Maria clone inspires them to open rebellion. With the city and everyone who lives there imperiled, only the actions of Freder and the real Maria can heal all wounds and unite the various factions of this volatile society of tomorrow.

WHY IT'S IMPORTANT:

Inspired, at least partially, by Fritz Lang's career-related trip to New York City, *Metropolis* is a breathtaking combination of super-spectacle (with "Biblical epic" flavoring) and populist social melodrama. It dazzled audiences of the day with astonishing special effects, sets and art direction, providing a vision of tomorrow's potentialities unlike anything previously attempted on film. Lang had already been acclaimed the world over as a visual perfectionist; *Metropolis* was unquestionably his mega-masterpiece, an imaginative statement about the pitfalls of power, the need to "get along," and, perhaps inevitably, the redemptive power of love.

Lang's city of tomorrow is off-the-scale colossal, the prototype for all subsequent cinematic visions of futuristic urban environments. But just as compelling and memorable is the austere "Machine Man," a gleaming asexual robot that figures significantly in the storyline. It is simply the most elegant and iconic science fiction android ever conceived, beating out George Lucas' creations (3P0 being a distant cousin) and James Cameron's skeletal Terminators. The fact that Machine Man actually "becomes" a twisted version of local heroine Maria only adds to the robot's mystique. A rather heavy religious angle is adhered to throughout *Metropolis*, starting with young Fredersen's vision of his father's mass-production machines as hellish instruments of Moloch, with sacrificed workers being tossed into fiery pits. Maria is clearly the Christian ethic personified, and an unmasked robot's climactic burning at the stake has all the flavor of a ritualistic purging. Years later, director Lang was a bit embarrassed by his screenwriter wife's "the heart must be the mediator between the mind and the hands" motif, omnipresent throughout and frequently criticized as being too "pat." But ultimately, it is precisely this simple and relatable message that justifies the film's grandiose, dehumanized view of tomorrow. Without Maria's selfless spirit of self-sacrifice, or young Fredersen's determined struggle for even-handed cooperation between warring classes, tomorrowland would be an unrelenting nightmare.

In 2010, almost an hour's worth of lost footage from *Metropolis* was unearthed in heavily-scratched 16mm form. Containing key scenes, close-ups, medium shots and other imperative material, it has since been re-inserted, enhancing Lang's already brilliant vision of a future plagued by crisis, but ultimately saved by simple hope.

ABOVE: Another day, another work shift; Lang found an eerie similarity between Hitler's concentration camps and the hopeless, wretched souls of Fredersen's future. RIGHT: super-city Metropolis in all its glory. Even today, Lang's vision of tomorrow continues to impress and inspire.

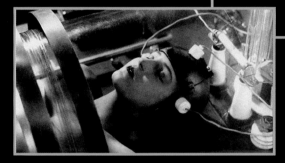

Loved by the masses, Maria (Brigitte Helm) is dramatically transposed to fulfill Joh Fredersen's diabolical plan.

More like a soul-swapping alchemist, Rotwang (Rudolf Klein-Rogge) is about to use his shiny new equipment to give his austere robot the appearance of a woman. The gender variant "Machine Man" clearly inspired George Lucas' C-3P0.

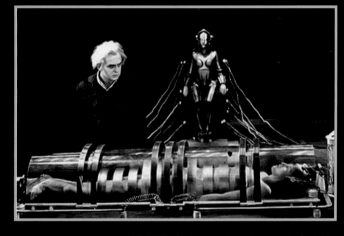

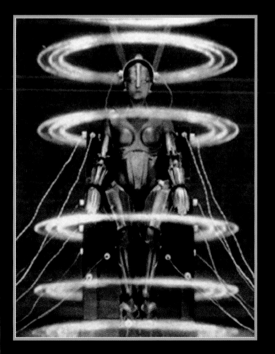

RIGHT: The humanity of Joh's son Freder (Gustav Frohlich), seen here taking over for an exhausted worker, fuels the plot and conflict of *Metropolis*.

ABOVE: Quite mad and most definitely a scientist, Rotwang had no problem sacrificing a hand to create his beloved robot, soon to be "blessed" with Maria's face. In many ways, Rotwang was a take-off on the alchemists featured in German horror films.

Versatile and beautiful Brigitte Helm plays various related roles, including that of the robot, or "Machine Man."

This page: *Metropolis (1927)*. Facing page: *Blade Runner (1982)*.

WHO MADE IT:

Warner Bros./The Ladd Company/Shaw Brothers (U.S.). Director: Ridley Scott. Producers: Micheal Deeley, Hampton Fancher, Brian Kelly, Run Run Shaw, Bud Yorkin. Writers: Hampton Fancher and David Peoples, based on the novel "Do Androids Dream of Electric Sheep? By Philip K. Dick. Cinematography (Technicolor): Jordan Cronenweth. Music: Vangelis. Visual Effects Supervisor: Douglas Trumbull. Starring Harrison Ford (Rick Deckard), Rutger Hauer (Roy Batty), Sean Young (Rachael), Edward James Olmos (Gaff), M. Emmet Walsh (Bryant), Daryl Hannah (Pris), William Sanderson (J.F. Sebastian), Brion James (Leon), Joe Turkel (Dr. Tyrell), Joanna Cassidy (Zhora).

WHAT IT'S ABOUT:

In Los Angeles of the future, retired cop/detective Rick Deckard is pressured into using his considerable "Blade Runner" skills to destroy four murderous replicants (androids) who are now fugitives seeking an extension of their limited lifespan. Looking into the Tyrell corporation that created them, weather-beaten, disillusioned Deckard becomes involved with Rachael, another sophisticated android from Tyrell who is strangely unaware of her artificial status. Ultimately, each of the four killer replicants is tracked down and executed by Deckard, until he squares off with their powerful leader, Roy Batty. Instead of slaughtering the bested detective, Batty saves his life so that he can recount the glorious virtues of his super-existence, something a despairing human like Deckard can never match.

WHY IT'S IMPORTANT:

The commercial and critical success of *Alien* was a tough act for filmmaker Ridley Scott to follow. His answer? A futuristic noir called *Blade Runner*, based on a Philip K. Dick story and starring *Star Wars* and Indiana Jones superstar Harrison Ford in the title role. At the time of release, reactions were more tepid than expected: "Art direction alone doesn't make a good movie," groused one critic. But over the years, very much like Kubrick's *The Shining*, the film has established itself as a genuine classic of its genre, even overtaking Scott's own *Alien* in popularity.

Perversely, the flaws of *Blade Runner* are still there, exacerbated by multiple versions of the film that tend to confuse its meaning. Scott's original theatrical version is probably the best, with Harrison Ford's narration helping to explain a somewhat convoluted plot while reminding viewers of the classic noir connection. Most significantly, it reflects the original point and theme of the movie: in a dehumanized future world, robots, even murderous ones, have more life spirit in them than many cynical humans, who have allowed their sense of hope to atrophy. It's a wonderful irony, driven home by Rutger Hauer's aggressive, highly physical performance (his "I've seen things…" final speech is a poetic classic), and Ford's traditional hang-dog look, well-suited to the part of a soul-sapped misanthrope assigned to end the life of an entity who is fully embracing this miraculous gift. Unfortunately, the gimmick notion of Ford's character Dekker being an android, which leads nowhere thematically, began to obsess Scott, and most of the later re-edits of his film reflect this pointless direction. What is the ultimate theme of *Blade Runner* in these versions? Nobody knows for sure, and what's worse, fans don't really seem to care. Because the film is still an ingenious visual spectacle, presenting a lavish but tainted vision of tomorrow that rivals the imagination of *Metropolis*. Scott's skills as a visualist are on full display, with fx wizard Douglas Trumbull pushing the technical strides made by John Dykstra and the ILM unit to new, artistically overwhelming heights. Scott also brilliantly blends the past (LA's landmark Bradbury Building) into this irresistible future mix, with grand old edifices sharing cityspace with towering new creations, just as they do in real life.

ABOVE: Deckard (Harrison Ford) and Gaff (Edward James Olmos). BELOW: Rachael (Sean Young). BELOW, RIGHT: Pris (Daryl Hannah).

Deckard's speeder zooms across futuristic LA, finally settling down to Earth so the ex-Blade Runner can corner his quarry. A fit Harrison Ford performed many of his own stunts.

Blade Runner is more than simply an action flick with badass super-villains – and also a good deal less, due to an aging director's ill-advised tampering that changes the meaning of his film. Stick with the original theatrical version, a flawed masterpiece made by a great artist at the peak of his creative powers.

LEFT: Rutger Hauer as murderous, poetic replicant Roy Batty.

Some of the astonishing production design delivered by Scott's artistic team, faithfully replicated (couldn't resist) for the film itself.

WHO MADE IT:

Metro-Goldwyn-Mayer (U.S.). Director/Producer: George Pal. Writer: David Duncan, based on the novel by H.G. Wells. Cinematography (Metrocolor): Paul Vogel. Music: Russ Garcia. Visual Effects: Wah Chang, Gene Warren, Tim Baar, Howard A. Anderson, Jim Danforth. Makeup: William Tuttle. Starring Rod Taylor (George, the Time Traveler), Yvette Mimieux (Weena), Alan Young (David/James Philby, Sebastian Cabot (Dr. Hillyer), Tom Helmore (Bridewell), Whit Bissell (Kemp), Doris Lloyd (Mrs. Watchett).

WHAT IT'S ABOUT:

Dissatisfied with his war-obsessed century, Victorian era scientist George designs a time machine, enabling the user to travel backward and forward via a crystal that penetrates the fourth dimension. Venturing years ahead, he encounters devastating wars in every generation... so George pushes dramatically forward, to the far distant future. Here, in a strange Garden of Eden-like environment, he discovers that the human race had divided itself after a worldwide nuclear war: those who chose to remain on the Earth's surface became helpless and childlike (the Eloi), while those who ventured underground devolved into grotesque, monster cannibals known as Morlocks. Loner George falls in love with an Eloi girl named Weena, and ultimately helps her people, bred like cattle by the ravenous Morlocks, to fight back and reclaim their human heritage.

WHY IT'S IMPORTANT:

A charming combination of Victorian fantasy and sci-fi speculation, *The Time Machine* is producer/director George Pal's most accomplished film, a winner in just about every creative department. Unlike his updated *War of the Worlds*, this picture embraces the past with wistful nostalgia, even as George the Time Traveler (check out that nameplate on his Machine) promptly bids the comfort of his Victorian existence farewell, hoping to build a better life for himself in a more progressive, less war-ravaged century. What he finds in the future, of course, is simply more conflict, ultimately between childlike humans and nocturnal, flesh-hungry mutant cannibals. But he also discovers romantic love in the form of Weena, something denied him in a conventional society unable to appreciate his unique abilities. In the pivotal leading role, energetic Rod Taylor is a more than perfect fit, deftly combining intellect and physicality as he two-fists his way through a plethora of extreme temporal challenges. The pure joy of exploration radiates from his handsome face; determined to be the catalyst for humanity's miraculous comeback, Taylor's equally convincing as a disillusioned, emotionally unsettled 19th Century loner. There's an interesting metaphor here about people needing to push themselves to the limit before they can find their finer lights. Although George talks a lot about improving his "natural" century with insights brought back from the future, it's clear that his heart really belongs in a far distant reality, one where love is patiently waiting and his ultimate humanist purpose can finally be fulfilled.

Like many Pal films, *The Time Machine* won an Academy Award for its ambitious special effects. While fourth-dimensional travel is accomplished with a delightful blend of time-lapse photography and stop-motion animation, it's the Machine itself that pretty much steals this show, along with its equally memorable mini-prototype. Very much a character in Pal's scenario, it reflects the inherent romanticism of its era and reminds viewers that this science fiction story has a classical side, even in the face of atomic satellites and radiation-ravaged Morlocks on the prowl.

Produced by an inspired filmmaker with palpable fondness for all things fantastic, this MGM classic remains the definitive dramatization of Wells' seminal work half a century after its creation. It is, in a word, timeless.

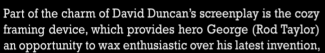

Part of the charm of David Duncan's screenplay is the cozy framing device, which provides hero George (Rod Taylor) an opportunity to wax enthusiastic over his latest invention, the time machine, of which he has a small experimental prototype (RIGHT INSERT) Patiently listening friends include Tom Helmore, Sebastian Cabot, and a sympathetic Alan Young (not pictured).

LEFT, ABOVE: England in 1966 is the victim of both atomic satellites and an angry nature's rebuttal with street-streaming molten lava. RIGHT: The "Talking Rings" help George understand what happened to humanity during his time-tripping.

Hell and Heaven: Monstrous Morlocks maintain the childlike Eloi as food stock.

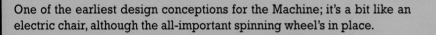

One of the earliest design conceptions for the Machine; it's a bit like an electric chair, although the all-important spinning wheel's in place.

5

STAR WARS 1977

(121) 2.20

A long time ago in a galaxy far, far away...

WHO MADE IT:

20th Century Fox (U.S.). Director: George Kucas. Producer: Gary Kurtz: Writer: George Lucas. Cinematography (Technicolor/DeLuxe): Gilbert Taylor. Music: John Williams. Special Effects Supervisor: John Dykstra. Starring Mark Hamill (Luke Skywalker), Carrie Fisher (Princess Leia Organa), Harrison Ford (Han Solo), Alec Guinness (Ben Kenobi), Peter Cushing (Grand Moff Tarkin), David Prowse (Darth Vader), James Earl Jones (Voice of Vader), Peter Mayhew (Chewbacca), Anthony Daniels (C-3PO), Kenny Baker (R2D2).

WHAT IT'S ABOUT:

Escaping from her Imperial enemies, Princess Leia prevents Darth Vader from retrieving the stolen technical readouts for the Empire's Death Star battle station, placing them within an ejected R2 unit. This little droid soon winds up with young, restless Tatooine farmer Luke Skywalker, who is persuaded to join the battle against Imperial aggression by desert rat Jedi knight Ben (Obi-Wan) Kenobi after the savage murder of Luke's guardians. Teaming up with brash space pirate Han Solo, Kenobi and his young allies penetrate Death Star and rescue the Princess; but Ben engages in an intense lightsaber duel with former pupil Darth Vader, and appears to vanish. After escaping, Skywalker, Solo and Leia regroup with the organized Rebels, who review the stolen Death Star readouts and discover an exploitable weakness. Leia's Rebels, with ace starfjghter Luke among them, launch a daring offensive against the now-orbiting space station. In the end, it's the spiritual power of the Force that brings victory to young Skywalker and his courageous companions.

WHY IT'S IMPORTANT:

At a time when most science fiction movies were downbeat and pretentiously message-laden, celebrated filmmaker George Lucas re-invented the genre in a way no one was expecting. Embracing his love for the *Flash Gordon* serials of yesteryear, Lucas hoped to infuse far-out fantasy with pure fun, sentiment, and the qualities that made Hollywood classics like *The Wizard of Oz* resonate for multiple generations. He wound up achieving this goal, and a great deal more: Like the Beatles, *Star Wars* changed popular culture forever. To some, this represented a most welcome cinematic renaissance; to others, it signaled the replacement of "real" movies with rollercoaster-like confections, and reduced science fiction to its most childish roots. Of the six movies Lucas made on this fanciful subject, his 1977 original remains the freshest and most honest. There's still that agreeably grainy, hand-held, rough-around-the-edges quality of *American Graffiti* at work here, before the pressures of big-budget moviemaking began to transform the series into a slicker product. A simple scene like frustrated young Luke's meal conversation with his guardians is alive with texture and sophistication absent from the later pictures. Although *The Empire Strikes Back* is often praised for being "dark," no scene in that sequel can rival's Luke's discovery of the charred bodies of those same guardians. Hamill plays the moment perfectly, internalizing his emotions of shock, disbelief and horror. Our heroes battling TIE fighters during their escape from the Death Star offers more than just "fast editing"; these cuts contain levels of satiric maturity (Leia and her furry ally Chewbacca turning their heads in unison) that gradually faded from the series. It's almost as if a superior cinematic vision was required in order to justify what many in the industry believed to be childish, campy material. Once this new "space fantasy" genre proved itself, the visual style and overall ambience could be more straightforward and functional. Seamlessly blending mythic fantasy, broad humor, and a new approach to high velocity special effects that movie audiences will never outgrow, *Star Wars* is a great movie that literally changed the way we live and think. There is no higher praise for an artist's work, and, as far as this critic's concerned, no more enjoyable way to spend an afternoon in a movie theater.

TWENTIETH CENTURY-FOX Presents
A LUCASFILM LTD. PRODUCTION
STAR WARS
Starring MARK HAMILL HARRISON FORD CARRIE FISHER
PETER CUSHING
and
ALEC GUINNESS
Written and Directed by GEORGE LUCAS Produced by GARY KURTZ Music by JOHN WILLIAMS
PANAVISION® PRINTS BY DE LUXE® TECHNICOLOR®
PG PARENTAL GUIDANCE SUGGESTED

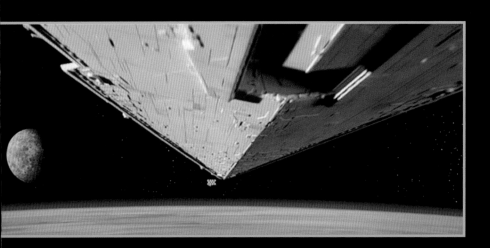

ABOVE: the overhead intro-shot that changed pop culture forever. In truth, *Star Wars* is as novel and powerful a motion picture as the best ever conceived for a mainstream audience, arguably the most influential action film since *The Great Train Robbery*.

Hero Han Solo (Harrison Ford) and his saucer-like spaceship, the Millennium Falcon, play a key role in *Star Wars*' breathless "Death Star trench" climax. ILM's groundbreaking fx earned a well-deserved Academy Award.

Inside the Empire's battle station with his youthful allies, Kenobi (Alec Guinness) clashes with Vader.

Oscar-winning veteran actor Alec Guinness relaxes with director George Lucas on set in Tunisia.

BEWARE THE STARE THAT WILL PARALYZE THE WILL OF THE WORLD

METRO-GOLDWYN-MAYER Presents
GEORGE SANDERS
BARBARA SHELLEY in

VILLAGE OF THE DAMNED

with
MICHAEL GWYNN
Screen Play by
STIRLING SILLIPHANT
WOLF RILLA GEORGE BARCLAY
Based on the Novel "The Midwich Cuckoos"
by JOHN WYNDHAM
Directed by
WOLF RILLA
Produced by
RONALD KINNOCH

WHO MADE IT:

Metro-Goldwyn-Mayer (U.K./U.S.). Director: Wolf Rilla. Producer: Ronald Kinnoch. Writers: Stirling Silliphant, Wolf Rilla, George Barclay aka Ronald Kinnoch, based on the novel *The Midwich Cuckoos* by John Wyndham. Cinematography (b/w): Geoffrey Faithfull. Music: Ron Goodwin. Starring George Sanders (Gordon Zellaby), Barbara Shelley (Anthea Zellaby), Martin Stephens (David Zellaby), Michael Gwynn (Alan Bernard), Laurence Naismith (Dr. Willers), Ricahrd Warner (Harrington), Jenny Laird (Mrs. Harrington), Sarah Long (Evelyn Harrington).

WHAT IT'S ABOUT:

For some inexplicable reason, all living creatures in the small hamlet of Midwich are rendered senseless for a brief time. Months later, every human female capable of childbirth winds up pregnant, and the resulting children are an enigmatic, highly-advanced breed, gifted with unique psychic abilities. Gordon Zellaby, surrogate father to little David, tries to solve the mystery of these children, while protecting them from increasingly apprehensive authority figures. In time Zellaby begins to suspect that energy from another planet caused the "time out" phenomena in Midwich, impregnating women with an alien "seed." Unable to temper the deadly-dangerous behavior of the Children with moral and ethical instruction, he finally uses the image of a brick wall to block their psychic control, destroying them all – and himself – with a concealed time-bomb.

WHY IT'S IMPORTANT:

Village of the Damned is the perfect science fiction movie, not an inch of fat on its rock-steady bones. Wyndham's novel *The Midwich Cuckoos* is a brilliant little terror tale to begin with; but this modestly-budgeted screen adaptation from MGM is even better, capturing all of Wyndham's spookiness but adding a mature, methodical pace and unique sense of wonder that's never been duplicated in a film of this genre.

Director Wolf Rilla caught lightning in a bottle with the casting of George Sanders as Dr. Zellaby, the intellectual soul and moral compass of the piece. A fine actor from Hollywood's heyday whose sardonic sense of humor and charmingly ironic persona made him an Oscar-winning superstar, Sanders is far more restrained than usual here, hooking the viewer on each new fascinating theory just as he himself is riveted by the thought-provoking enigma in his midst. As "father" to little David, leader of the super-tykes, Sanders' Zellaby is cool intelligence personified, the ultimate patient scientist – but he's also a proud surrogate papa, pleased that his handsome young son may become another Einstein ("potentially greater"). By establishing Zellaby early on as a caring husband to younger wife Anthea (Barbara Shelley), their sudden parenting dovetailing beautifully with Midwich's unnatural births, he is fully grounded as a mature, sympathetic man with a strong sense of morality. This is most important when events start spiraling out of control; the audience is reassured that, whatever it takes, our scientist-hero is committed to doing the right thing. From the opening scenes of Midwich's "winking out" (beautifully directed, with no background music), to the exquisite finale, Rilla's film holds our attention and never lets go. That business early on with the little Chinese puzzle demonstrating both the aliens' superior intellect and communal mind is arguably the smartest scene ever conceived for a science fiction movie. And as for those glowing eyes, this optical gimmick was added at the last minute for some much-needed exploitation. But far from compromising a grown-up story, as some critics contend, they simply add a juicy, welcome element of sci-fi melodrama to an unassailably brilliant think piece.

ABOVE: Midwich is suddenly asleep, and the authorities are baffled. RIGHT: The Children and their cold-as-ice leader, David Zellaby (Martin Stephens, FAR RIGHT). BELOW: Anthea Zellaby (Barbara Shelley) can only get so close to her meta-human offspring, who is incapable of normal emotions.

The Midwich phenomenon is like an intellectual artichoke, with Zellaby and company rationally peeling away each fascinating leaf for movie audiences to savor. BELOW, INSERT A: Zellaby thinks of a "brick wall" to shield his deadly secret. INSERT B: Have the aliens escaped death? Think of these final zooming eyes as a metaphoric warning… it can all happen again tomorrow.

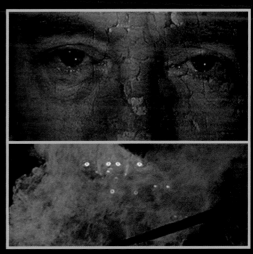

LEFT: *Children of the Damned* (1963). RIGHT: John Carpenter's 1997 remake.

3 FIVE MILLION YEARS TO EARTH 1967 ⟨97⟩ 1.66

aka Quatermass and the Pit

WHO MADE IT:

Seven Arts-Hammer Films (U.K.)/20th Century-Fox (U.S.). Director: Roy Ward Baker. Producer: Anthony Nelson Keys. Writer: Nigel Kneale, based on his BBC TV serial "Quatermass and the Pit." Cinematography (color): Arthur Grant. Music: Tristram Cary. Special Effects: Les Bowie. Starring James Donald (Dr. Mathew Roney), Andrew Keir (Prof. Bernard Quatermass), Barbara Shelley (Barbara Judd), Julian Glover (Colonel Breen), Duncan Lamont (Sladden), Bryan Marshall (Captain Potter), Peter Copley (Howell), Edwin Richfield (Minister).

WHAT IT'S ABOUT:

Subway workers in London uncover fossil skeletons of ancient man, along with what appears to be an unexploded bomb or missile. Paleontologist Dr. Roney joins forces with space expert Dr. Bernard Quatermass to solve the mystery of this device. As fantastic events escalate (workmen are suddenly "possessed"), Quatermass begins to suspect that the this bomb is actually an ancient spaceship, a theory confirmed by the discovery of long-dead, but preserved, insectlike aliens within its hull. Using a mind-recording device, the scientists deduce that we owe our human condition to the intervention of advanced alien insects from a dying world, who tried to maintain their culture by advancing Earthy apes through genetic surgery during prehistoric times. Being near this ancient ship rekindles atrophied powers from the past, possessing all who come near it and threatening to turn modern London into a reborn Martian colony.

WHY IT'S IMPORTANT:

Well-adapted from his popular BBC-TV serial, *Five Million Years to Earth* represents author Nigel Kneale's approach to science fiction in its purest form, a riveting and unforgettable deconstruction of natural history, human genetics (we're all part Martian) and what we commonly refer to as the supernatural. Never before was such an all-encompassing parallel view of the human condition presented in a movie. Although the depth of these concepts calls for a lavish, major studio treatment, Hammer and director Roy Ward Baker managed to whip up a satisfying epic on a relative shoestring, the sheer imaginative power of Kneale's ideas transcending budgetary limitations. The plot centers around a strange, missile-like object unearthed during the excavation of a London subway tunnel. Found in and around this machine are precious fossils of prehistoric man-apes, and it's no-nonsense rocket expert Bernard Quatermass (Andrew Keir) who finally makes the astonishing connection: this device is actually a dormant spaceship that crash-landed in prehistoric times, and its dead-but-preserved insectlike occupants are visitors from planet Mars. Moreover, these horned aliens experimented on primitive Earth simians, evolving them into a sentient species that came to be called human (*2001* shares the same basic premise). It isn't long before ancient, destructive psychic powers are rekindled by the thing in the pit, culminating in its metamorphosis as "the horned devil" from ancient legend. Of all the jaw-dropping concepts and wildly imaginative ideas that Kneale dishes out, perhaps the most intriguing is this forged connection between supernatural phenomena (ESP, telekinesis, demonic possession) and extraterrestrial influence. Not only are psychic skills "latent abilities" we humans have carried over from prehistoric times, but witchcraft, ghost phenomena, and even mankind's image of the devil (a fearful horned entity) stem from our collective terror of ancient Martian masters, humanity's "creators." Using their knowledge of mythology ("The Devil's enemy was iron!"), Quatermass and forward-thinking colleague Dr. Roney (James Donald) are able to thwart this diabolical modern threat.

RCE MORE POWERFUL THAN 1,000 H-BOMBS UNLEASHED O DEVASTATE EARTH! WORLD IN PANIC! CITIES IN FLAMES!

FIVE MILLION YEARS TO EARTH

COLOR BY DELUXE

Starring JAMES DONALD · ANDREW KEIR · BARBARA SHELLEY · JULIAN GLOVER   Produced by ANTHONY NELSON KEYS   Directed by ROY BAKER   Screenplay by NIGEL KNEALE   A SEVEN ARTS-HAMMER PRODUCTION

ABOVE: uncovering the mystery device. Almost invisible when first released, *Five Million Years to Earth* built its reputation steadily over the years, introduced to larger audience via television showings.

Kneale's classic continues to blow away audiences with its ingenious ruminations about our confounding, volatile species and the mysterious forces that formed it.

Colonel Breen (Julian Glover) is roasted alive by the glowing, "living" spaceship.

Quatermass (Andrew Keir), Potter (Bryan Marshall), Judd (Barbara Shelley).

A resolved Roney (James Donald) faces the Horned Devil of ancient lore, now a threat to modern London.

Happy Birthday, Dr. Quatermass! Andrew Keir and Barbara Shelley celebrate on the *Five Million Years to Earth* set (Keir was 42).

An epic drama of dventure and exploration

Space Station One: your first step in an Odyssey that will take you to the Moon, the planets and the distant stars.

2001: a space odyssey

MGM PRESENTS A STANLEY KUBRICK PRODUCTION

CINERAMA Super Panavision® and Metrocolor

WHO MADE IT:

Metro-Goldwyn-Mayer (U.K./U.S.). Director: Stanley Kubrick. Producer: Stanley Kubrick, Victor Lyndon (uncredited). Writers: Stanley Kubrick, Arthur C. Clarke, based on the short story "The Sentinel" by Arthur C. Clarke. Cinematography (Technicolor/Metrocolor): Geoffrey Unsworth. Music: Various. Visual Effects: Tom Howard, Douglas Trumbull, Wally Veevers. Starring Keir Dullea (Dr. Dave Bowman), Gary Lockwood (Dr. Frank Poole), William Sylvester (Dr. Heywood R. Floyd), Daniel Richter (Moon-Watcher), Douglas Rain (Voice of HAL 9000), Leonard Rossiter (Dr. Andrei Smyslov), Edward Bishop (Shuttle Captain).

WHAT IT'S ABOUT:

In prehistoric times, primitive simians encounter a mysterious extraterrestrial monolith that evolves these creatures into more advanced, ultimately human beings. Centuries later, Man has conquered space travel, and discovers a similar monolith excavated from within the moon's surface. This strange artifact sends a cryptic radio emission to Jupiter, inspiring a space mission to the distant planet commanded by David Bowman, and watched over by supercomputer HAL. During the course of this journey, HAL makes some inexplicable technical mistakes, and ultimately murders all members of the crew except for Bowman, who eventually manages to disconnect the electronic brain. Entering Jupiter's orbit, Bowman watches wide-eyed as he's engulfed in the colorful swirls of an alien dimensional warp. Now aged in an Earth-like setting on Jupiter, he transforms yet again, into an embryo-like Star Child, forever watching over his home world.

WHY IT'S IMPORTANT:

When *2001* was released in 1968, critical and viewer reactions were divided: some considered Stanley Kubrick's mega-opus a crashing bore, while others deemed it the most artistic movie ever made. Time has validated Kubrick's ambitious vision. In terms of special effects, *2001*'s widescreen vistas are light years ahead of anything previously attempted (take that, *Forbidden Planet*), and predate Lucas and Spielberg's sci-fi extravaganzas by a full decade. But this movie's more than just a visual tour-de-force; it's an unique interstellar enigma, exploring alien-assisted Darwinism, the dangers of a computer-controlled civilization, and man's insatiable need to connect with God, symbolically speaking. Audiences expecting traditional plotting, characters and dialogue are bound to be thrown by Kubrick's off-rhythm structure, which jumps from the Dawn of Man as a sentient species to orbiting space stations in the blink of an eye (and with the toss of a tibia). Movies in general were changing dramatically in the late 1960s, with daring, previously taboo subjects and more flamboyant styles of filmmaking eagerly taking center stage. *2001* was a key part of that movement. Although the film's metaphysics and ambiguous ending threw some viewers ("Instant Ingmar," complained Andrew Sarris), no one found fault with the groundbreaking visuals, most notably Douglas Trumbull's jaw-dropping special effects. By the time *2001* moves into its eye-straining third act, an avalanche of varied fx techniques are called upon to represent Dave Bowman's cosmic journey through the alien "star gate." This POV light show is the highlight of *Space Odyssey* for many viewers, especially those under the influence of a popular '60s hallucinogen. Adding to the experience is a soundscape that rejects Hollywood music scoring in favor of unhummable, atonal compositions by Gyorgy Ligeti and, most famously, Richard Strauss' *Thus Spoke Zarathustra*, a declarative, five-note theme that not only epitomizes the innovative boldness of *2001*, but also came to represent human progress in general. The notion of scientifically advanced aliens evolving apes into human beings and sparking sentient civilization was not a new one in 1968 (*Five Million Years to Earth* probed the same subject with even more specific focus twelve months earlier). But it was certainly fresh enough, and *2001*'s methodical, mostly dialogue-free approach to exploring this captivating notion is pure Kubrick... and total cinematic genius.

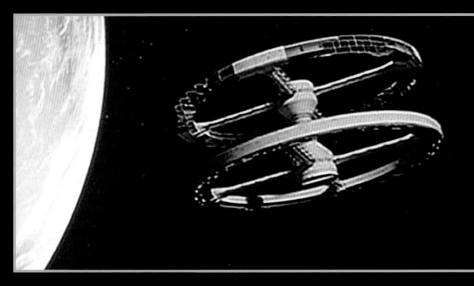

ABOVE: Prehistoric apes have been given advanced intelligence, and the first thing they do with it is devise better methods of killing. When Man gets to outer space centuries later, he's still in high-killing mode, using orbiting bombs for protection. Kubrick counterpoints this brilliantly with his use of the deceptively serene Blue Danube on the soundtrack.

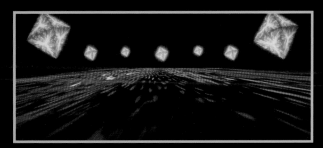

ABOVE, LEFT: The discovery of Monolith #2 (or is it still #1?) leads to the Jupiter mission, where HAL apparently goes berserk (here, Gary Lockwood and Keir Dullea discuss his fate). RIGHT: Bowman finds his way back into the Discovery, endures an alien-escorted vortex trip, and winds up the luminous Star Child.

Stanley Kubrick and stand-in scientists in an early version of the lunar monolith sequence.

FORBIDDEN PLANET 1956 98 2.55

WHO MADE IT:

Metro-Goldwyn-Mayer (U.S.). Director: Fred M. Wilcox. Producer: Nicholas Nayfack. Writer: Cyril Hume, from a story by Irving Block and Allen Adler, inspired by William Shakespeare's "The Tempest." Cinematography (Eastman Color): George J. Folsey. Music aka Electronic Tonalities: Bebe Barron, Louis Barron. Special Effects: A Arnold Gillespie, Joshua Meador, Warren Newcombe, Irving G. Ries. Robot Design: Robert Kinoshita. Id Animator: Bob Trochim. Starring Walter Pidgeon (Dr. Edward Morbius), Anne Francis (Altaira 'Alta' Morbius), Leslie Nielsen (Commander J.J. Adams), Warren Stevens (Lt. 'Doc' Ostrow), Jack Kelly (Lt. Jerry Farman), Richard Anderson (Chief Quinn), Earl Holliman (Cook), Marvin Miller (Robby's voice).

WHAT IT'S ABOUT:

Spaceship commander J.J. Adams and his crew set down on planet Altair-4 to investigate the fate of settlers who landed there decades earlier. The only survivors are philologist Edward Morbius and his beautiful daughter, Altaira. Dr. Morbius explains how his colleagues succumbed to an invisible, marauding planetary force. He also reveals the truth of his scientific studies, discussing the rise and fall of an indigenous species known as the Krell, who perfected a technology that enabled them to create solid matter by sheer thought, then inexplicably destroyed themselves in a single night. It eventually becomes clear that Morbius, his brain capacity amplified by Krell machinery, is repeating their tragic mistake by manifesting the tangible embodiment of his inner frustrations, a "monster from the id," to kill Adams and his men. With daughter Altaira now bonded with the commander, Morbius must finally face his enraged inner demon, given limitless power by Krell machinery.

WHY IT'S IMPORTANT:

Forbidden Planet has all the opulence one expects from an MGM outing – grand special effects, astonishing production design, an A-list star of dignity, even the decade's most iconic robot. What is totally unexpected is the depth of intellectual content. Yes, it was certainly clever of *Planet*'s screenwriters to use Shakespeare's *The Tempest* as the basis for their plotline. But even more remarkable are the scientific and cultural discoveries of planet Altair-4, specifically the revelation about an advanced race's ignominious extinction. Right from the start, *Planet* breaks new ground by pretty much inventing *Star Trek*'s formula of a united Earth spaceship seeking out new life and new civilizations (even *Trek*'s hyperdrive is addressed). The new arrivals threaten Morbius' "egomaniac empire" on Altair-4 and, very specifically, his exclusive relationship with comely daughter Altaira (Anne Francis). Indeed, this is probably the first time in movie history that an MGM love triangle suggests incest, however obliquely. But *Planet*'s audaciousness doesn't stop there. If a Godlike sentient species is still under the thumb of primal hates and jealousies when the safeguards of civilization are removed, where does that leave a far less Godlike, far more imperfect species like the human race? Even if we're lucky enough to evolve into saintly altruists, we'll still be at each other's throats given half the chance. Now that's a bleak assessment.

Still, *Forbidden Planet* never gets bogged down by heavy theorizing. Blessed with an adventuresome plotline and colorful production values, the film deftly delivers all the prerequisite pleasures of a rousing space adventure. But it also happens to be sci-fi cinema's most imaginative and intellectually-stimulating portrait of sentient arrogance, bravely holding a mirror to our darkest realities.

ABOVE: Commander Adams (Leslie Nielsen, with mike) and his two best buds, "Doc" Ostrow (Warren Stevens, center), and Lt. Jerry Farman (Jack Kelly). As *Star Trek* writer David Gerrold once pointed out, Adams and Captain James T. Kirk would feel quite at home on each other's ships. RIGHT: Adams' space cruiser looks suspiciously like an iconic '50s flying saucer as it sets down on the alien landscape of Altair-4.

ABOVE: Boy-crazy Altaira (Anne Francis), doting Dr. Morbius (Walter Pidgeon). RIGHT: The cook (Earl Holliman) asks new friend Robby for a favor (burp).

Monster from the Id: An unconscious Dr. Morbius "whistles up" this primordial nightmare when his daughter Altaira defies him, falling in love with Commander Adams.

Morbius tells all about the Krell, an extinct, Godlike species.

Suicide act: "I give you up!"

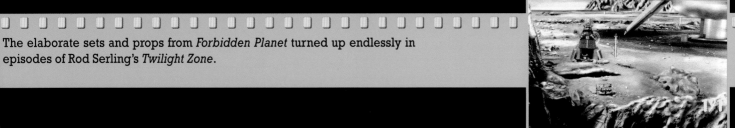

The elaborate sets and props from *Forbidden Planet* turned up endlessly in episodes of Rod Serling's *Twilight Zone*.

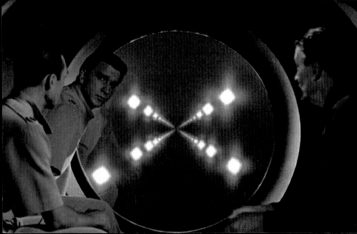

LEGACY OF THE KRELL

Will Humanity Repeat Their Tragic Mistake?

Pity the Krell. "After a million years of shining sanity, they could hardly understand the power that was destroying them," offers contrite Dr. Morbius. It's a sad bit of irony that we less-advanced humans can figure out their problem, and partially because of the moral lesson dramatized in *Forbidden Planet*.

Everything we know about this "all but divine" race inspires awe and admiration. In spite of the Krell's technological constructs (such as all the scientific wonders presented here), we get the impression that these super-advanced entities were humble and pure; even their music suggests a kind of soothing intellectualism. Yet we're aware that, in one fateful night, the species turned preternaturally savage and destroyed itself. Ages of civilization could not restrain the latent devil in each and every Krell. "We are all part monster in our subconscious," Adams correctly points out. "So we have laws and religion (to keep that side of ourselves in check)…"

But here's where the issue gets problematic, even irritating. You'd think that after eons of producing nothing but Good, the Krel could maybe kick back for twenty-four hours and take their decent natures for granted. Doesn't work that way. We're all part monster, inherently damaged goods; and even if we humans evolve into angels a billion years from now we'll still be part monster, at least according to *Forbidden Planet*'s screenwriters. It's a daunting and damning point-of-view being offered up here. Even David McCallum's big-brained futureman from *Outer Limits*' "Sixth Finger" evolves beyond the need for violence or revenge. But this movie's philosophy is bleaker. So, what can we "part monsters" do?

ALL PHOTOS: Morbius (Walter Pidgeon) takes Commander Adams (Leslie Neilsen) and Dr. Ostrow (Warren Stevens) on an awe-inspiring tour of Krell technology.

Says Commander Adams of Morbius' tragic lesson: "...it will remind us that we are, after all, not God." Or, put in less poetic terms, that we aren't Perfect. Because the minute we start believing we are, that's the minute everything starts going straight to Hell.

So this is what we have learned from *Forbidden Planet*, and what the all-but-divine Krell so carelessly forgot. No matter how much the human race accomplishes, no matter how "great" we eventually become, we are by nature emotionally unsettled, capable of monstrous wrongs for the best of reasons. People hate facing this.

But denying it is the first step toward self-destruction, just as pride comes before a fall. And that, more than anything, is the enduring legacy of a species known as Krell, and why we celebrate the remarkable movie that introduced it to us.

AFTERVIEW

BUBBLING UNDER THE TOP 100: *Signs* (M. Night Shyamalan, 2002), *Cloverfield* (Matt Reeves, 2008), *Starship Troopers* (Paul Verhoeven, 1997), *Cocoon* (Ron Howard, 1985), Solaris (Andrey Tarkovskiy, 1972), *Kronos* (Kurt Neumann, 1957), *Avatar* (James Cameron, 2009), *Four-Sided Triangle* (Terence Fisher, 1953), *Inception* (Christopher Nolan, 2010), *Magnetic Monster* (Curt Siodmak, 1953), *Sunshine* (Danny Boyle, 2007), *Charley* (Ralph Nelson, 1968), *Contact* (Robert Zemeckis, 1997), *1984* (Michael Anderson Jr., 1956), *The Brother from Another Planet* (John Sayles, 1984), *Fire in the Sky* (Bob Lieberman, 1993), *Fiend Without a Face* (Arthur Crabtree, 1958).

MOST CLEVER PREMISE FOR A SCI-FI MOVIE: miniaturizing scientist-surgeons and injecting them into a person's bloodstream so they can operate from within (*Fantastic Voyage*). Runner-up: extracting DNA from mosquitoes encased in prehistoric amber in order to recreate living dinosaurs (*Jurassic Park*).

SIMPLY IN A CLASS BY ITSELF: *A Trip to the Moon* (1902, Georges Méliès), the very first sci-fi film.

MOST MEMORABLE LINES OF DIALOGUE IN A SCI-FI MOVIE: 1. "Klaatu barada nikto" (*The Day the Earth Stood Still*). 2. "May the Force be with you!" (*Star Wars*). 3. "Keep watching the skies!" (*The Thing '51*). 4. "E.T. phone home!" (*E.T.*). 5. "I'll be back" (*The Terminator*).

TOP TEN ICONIC ALIEN CRAFT: 1. The Starship Enterprise. 2. The Millennium Falcon. 3. TIE Fighters. 4. The *Close Encounters* Mothership. 5. Martian War Machine '53. 6. The Discovery (*2001*). 7. Harryhausen's Flying Saucers. 8. Luna (*Destination Moon*). 9. *Just Imagine* spaceship. 10. Klaatu's Saucer.

TOP TEN ICONIC SCI-FI ENTITIES: 1. The Robot Maria (*Metropolis*). 2. Darth Vader. 3. The Alien (*Alien*). 4. The Metaluna Mutant (*This Island Earth*). 5. The Predator. 6. Robby the Robot. 7. E.T. 9. The Creature from the Black Lagoon. 10. The Terminator.

TOP TEN SCI-FI MOVIE SOUNDTRACKS: 1. *Star Wars/Empire* (John Williams). 2. *Forbidden Planet* (Louis & Bebe Barron). 2. *The Day the Earth Stood Still* (Bernard Herrmann). 3. *Planet of the Apes* (Jerry Goldsmith). 4. *The Thing from Another World* (Dimitri Tiompkin). 5. *The Power* (Miklos Rozsa). 6. *Blade Runner* (Vangelis) 7. *The Time Machine* (Russ Garcia) 8. *Fahrenheit 451* (Herrmann). 9. *World Without End* (Leith Stevens) 10. *Crack in the World* (John Douglas).

THE TOP TEN SCI-FI SFX CREATORS

GEORGES MÉLIÈS. From 1896 to 1912, Georges Méliès captivated audiences with his charming and wildly creative celluloid imaginings. Credited with developing optical techniques such as the "fade," "dissolve," and the perfection of fast and slow motion, Méliès was also ahead of his time in combining various specialeffects methods to achieve a specific goal. His most famous work, *A Trip to the Moon* (1902), offered everything fromcut-out landscapes to an actor portraying the moon, wearing heavy whipped cream makeup and wincing in pain as the bullet-like spaceship impacts. It's little wonder mastermagician Méliès was dubbed "the Jules Verne of movies."

RAY HARRYHAUSEN. One of the most famous names in fantasy special effects, Harryhausen's beloved stop-motion creations are legendary. Working alone with miniaturefigures, patience and passion his indispensible allies, heproduced such seminal works as Mighty *Joe Young, The Beast from 20,000 Fathoms, Earth vs. the Flying Saucers, 20 Million Miles to Earth, The 7th Voyage of Sinbad, Mysterious Island, Jason and the Argonauts, First Men in the Moon, One Million Years B.C., Valley of Gwangi, Clash of the Titans*, and others.

DOUGLAS TRUMBULL. Some fx creators are competent technicians, others are artists with something unique to express through their specialized craft. It was Doug Trumbull's striking futuristic vision that helped to establish the specific personality of science fiction classics like Kubrick's *2001: A Space Odyssey* and Spielberg's *Close Encounters of the Third Kind*. Oscar-winning Trumbull pushed early computer technology to the max and mated it seamlessly with traditional photo-chemical procedures. Other films include *Star Trek: the Motion Picture* and *Blade Runner*. He also directed the movies *Silent Running* and *Brainstorm*.

ILM (INDUSTRIAL LIGHT & MAGIC). Dennis Muren pictured. Probably the most famous special effects production house in the world, ILM was created by George Lucas during the making of his seminal fx extravaganza, *Star Wars*. Luminaries such as John Dykstra, Muren, Phil Tippett, Richard Edlund and countless others have contributed to the company, which has always been on the cutting-edge of computer-driven fx. Films include all of Lucas and Spielberg's work, the *Star Trek* movies, *The Witches of Eastwick, Field of Dreams, The Abyss, Mission Impossible, Titanic, Starship Troopers, Chronicles of Narnia*, the *Harry Potter* series, and countless others.

WILLIS O'BRIEN. The pioneering genius who introduced stop-motion photography to mainstream audiences, Willis O'Brien first awed one and all by bringing "living" dinosaurs to life in 1927's silent *The Lost World*. Blown away by the realism and melodrama provided by this fx approach, producer Merian C. Cooper hired him as chief technician on RKO's *King Kong*, and the rest is cinematic history. Key influence and mentor to animation protégé Ray Harryhausen, O'Brien went on to supervise the impressive effects for *Last Days of Pompeii, Mighty Joe Young, The Beast of Hollow Mountain, The Black Scorpion*, and *The Giant Behemoth*.

THE STAN WINSTON STUDIO. Beginning his career on television as a makeup artist in the '70s, Stan Winston (pictured) eventually became one of the most important names in Hollywood special effects, winning four Oscars for his work. High-profile assignments included *The Terminator* films and *Aliens* for James Cameron, John Carpenter's *The Thing, Batman Returns, Jurassic Park* and *Iron Man*. Many accomplished fx artists have worked for Winston, including Alec Gillis and Tom Woodruff Jr., who eventually formed their own highly-successful company. Stan Winston also enjoyed a brief career as movie director, helming the cult classic *Pumpkinhead*.

THE BUD WESTMORE UNIT. Part of the legendary Westmore Hollywood makeup dynasty, handsome Bud joined Universal in the late 1940s and assembled a first-class team of design/makeup/sculpting experts. This group included Jack Kevan, Millicent Patrick, Chris Moeller, John Chambers and others. In the 1950s and into the '60s, Universal kept these talented artists busy with projects like *Creature from the Black Lagoon, It Came from Outer Space, This Island Earth, Revenge of the Creature, The Mole People, Tarantula, The Creature Walks Among Us, Monster on the Campus, The List of Adrian Messenger, Munster Go Home*, and several others.

WAH CHANG. Often associated with fellow artist Gene Warren, Wah Chang lent his brilliant designing and sculpting expertise to a number of classic sci-fi properties. He created the Time Machine for George Pal in 1960 and earned an Academy Award. Other notable creations include the maquette used as prototype-reference for Disney's *Pinocchio*, props for the original *Planet of the Apes*, and groundbreaking conceptual designs for TV's *Outer Limits* and *Star Trek*. In the early '60s Chang formed his own company, Project Unlimited, which employed future fx superstars like Tim Barr and Jim (*When Dinosaurs Ruled the Earth*) Danforth.

EIJI TSUBURAYA. Japan's answer to American monster-makers Willis O'Brien and Ray Harryhausen, Eiji Tsuburaya was the special effects master who realized Godzilla and countless giant sci-fi creatures for the big screen. Although his specialty was miniature designing and he rejected costly, time-consuming stop-motion animation in favor of textured monster suits, his films became iconic classics, and the Japanese movie industry flourished when these pictures succeeded worldwide. Credits include *Godzilla, Rodan, The H-Man, Secret of the Telegian, Mothra, King Kong vs. Godzilla, Attack of the Mushroom People*, and *Ultraman*.

PAUL BLAISDELL. Just as producer/director Roger Corman was the King of B-movies, designer/sculptor Paul Blaisdell became the Hollywood fx artist most likely to whip up an iconic sci-fi monster for a fraction of what the majors charged. Feisty independent studios gave him lots of work in the '50s: *The She Creature, Day the World Ended, It Conquered the World, The Amazing Colossal Man, It! The Terror from Beyond Space*, among others. Finished costumes for his characters were hand-painted and personally worn by the committed Blaisdell. His best pal and assistant, Bob Burns, is a noted film historian and high-profile memorabilia collector.

THE TOP TEN SCI-FI MOVIE DIRECTORS

1. STANLEY KUBRICK. 2001, A Clockwork Orange
2. FRITZ LANG Metropolis, Woman in the Moon
3. STEVEN SPIELBERG. Close Encounters, E.T.
4. GEORGE LUCAS. Star Wars, THX-1138
5. JAMES CAMERON. The Terminator, Aliens
6. JACK ARNOLD. The Incredible Shrinking Man
7. JOHN CARPENTER. The Thing, Dark Star
8. GEORGE PAL. The Time Machine
9. BYRON HASKIN. War of the Worlds, Robinson Crusoe on Mars
10. KURT NEUMANN. The Fly, Rocketship X-M